THE ESSENTIAL
DEMING

THE ESSENTIAL
DEMING

Leadership Principles
from the
FATHER OF QUALITY

W. Edwards Deming

EDITED BY JOYCE NILSSON ORSINI, PHD

New York   Chicago   San Francisco   Lisbon   London
Madrid   Mexico City   New Delhi   San Juan
Seoul   Singapore   Sydney   Toronto

Copyright © 2013 by The W. Edwards Deming Institute. All rights reserved. Printed in the United States of America. Except as permitted under the United States Copyright Act of 1976, no part of this publication may be reproduced or distributed in any form or by any means, or stored in a database or retrieval system, without the prior written permission of the publisher.

10   LHN   23

ISBN   978-0-07-179022-2
MHID   0-07-179022-5

e-ISBN   978-0-07-179021-5
e-MHID   0-07-179021-7

Library of Congress Cataloging-in-Publication Data

Deming, W. Edwards (William Edwards).
   The essential Deming : leadership principles from the father of quality/ by W. Edwards Deming.
      p. cm.
ISBN 978-0-07-179022-2 (alk. paper)—ISBN 0-07-179022-5 (alk. paper)
1. Total quality management. 2. Leadership. 3. Industrial management.
I. Title.
HD62.15.D459 2013
658.4'092—dc23   2012032544

McGraw-Hill books are available at special quantity discounts to use as premiums and sales promotions or for use in corporate training programs. To contact a representative, please e-mail us at bulksales@mcgraw-hill.com.

This book is printed on acid-free paper.

Contents

————◆————

Preface

Dr. W. Edwards Deming published books and articles in academic journals and the popular press, with frequent letters to the editors. He wrote papers for colleagues and students, and conducted hundreds of studies for clients. He also left a number of undistributed draft papers and personal letters to colleagues and businesses, as well as to his clients. He delivered abundant four-day seminars to tens of thousands of people, and spoke frequently at conferences. He criticized the status quo, and was outspoken about government and corporate policies alike. Many of his ideas are standard in business today. Many more need yet to be adopted.

Chronologically, during the late 1920s through about 1940, Deming's writings were based in physics. For the next forty years his written works centered in statistics and sampling theory. It was during his last thirteen years (1980–1993), roughly, that he focused on the transformation of management.

Nuggets of management theory appear in Deming's early statistical work that pop up again forty years later in his management writings. I believe Deming's theory of management is the culmination of his life's work—everything is in it.

This book is about Deming's theory of management, in his own words, gleaned from articles and papers he wrote, and speeches he gave at conferences and seminars?—little-distributed until now.

My approach: I have reviewed the Deming Collection of materials in the Library of Congress Manuscript Division in Washington

DC, materials that Deming gave to me over the years, and copies of papers he handed out in classes, at various conferences, and that I have gathered from other sources. I have also reviewed hundreds of hours of video and audio recordings of his lectures to students and at conferences. More than half of Deming's works are very statistical and not directly appropriate in this book for more general audiences.

After skimming thousands of documents, I reviewed in detail some 850 articles, letters, papers, cases, lectures, speeches, and notes by Deming that contained potential material for this book. I've selected about a hundred of them for inclusion in whole or in part in this book. None of the works were in electronic format, so they had to be digitized. Several documents were sixth or seventh carbon copies, extremely difficult to read—but worth the effort to include them, I believe. Twenty of the conference films and one of the audiotapes were transcribed for excerpts to include in this book as well.

In this review of Deming's works, I found that he had a propensity to reuse the same (identical) paragraphs in different articles – sometimes identical titles, too, on different articles. Although he had some new content in each article, sometimes more than half of the content would be culled from other articles. Many papers were written in precomputer time, so I could see the "cut and paste" sections on the originals of some of the articles. Deming also paraphrased prior writings in new articles. Within a speech, especially, he often looped around and repeated the same content two or three times for effect. The looping has been removed. To minimize duplication of content in different articles included in this book, the editor took a heavier hand. As a result, the book contains very few complete articles.

Deming never missed an opportunity to include statistical theory. So, a fair amount of editing was done in this area of his papers, as well, save for some light words on statistics in Chapter 7. One cannot talk about prediction without including the rudiments of statistical theory.

Deming's inimitable style of writing has not been removed deliberately. Deming eschewed contractions and used two words instead (e.g., "can not," "cannot," instead of can't). He used the British spelling of some words (e.g., connexion, enquire, lustre). These were often replaced by American editors, but not by all. I did not go back into edited pieces and reinstate his original style. Nor did I alter his original style when encountered, so you will see differences between articles in this respect. You will, no doubt, discover other idiosyncrasies in Deming's writing.

Deming did not use the same elements of style or structure for every article. At first, I attempted to make all of the articles consistent with regard to style, so as not to disconcert the reader. That was a fiasco. Deming used style to shape the substance. The articles herein are each in their original style.

The choice of where to place each article in this book was difficult. I could make arguments for placing some articles in any one of several chapters. In the end, articles are placed where I believe they will serve the reader best.

The contents of this book are Deming's words. I have not added my own words, except where noted in introductory statements. This book is not a substitute for Deming's books, *Out of the Crisis* and *The New Economics for Industry, Government, Education*. *The Essential Deming* necessarily includes some of Deming's ideas that came to be included in these two earlier works, but not all. This book is written for those people who wish to see more of what Deming had to say about management in this world we live in, beyond these two earlier books.

I wish to thank Niki Papadapolous, then an editor at McGraw-Hill, for her idea to create this book, and Knox Huston, who is senior editor at McGraw-Hill, for his skillful help and suggestions in preparation of this book for publication. I wish to thank my friend and colleague, the Honorable Lawrence U. Costiglio for his collaborations, suggestions, and recommendations at every stage of the development of the book.

Joyce Nilsson Orsini
2012

1

The World Is Being Ruined by Best Efforts

(Best Efforts Without Guidance Lead to Failure)

People sometimes find themselves in a situation where things don't go right. The best employees find ways to "correct" the problem. I put the word correct in quotes because often the corrections wind up making things worse. Not because of mal-intent or lack of follow-through. If the problem is caused by the way the process is designed (a management responsibility), the tweaking done by the employee may alter the system in such a way that future products or services are even worse. The correction addresses the wrong problem and winds up doing more harm than good. It's counter-intuitive to believe that your best workers, doing their best, could make things worse. Best efforts won't cut it; better management of the system is needed.

This chapter contains articles that Deming wrote between 1978 and 1992, trying to help management take responsibility for actively managing. He recognized that many of the bad practices were so ingrained that they would take decades to be rid of. He also realized that many executives had no idea how much trouble they were in. He likened the situation in America to that in Japan in the late 1940s.

At the end of the chapter are articles specifically on problems with the merit pay system, competition and monopolies, and quality control (QC)-Circles.

Deming wrote this note to himself to capture his thought that the United States is in a state of crisis, much as Japan had been after World War II. But unlike the Japanese, the United States doesn't know they're in a crisis.

The Invisible Crisis

Japan was in a crisis. The crisis was visible, the country blown to bits, destroyed by fire. Our country is in a worse crisis because it is invisible. Japanese top management asked me in 1950 to come to help. Japan soon became an economic power. The secret:

Management of a system, cooperation between components, not competition. Management of people.

We suffer from evil styles of management, such as ranking people, divisions, plants (creating competition between people), management by results, failure to understand cooperation in a system in which everybody wins.

Transformation is required: not mere change. Transformation requires Profound Knowledge.

From a note written April 4, 1992.

Fourteen years earlier, in a letter to the dean of a university, Deming discusses the many road-blocks that stand in the way of improvement of American industry. He talks about the joint efforts of the production-worker and management in Japan and the mistaken notion that the Japanese copy from others. If they are copying, how did they get so far ahead?, he wondered.

Poor performance in American companies lies, at least in part, in the failure of American management to keep abreast of modern methods of management and innovation, Deming believed. Relations between the American production-worker and American management "presents a sad spectacle" he states in this communication.

Irrational Explanations and Excuses

A road-block stands in the way of improved productivity in American industry, so badly needed in view of America's unfavorable balance of trade. The road-block is the irrational explanations and excuses offered by most Americans, including unfortunately most leaders of industry, for the success of the Japanese, and for the competitive position of their products. It would be better to face up to the facts, and try to understand better the reasons for the miracle of Japanese efficiency and quality. The miracle of economic growth in Japan has been the envy and a model for other industrial economies.

Most Americans, from top management on down to the rank and file, even as consumers, have a badly distorted image of Japanese industry. It seems incredible to Americans that the Japanese could out-smart Americans, not by low wages, not by longer hours, but by sheer efficiency and brilliant innovation. Accusation that Japanese firms dump their products on American shores below cost, through subsidy or preferential treatment by the Japanese government, and accusation of other so-called unfair techniques by Japanese industry, are mostly unfounded. There is also prevalent amongst Americans the idea that importation of Japanese products lowers our standard of living by taking jobs away from Americans, when the fact is that without Japanese products the standard of living of most Americans, especially those of lower income, would today be considerably lower than it is.

Everyone knows that the economy of the United States has not maintained leadership in productivity that the world requires for balance of commerce. There are doubtless many reasons for this poor performance, but one of them surely lies in the failure of American management to keep abreast of modern methods of management. Innovation in America has not kept up with the Japanese. Relations between the American production-worker and American management presents a sad spectacle.

By contrast, in Japan, the contribution of the production-worker and the contribution of management are a joint effort. All people work together toward the same end, even though the motivation may in some part be selfish. The greater the productivity, the better the economic lot of everybody. This is a simple principle and it is learned in Japan at an early age.

There is, in addition, the supposition in the minds of most Americans that Japanese manufacturers exist by copying the techniques and products of other countries. The Japanese are clever and can indeed, copy.

Whose trains did the Japanese copy? And where did they get the idea that trains should run on time within 15 seconds? (I do not mean 15 minutes.) Whose TV did Sony copy? Whose cameras? I hold in my hand a Casio hand-calculator, weight two ounces, one-quarter inch thick, with a digital clock that keeps time within two seconds per month. Could American manufacturers make it? Yes. Then why don't they? The Japanese beat them to it.

Failure of Americans to understand that the Japanese have also superior ability in innovation and that they have developed superior management and channels of trade is one of the barriers to better efficiency in American production, and to innovation in America. It would be far better for the leaders of industry in America to admit that most (not all) Japanese products are better and more dependable than the competitive American product, and that Japanese production is in general more efficient than American production.

The mail service in Japan is enviable: a letter that I posted to myself on the street at 7:25 p.m., just for a test, was waiting for me at my hotel at 10 o'clock that same evening. Obviously the Japanese postal system did not copy ours. Japanese homes have been 99 per cent electrified from a year or two after the close of the war.

I make the above assertions on the basis of work with Japanese industry that dates from 1950, 14 trips so far, a 15th to occur in October 1978, and with even longer experience with a cross-section of American industry. I may remind you that, according to Japanese testimony, it was the statistical control of quality that brought about the revolution in quality and efficiency of production in Japan, which began in 1950. These methods affect all aspects of production, from raw material to finished product, plus consumer research and re-design of product, and design of new products. One feature, especially applicable to production, is techniques by which to distinguish between (a) special causes of variation of quality and economic loss, which the worker himself can correct on statistical signal, and (b) faults of the system, which only management can correct. Statistical methods thus assist management and production-worker in Japan to pull together.

The boost in morale, and in production as well, of the production-worker in America, if he were to perceive a genuine attempt on the part of management to improve the system and to hold the production-worker responsible only for what the production-worker is responsible for and can govern, and not for handicaps placed on him by the system, would be hard to over-estimate. It has not been tried, I believe, outside Japan.

As an example, most people are not aware that the basic reason for recalls for a defective part in an automobile is chargeable to management, not to sloppy workmanship. The fault is in design, not workmanship. Design is the function of management, not of the production-worker.

There were other new principles of administration that Japanese management learned from an American in 1950. Results were obvious within six months in some companies. Within 15 years Japanese quality and efficient productivity had upset the monetary system of the world.

These principles, imported from America, used and refined in Japan, are at hand for anybody to learn and to use, including Americans.

Another unfortunate drag on American management is American schools of business that lead students to suppose that a manager need not know anything. There is in most American schools of business a loss of respect for the fundamentals of knowledge such as economics, history, theory of law, psychology, mathematics, statistical methods. Substitution of the computer for fundamentals will take its toll on American production.

From a Memorandum to the
Dean of the School of Business Administration,
The American University,
August 23, 1978.

In this excerpt Deming puts the blame for poor performance squarely on the shoulders of top management. What is needed cannot be delegated, and cannot be done by the workforce, who are already doing their best.

Everyone Is Already Doing His Best

The wealth of a nation depends on its people, management, and government, more than on its natural resources. The problem is where to find good management. It would be a mistake to export American management to a friendly country.

A long road lies ahead of American industry—10 to 25 years—to regain a stable state of competitive position. Many changes are required. The quarterly dividend, and brief tenure in management positions, have defeated the competitive position and the standard of living that Americans have heretofore supposed could only move to still higher levels.

Paper profits, the yardstick by which stockholders and Boards of Directors often measure performance of top management, make no contribution to material living for people anywhere, nor do they improve the competitive position of a company or of American industry.

Paper profits do not make bread: improvement of quality and productivity do. They make a contribution to better material living for all people, here and everywhere.

It is not enough for everyone to do his best. Everyone is already doing his best. Efforts, to be effective, must go in the right direction.

It is not enough that top management commit themselves for life to quality and productivity. They must know what it is that they are committed to – i.e., what they must do. These obligations can not be delegated. Mere approval is not enough, nor New Year's resolutions.

Only top management can bring about the changes required. Failure of top management to act on any one of the 14 points listed [in Chapter 4] will impair efforts on the other 13.

From "Obligations of Management in the New Economic Age,"
The Institute of Management Sciences in Osaka,
July 24, 1989.

Deming points out some of the deficiencies and fallacies of suggestions that are generally put forth for bringing about improvement. He believed that every one of them ducks the responsibility of management. He makes the point that hard work and best efforts by themselves will not produce quality, that knowledge is required.

The Usual Suggestions Fall Short

Where are we? How are we doing? Let us think about the U.S., or about all North America, not just about our own selves, nor just about our company, nor about our own community. How is the U.S. doing in respect to balance of trade? The answer is that we are not doing well.

North America has contributed much to new knowledge and to applications of knowledge. The U.S., by efficient product and natural resources, beginning around 1920 and for decades, put manufactured products in the hands of millions of people the world over that could not otherwise have had them. Our quality was good enough to create appetite for our goods and services.

For a decade after the War, North America was the only part of the world that could produce manufactured goods to full capacity. The rest of the industrial world lay in ruins from the War. They were our customers, willing buyers. Gold flowed into Fort Knox.

Everyone expected the good times to continue and to wax better and better. It is easy to manage a business in an expanding market, and to be hopeful. In contrast with expectations, we find, on looking back, that we have been on an economic decline for three decades. It is easy to date an earthquake, but not a decline.

What happened? It is hard to believe that anything is different now than in 1950. The change has been gradual, not visible week to week. We can only see the decline by looking back.

A cat is unaware that dusk has settled upon the earth, but the cat in total darkness is as helpless as any of us.

Some industries are doing better than ever. There are more automobiles in the U.S. than ever before, and more travel by air. Do such figures mean decline or advance? An answer would have to take into account that in 1958 we had inter-city trains. There was a choice, air or train. Now, we have only limited train service, air or automobile; go by air or by automobile.

There was until a few years ago a favorable balance of trade in agricultural products—wheat, cotton, soybeans, to name a few—but no longer. Imports of agricultural products have overtaken exports, and as someone in one of my seminars pointed out, if we could put illicit drugs into the accounting, our deficit in agricultural products would show up worse than the published figures.

One of our best exports, one that brings in dollars, is materials for war. We could greatly expand this income but for moral reasons. American aircraft have about 70% of the world market, and bring in huge amounts of dollars. Another big earner of dollars is scrap metal. We can't use it, so we sell it. Close on to it is scrap cardboard and paper. Timber brings in dollars. Timber is important, renewable. Equipment for construction is an important export, so I understand. American movies, a service, bring in dollars. Banking and other services were at one time important, but no longer. The biggest U.S. bank is today far down the list of biggest banks in the world. Banking is now known mostly for losses on bad loans. (As an aside, quality in banking might be improved.)

We ship out, for dollars, iron ore, partially refined, aluminum, nickel, copper, coal, all nonrenewable. Scrap metal is nonrenewable.

Have we been living on fat? We have been wasting our natural resources, and worse, as we shall see, destroying our people. We need them.

Our problem is quality. Around 1958, Japanese goods started to flow in. The price was good, and the quality was good, not like the shoddy quality that came from Japan before the War and just after, cheap but worth the price. Preference for imported items—some at least—gradually climbed and became a threat to North American industry.

Were Americans caught napping? Are we still napping? Our problem is quality. Can't we make quality? Of course, and some American products are superior. We are thankful for them. Unfortunately, some good American products have little appeal beyond our borders, good paper clips, for example.

It will not suffice to have customers that are merely satisfied. A satisfied customer may switch. Why not? He might come out better for the switch.

What a company requires to get ahead is loyal customers, the customer that comes back, waits in line, and brings a friend with him.

What state of company is in the best position to improve quality? The answer is that a company that is doing well, future assured, is in excellent position to improve quality and service, thus to contribute to the economic condition of itself and of all of us, and has the greatest obligation to improve. A monopoly is in the best position to improve year by year, and has the greatest obligation.

A look at some of the usual suggestions for quality. There is widespread interest in quality. Suppose that we were to conduct next Tuesday a national referendum:

Are you in favor of quality?
(Be honest in your answer.)
Yes _____ No _____

The results would show, I believe, an avalanche in favor of quality. Moreover, unfortunately, almost everybody has the answer on how to achieve it. Just read Letters to the Editor, speeches, books. It seems so simple. Here are some of the answers offered, all insufficient, some negative in results.

Automation
New machinery
Computers
Gadgets
Hard work
Best efforts
Make everybody accountable
M.B.O., management by objective, management by the numbers, actually tampering
M.B.R., management by results
Merit system (actually, destroyer of people)
Incentive pay. Pay for performance
Work standards (quotas, time standards)
    They double the cost of production be they for manufacturing or for service (bank, telephone company)
    They rob people of pride of workmanship, the emphasis being on numbers, not on quality
    They are a barrier to improvement
Just in time
Zero defects. Zero defect days
Meet specifications
Motivate people

Some remarks. The deficiencies and fallacies of the suggestions listed above will be obvious. Every one of them ducks the responsibility of management, requiring only skills, not knowledge about management.

Why do the above suggestions fall short? A little ingredient that I call profound knowledge is missing from all the above suggestions. There is no substitute for knowledge. Hard work and best efforts will by themselves not produce quality nor a market. We shall soon come to suggestions for the missing ingredient, profound knowledge.

If the reader could follow me around in my consultations, he would perceive that much automation and much new machinery is a source of poor quality and high cost, helping to put us out of business. Much of it, if it performs as intended, is built for twice the capacity that is needed. Some of it is poorly designed, such as make → inspect → make inspect → make inspect → … where inspection may not be economically the best procedure. Moreover, the apparatus for inspection usually gives more trouble than the apparatus for make.

Just in time, along with low inventory, is good, of course. Unfortunately, efforts usually start at the wrong end. The place to start is with processes and movements of materials used. Once processes and movements are in statistical control, the plant manager will know how much of this and that that he will need by 3 o'clock tomorrow. Quantity and quality will be predictable.

Zero defects, meet specifications, incoming and outgoing, are not good enough. Of course, we wish not to violate specifications, but to meet specifications is not enough. The pieces in an assembly must work together as a system. Assemblies must work together as a system. I may refer to page 476 in the book, *Out of the Crisis:*

Principle 3. Tests of components in stages of development can not provide (a) assurance that they will work together satisfactorily as a system in service; nor (b) the average run between failures of the system; nor (c) the type and cost of maintenance that will be required in service.

A company advertised that the future belongs to him that invests in it, and went ahead and spent $45,000,000,000 for new machinery. Most of it turned out to be a binge into high costs and low quality, but it must be said in defense of the management that they were obviously taking a long view into the future, not trying to capture short-term profits.

One could announce an important theorem: we are being ruined by best efforts directed the wrong way. We need best efforts directed by a theory of management.

Wrong way. The President of a company put quality in the hands of his plant managers. The results in time became obvious and embarrassing. Quality went down, as was predictable. A plant manager can not possibly know what quality is, and even if he did, he could do nothing about it. He is helpless. He can only try to do his job, and to confirm specifications.

The President of a company wrote that

> Our people in the plants are responsible for their own product and for its quality.

They are not. They can only try to do their jobs. Their product and its quality are the responsibility of the man that wrote the article, the President of the company.

The management of a company put this slogan in the hands of all employees:

> The operator is responsible for the quality of our products.
> The inspector shares this responsibility.

Again, the operator is not responsible for the quality of his product. The product is the responsibility of the management.

Moreover, responsibility divided between operator and inspector, as it is here, assures mistakes and trouble.

The management in both of these examples rid themselves of their responsibility by handing it over to people that are helpless to define quality and to improve processes. Another example: a group of consultants in management advertised thus:

> Computerized quality information systems provide the vital link between high technology and effective decision making.

I wish that management were as simple as that.

The big losses. Too often, the financial people in a company merely beat down costs, on the thought that any cost is too high. Why do they write cheques for machinery that violates good practice?

It is vital for management to manage the big losses. One should of course chase the nickels and dimes, but it is futile to chase nickels and dimes and at the same time neglect the biggest losses. The biggest losses, as Dr. Lloyd S. Nelson said years ago, are unknown and unknowable. Most of them are not even under suspicion.

What are the big losses? Answer: the so-called merit systems—actually, destroyer of people; M.B.O., management by the numbers, quotas, failure to optimize the various activities and divisions of a company as a system, business plans in terms of a matrix of targets without regard to the whole plan as a system of improvement. Further Losses come from

Worker training worker
Executives working with best efforts, trying to improve quality, the market, and profit, but working without guidance of profound knowledge

Tampering

Failure to optimize efforts of people and divisions within the company, accepting, instead, suboptimization—everyone trying to maximize the profits of his own division—and the consequent losses

Failure of customers and suppliers to work together for ever greater and greater satisfaction of quality, lower costs, everybody wins

Knowledge about the Taguchi loss function is necessary for management. It is management's job to discover which quality-characteristic is most critical, conquer it, then to move on to the next one.

From "Obligations of Management in the New Economic Age," The Institute of Management Sciences in Osaka, July 24, 1989.

The transformation of the American style of management is not a job of reconstruction nor revision. It requires a whole new structure, from foundation upward. Deming outlines some of the failures, the need to halt the decline, seven deadly diseases, the long road to recovery, and some notes on the government and service industry.

A New Structure Is Required

Failure of management to plan for the future and to foresee problems has brought about waste of manpower, of materials, and of machine-time, all of which raise the manufacturer's cost and price that the purchaser must pay. The consumer is not always willing to subsidize this waste. The inevitable result is loss of market. Loss of market begets unemployment.

Performance of management should be measured by potential to stay in business, to protect investment, to ensure future dividends and jobs through improvement of product and service for the future, not by the quarterly dividend.

It is no longer socially acceptable to dump employees on to the heap of unemployed. Loss of market, and resulting unemployment are not foreordained. They are not inevitable. They are man-made.

The basic cause of sickness in American industry and resulting unemployment is failure of top management to manage. He that sells not can buy not. The causes usually cited for failure of a company are costs of start-up, overruns on costs, depreciation of excess inventory, competition—anything but the actual cause, *pure and simple bad management.*

What must management do? Management obviously have a new job. Where can management learn about the transformation that is necessary? Management can not learn by experience alone what they must do to improve quality and productivity and the competitive position of the company.

Everyone simply doing his best is not the answer, either. It is first necessary that people know what to do. Drastic changes are required. The first step in the transformation is to learn how to change: that is, to understand and use the 14 points and to cure the seven deadly diseases.

The 7 Deadly Diseases

The application of the 14 points will transform the American style of management. Unfortunately, deadly diseases and obstacles still stand in the way of transformation. The following seven diseases afflict most American companies:

1. *Lack of constancy of purpose* to plan product and service that will have a market and keep the company in business, and provide jobs.

2. *Emphasis on short-term, profits:* short-term thinking fed by fear of unfriendly takeover, and by push from bankers and owners for dividends. Short-term profits are not a reliable indicator of performance of management. Anybody can pay dividends by deferring maintenance, cutting out research, or acquiring another company.

   Dividends and paper profits, the yardstick by which managers of money and heads of companies are judged, make no contribution to material living for people anywhere, nor do they improve the competitive position of a company or of American industry. Paper profits do not make bread: improvement of quality and productivity do.

3. *Evaluation of performance,* merit rating, or annual review. These traditional appraisal systems reward people who do well in the system. They do not reward attempts to improve the system.

4. *Mobility of management.* The job of management is inseparable from the welfare of the company. Mobility from one company to another creates prima donnas for quick results. Mobility annihilates teamwork, so vital for continued existence. A new manager comes in. Everyone wonders what will happen. Unrest becomes rampant when the board of directors go outside the company to bring someone in for a rescue operation. Everyone takes to his life preserver.

   Mobility of labor in America is another serious problem. A strong contributing factor is dissatisfaction with the job, inability to take pride in the work. People stay home or look around for another job when they can not take pride in their work. Absenteeism and mobility are largely creations of poor management.

5. *Management by use only of visible figures.* He that would run his company on visible figures alone will in time have neither company nor figures. The most important figures for management (such as the multiplying effect on sales that comes from

a happy customer, and the opposite effect from an unhappy customer) are either unknown or unknowable, but successful management must nevertheless take account of them.

6. *Excessive medical costs.* As William E. Hoglund, manager of the Pontiac Motor Division, put it to me one day, "Blue Cross is our second largest supplier." Six months later he told me that Blue Cross had overtaken steel. The direct cost of medical care is $400 per automobile.

7. *Excessive costs of liability,* swelled by lawyers that work on contingency fees.

Long Road to Recovery

Long-term commitment to new learning and new philosophy is required of any management that seeks transformation. The timid and the fainthearted, and people that expect quick results, are doomed to disappointment.

Solving problems, big problems and little problems, will not halt the decline of American industry, nor will expansion in use of computers, gadgets, and robotic machinery. Benefits from massive expansion of new machinery constitute a vain hope. Massive immediate expansion in the teaching of statistical methods to production-workers is not the answer either, nor are wholesale flashes of quality control circles.

Management by walking around is hardly ever effective either. The reason is that someone in management, walking around, has little idea about what questions to ask, and usually does not pause long enough at any spot to get the right answer.

All these activities make their contribution, but they only prolong the life of the patient: they can not halt the decline. Only transformation of the American style of management, and of governmental relations with industry, can halt the decline and give American industry a chance to lead the world again.

A. V. Feigenbaum estimated that from 15 to 40 percent of the manufacturer's costs of almost any American product that you buy today is for waste embedded in it—waste of human effort, waste of machine-time, nonproductive use of accompanying burden. No wonder that many American products are hard to sell at home or abroad.

If I were a banker, I would not lend money for new equipment unless the company that asked for the loan could demonstrate by statistical evidence that they are using their present equipment to reasonably full capacity, and are at work on the 14 points and on the 7 deadly diseases.

Government and Service Industries

Eventually quality improvement will reach government and the service industries as well—hotels, restaurants, transportation of freight and passengers, wholesale and retail establishments, hospitals, medical service, care of the aged, perhaps even the U.S. mail. I make no distinction between manufacturing and service industries. All industries, manufacturing and service, are subject to the same principles of management.

All must adopt a new style of management. Not only is the style of American management unfitted for this economic age, but many government regulations and the Justice Department's Antitrust Division are out of step, propelling American industry along the path of decline, contrary to the well-being of the American people. Dependence on protection by tariffs and laws to "buy American" only encourages incompetence. And unfriendly takeovers and leveraged buyouts are a cancer in the American system. Fear of takeover, along with emphasis on the quarterly dividend, defeats constancy of purpose. Without constancy of purpose to stay in business by providing products and services that have a market, there will be further downturn and more unemployment.

When we size up the job ahead, it is obvious that a long thorny road lies ahead—decades. American business and industry can no longer afford job hopping—here a while and gone, from the management of one company to the management of another. Management must declare a policy for the future, to stay in business and to provide jobs for their people, and more jobs. Management must understand design of product and of service, procurement of materials, problems of production, process control, and barriers on the job that rob people of their birthright, the right to pride of workmanship.

There is hope for the future. In fact, one requirement for innovation is faith in the future. Innovation, the foundation of the future, can not thrive unless the top management has declared unshakeable commitment to quality and productivity. The management of a number of American companies are at work on the 14 points and on the diseases that afflict them. Substantial results are already recorded. But the complete transformation will take time. We are certainly not yet out of the crisis.

From "Transformation of American Management,"
Executive Excellence,
January 1987.

Many people work without sufficient knowledge, little guidance, and focus in the wrong place. Deming discusses in this article the drastic changes he believed necessary in American companies.

Everyone Doing His Best Is Not the Answer

The biggest problem that most any company in the Western world faces is not its competitors, nor the Japanese. The biggest problems are self-inflicted, created right at home by management that are off course in the competitive world of today.

Systems of management are in place in the Western world that for survival must be blasted out; new construction commenced. Patchwork will not suffice.

Everyone doing his best is not the answer. Everyone is doing his best. It is necessary that people understand the reason for the changes that are necessary. Moreover, there must be consistency of understanding and of effort.

There is much talk about the need to improve quality and productivity. Moreover, everyone knows exactly how to go about it. It is for other people to accomplish, not for me.

In the eyes of many people in management, the big trouble is that a lot of employees in operations and in management as well are careless and neglectful on the job. One writer has the solution—hold all employees accountable for job behaviour as well as for the results expected of them. The fact is that performance appraisal, management by the numbers, M.B.O., and work standards, have already devastated Western industry. More of the same could hardly be a solution.

The annual rating of performance has devastated Western industry. Work standards double the cost of the operations that they are applied to.

Other writers see information as the solution. Anyone can improve his work, they say, if he has enough information. The fact is that a figure by itself provides no information, has no meaning, no interpretation, in the absence of theory. In short, there is no substitute for knowledge, and a figure by itself is not knowledge.

Other people put their faith in gadgets, computers, new machinery, and robotic machinery. Solving problems is not the answer, nor improvement of operations. They are not the transformation required.

It will not suffice to match the competition. He that declares his intention to meet the competition is already licked, his back to the wall. Likewise, zero defects are a highway down the tube.

The sad truth is that all the parts of an apparatus may meet the specifications, yet the apparatus may be unsatisfactory or may even be a total failure. It is necessary in this world to outdo specifications, to move continually toward better and better performance of the finished product.

Likewise, it will not suffice to have customers that are merely satisfied. Satisfied customers switch, for no good reason, just to try something else. Why not? Profit and growth come from customers that can boast about your product or service—the loyal customer. He requires no advertising or other persuasion, and he brings a friend along with him.

Western management has for too long focused on the end product—get reports on people, productivity, quality, sales, inventory. It is necessary that management shift the focus to management's responsibility for the source of quality and service, viz., design of product and of the processes that turn out the product and service. Management in the Western world have too long been driving the automobile by keeping an eye on the rear view mirror (Myron Tribus).

Recognition of the distinction between a stable system and an unstable one is vital for management. A stable system is one whose performance is predictable; it appears to be in statistical control.

Plots of weekly proportions of people absent from the job, number of accidents, frequencies of complaints of customers, costs of warranty, sales, outgoing quality, costs, scrap, rejections, accounts overdue by four weeks or more, will show where the responsibility for improvement lies. It is instructive to look at a plot of proportion of people week by week over the past two years. Does the plot show a stable system? If yes, then only the management can reduce it.

Incidentally, such plots make clear the futility and fallacy of management by the numbers. A goal that lies beyond the capability of the system can not be achieved except at the destruction of other systems in the company. What is needed for management is not goals, but constant improvement of design and of processes at the source, the responsibility of management.

From Report No. 14 "Drastic Changes for Western Management,"
Center for Quality and Productivity Improvement,
University of Wisconsin-Madison,
June 8, 1986.
Republished with minor changes in Executive Excellence,
The Institute for Principle-Centered Leadership,
February 1987.

Poor performance in American companies lies, at least in part, in the failure of American management to keep abreast of modern methods of management and innovation, Deming believed. Relations between the American production-worker and American management presents a sad spectacle, he states in this article.

We've Been Sold Down the River

I. Need for Quality

American industry dominated the world for decades. Exports of manufactured product were at a high level for a decade after the War. The War had demolished the rest of the industrial world. The world waited in line to buy whatever North America could produce. Everyone in America expected the good times to continue. Instead, came decline. What happened?

The U.S. has suffered ever-increasing deficit in trade for twenty years. Export of agricultural products has in the past helped to defray our deficit, but no longer. Customers that buy our wheat are complaining about dirt and poor quality. Imports of agricultural products to the U.S. are now equal to exports, and would show a deficit were figures on imports of illicit drugs available for the balance sheet.

The basic cause of the decline is that the quality of many American products is not competitive, and never was. Mass production, generations ago, was a contribution, from America toward better living the world over. Quantity was important; quality was not. Today, the problem in America is quality. The purpose here is to start to learn what to do to improve quality.

Devaluation of the dollar against the yen is a disappointment, as anyone could predict. If I wish to sell this table, and nobody wishes to buy it, reduction in price will not sell it.

Devaluation of the dollar is not the road to better business. Better quality is. We are in a completely different position than we were in during the good times after the War.

The ills of American industry come from wrong styles of management. Unfortunately, wrong styles of management move freely across the international borders.

Wrong styles of management and bad practices have grown up and taken root in the Western World. They must be blasted out and replaced by new construction, directed at quality and productivity. Emphasis in America has lately been on finance, the quarterly dividend, manipulation and maneuvering of assets. Traditional ways of doing business must change. For example, advances in quality require long-term relationships between customer and supplier, and abandonment of traditional ways of doing business on competition by price tag. Quality must be stable and capable, with continual improvement.

II. Examples of Bad Practice

Top management abandoning their responsibility for quality, occupied with finance, quarterly dividend, price of the company's stock, churning money, short-term planning, suboptimization.

Lack of policy for quality. Quality, if it is to exist, must be directed from the Board Room.

Quality requires operational definitions at every stage, including the requirements of quality for the customer. Quality requires organization for quality. Organization for quality requires profound knowledge of statistical theory.

Incentive pay

Doing business on price-tag, on the supposition that the performance of two items that meet the specifications will be equal and that competition solves all problems.

Detailed action on reports of people, quality, sales, complaint of a customer, overdue account, etc., instead of action in the board room directed at improvement.

The annual appraisal of performance, or the so-called merit system. Of all the forces of destruction that have beset American industry, this one has dealt the most powerful blow. It destroys people, our most important asset. Ways are clear toward better administration.

Management by objective. Management by the numbers.

The supposition that quality follows inevitably from hard work and best efforts.

The supposition that quality is assured by improvement of operations, solving problems, and stamping out fires.

III. Failure of Management to Accept Responsibility for Quality

There is prevalent the unfortunate supposition that improvement of quality is assured by improvement of operations. The truth is that all operations in a company may be carried on without blemish while the company fails, producing very well a product with no sale. It is a mistake to suppose that quality can be achieved solely by hard work, by best efforts, by improvement of operations, solving problems, stamping out fires.

Hard work will not ensure quality. It is necessary to understand the theory of management, then put forth best efforts. A theory of management now exists.

It is obvious that experience is not the answer. The U.S. ranks highest in experience, measured in man years. Experience by itself teaches nothing unless guided and compared with theory of subject-matter and statistical theory.

Gadgets, automation, computers, information power, robotic machinery, high technology, are not the answer, nor zero defects. Much new machinery turns out to be the source of headaches and high cost. Money will not buy quality. There is no substitute for knowledge. New machinery should be planned in accordance with the theory of management. The possibility to make changes to improve processes must be built in.

Satisfied customers are not the answer. A satisfied customer may switch. Profit and merit come from loyal customers. A loyal customer waits in line and brings a friend with him.

It is the obligation of the producer to foresee the needs of his customer, and to produce for him new design, new product, new service.

We in America have been sold down the river on competition. Competition in the right place is essential, but competition in America has been over-extended. Management of companies do not work together on common problems, fearful of the Anti-Trust Division. Worship of competition broke up the telephone system that we enjoyed, perhaps our only exhibit of world quality. We have now no telephone system, no one responsible for the quality of service.

From "On the Statistician's Contribution to Quality,"
presented at the meeting of the International
Statistical Institute, Tokyo,
September 8–11, 1987.

Perhaps the most controversial of Deming's ideas for improvement is to abolish the merit pay system that he referred to as a "destroyer of people." This article addresses the problems with annual appraisals of people and the need for better leadership instead.

The Merit System: The Annual Appraisal: Destroyer of People

The aim of this paper is elaboration of the third disease—the merit rating, annual appraisal of people in management. Many companies in America have systems by which everyone in management or in research receives from his superiors a rating every year. On the basis of this rating, employees are ranked for raises—for example, outstanding high, outstanding, etc., on down to unsatisfactory. Management by fear would be a better name. This practice, by destroying people, has successfully devastated Western industry. The basic fault of the annual appraisal is that it penalizes people for normal variation of a system.

The merit rating nourishes short-term performance, annihilates long-term planning, builds fear, demolishes teamwork, [and] nourishes rivalry and politics. It leaves people bitter, crushed, bruised, battered, desolate, despondent, dejected, feeling inferior, some even depressed, unfit for work for weeks after receipt of rating, unable to comprehend why they are inferior. It is unfair, as it ascribes to the people in a group differences that may be caused totally by the system that they work in.

The idea of a merit rating is alluring. The sound of the words captivates the imagination: pay for what you get; get what you pay for; motivate people to do their best, for their own good.

The effect is exactly the opposite of what the words promise. Everyone propels himself forward, or tries to, for his own good, on his own life preserver. The organization is the loser.

The merit rating rewards people that conform to the system. It does not reward attempts to improve the system. Don't rock the boat.

Moreover, a merit rating is meaningless as a predictor of performance, except for someone whose performance has placed him outside the system.

Traditional appraisal systems increase the variability of performance of people. The trouble lies in the implied preciseness of rating schemes. What happens is this. Somebody is rated below average, takes a look at people that are rated above average. He tries to emulate people above average. The result is impairment of performance.

More on Leadership

Good leadership requires investigation into possible causes that have placed someone outside the system. There is rational basis to predict that anyone outside the system on the good side will perform well in the future: he deserves recognition. The reasons why someone outside the system is on the bad side may be permanent; it may be ephemeral. Someone that can not learn the job would provide an example of a permanent cause. The company that hired him for this job, hence has a moral obligation to put him into the right job. Likewise, someone that is worried about his health, or about someone in the family, may show poor performance. Counseling will in some cases restore confidence and performance.

What about repetition of a pattern? What we are saying is that apparent differences—even huge differences—could be caused entirely by a constant cause system.

A useful criterion for recognition of outstanding performance is unquestionable demonstration of improvement year by year over a period of seven or more years, in skill, knowledge, leadership. The opposite criterion, namely, persistent deterioration over a period of seven years, may indicate people that are in need of help.

All this may be mere dreamland, because no group of people will all stay in the same jobs so long a time. In some applications, however, the period of time may be compressed, which it naturally will be with production-workers. For them, there may be data by the week on number of items produced. Seven or more successive weeks may give trustworthy indication of relative performance.

"It can't be all bad." Abolishment of the annual rating of performance is delayed by the top management in some quarters by refuge in the obvious corollary that "It can't be all bad. It put me into this position." This is a trap that is easy to fall into. Every man that I work with is in a high position and is great, worth working with and arguing with. He reached this position by coming out on top in every annual rating, at the ruination of the lives of a score of other men. There is a better way.

Modern Principles of Leadership

Modern principles of leadership will replace the annual performance review. The first step in a company will be to provide education in leadership. The annual performance review may then be abolished. Leadership will take its place. This is what Western management should have been doing all along.

The annual performance review sneaked in and became popular because it does not require anyone to face the problems of people. It is easier to rate them; focus on the outcome. What Western industry needs is methods that will improve the outcome. Suggestions follow.

1. Institute education in leadership; obligations, principles, and methods.
2. More careful selection of the people in the first place

3. Better training and education after selection

4. A leader, instead of being a judge, will be a colleague, counseling and leading his people on a day-to-day basis, learning from them and with them. Everybody must be on a team to work for improvement of quality.

5. A leader will discover who if any of his people is (a) outside the system on the good side, (b) outside on the poor side, (c) belonging to a system. The calculations required are fairly simple if numbers are used for measures of performance. (Books on the statistical control of quality explain the calculations.) Ranking of people (outstanding down to unsatisfactory) that belong to the system violates scientific logic and is ruinous as a policy.

   In the absence of numerical data, a leader must make subjective judgment. A leader will spend hours with every one of his people. They will know what kind of help they need. There will sometimes be incontrovertible evidence of excellent performance, such as patents, publication of papers, invitations to give lectures, recognition of peers.

   People that are on the poor side of the system will require individual help.

   Monetary reward for outstanding performance outside the system, without other more satisfactory recognition, may be counterproductive.

6. The people of a group that form a system will all be subject to the company's formula for raises in pay. This formula may involve (e.g.) seniority. It will not depend on rank within the group, as the people within the system will not be ranked No. 1, No. 2, No. Last. (In bad times, there may be no raise for anybody.)

7. Hold a long interview with every employee, three or four hours, at least once a year, not for criticism, but for help and better understanding on the part of everybody.

8. Figures on performance should be used not to rank the people in a group that fall within the system, but to assist the leader to accomplish improvement of the system. These figures may also point out to him some of his own weaknesses (Michael Dolan, Columbia University, March 1986).

   Improvement of the system will help everybody, and will decrease the spread between the figures for the performances of people.

   The day is here when anyone deprived of a raise or of any privilege through misuse of figures for performance (as by ranking the people in a system) may with justice file a grievance.

The Merit System: The Annual Appraisal:
Destroyer of People,
post 1986.

Monopolies have the best chance of any type of company to provide maximum service to the world, Deming believed. In this paper, Deming talks about monopolies, the U.S. anti-trust division, gives several examples of companies that were broken up and thereafter provided poorer service, and suggests a better role for monopolies and the U.S. antitrust division.

Myths on Competition and Monopolies

Let's think in terms of two worlds. In world one, the aim of the company or group of companies is to stay in business for the long term and to provide maximum benefit to themselves, their stockholders, their customers, their suppliers, and to society. In other words a company is a component in a system.

In this world, if a monopoly, or any two or more companies or institutions could dominate a market, any two of us, any six of us, would dominate a market. If we could put our heads together for uniform prices, we'd be fools to set the price a cent higher than what would optimize, in the long run, the whole system. We'd only drive business away. We should set the price as low as possible for our own benefit. We should see ourselves, our customers, suppliers, employees, environment and the communities that all these people work in as part of the system. They would only cheat themselves out of profit in the long run, if they set the price one cent higher than would optimize the whole system.

The function of the anti-trust division should be education, to explain this principle to achieve maximum benefits from monopolies and cartels. It would be far better than for them to spend their time searching for imaginary violators. Will they ever learn? Can we learn? Of course we can. Nonsense to say that we can't learn. But sure, it's different from what we've been taught. We've been sold down the river. Sure there should be an open forum on prices. Producers and consumers would work together on prices, to exchange figures and points of view. Any customer should have the privilege to review and protest a suggested price.

In world two, for the company's short-term profit, it sets the price as high as the traffic will buy and get out. Make a big profit and get out. Get over the border. A useful function of the anti-trust division would also be education here. Plus protection of society. Can't we learn? Of course we can learn.

A monopoly has the best chance to be of maximum service to the world. And has a heavy obligation to do so. Maximum service requires of course, enlightened management. The contributions to our welfare from monopolies have been great. We need think only of the contributions of the Bell Telephone Laboratories. A monopoly. Responsible to nobody. I passed by it twice yesterday; the building was at 463 Rush Street in New York. Just a building. A piece of real estate. In use. Nobody that passes by, I believe, knows what came out of that place. A monopoly. Responsible to nobody but themselves. They're owned 50/50 by AT&T and Western Electric. A monopoly. What would the world be without the Bell Telephone Laboratories as it was? All of us together could write down a long series of contributions. Harold Dodge, on inspection. Walter Shewhart, who gave to the world more than control charts. William Shockley and others gave us the transistor, out of which came the integrated circuit. We would not be here had it not been for the Bell Telephone Laboratories, a monopoly.

Everybody in the United States is an innocent victim of the anti-trust division. Think of the telephone system that we had, up until 1984. A monopoly it was. Our telephone system was the envy of the world. What have we now? Another wrong, I believe, of the anti-trust division was to break up years ago, AT&T and Western Union. They combined around 1902 or 1903.... When I first started teaching in New York University, 1946, the stone at 195 Broadway still read on it, "The American Telephone and Telegraph Company and The Western Union Company." They still had not changed the stone. The two together dominated communication. It is up to us to conclude that that's wrong. It may have been the best way.

The anti-trust division brought suit against MIT, Yale, Columbia, Harvard, for getting together on financial aid to students. Think of the benefit to students that the universities tried to bring about. The President of MIT may go to jail. His companion may be the president of Yale, as they both go to jail. We're trying to provide a service. They should be encouraged to get together. Think of the simplicity. How they could work together. And students, instead of shopping around, would know what to expect. Everybody would win. Can people of this country ever learn? Can we unlearn what's wrong? A serious question. Our life depends on it, whether we can learn or not.

It's not enough to be a monopoly. The monopoly must have an aim and be managed as a system. The components of the system cannot manage themselves. An example of a monopoly is the DeBeers consortium, which over a century, has dominated the supply of diamonds, and the prices of diamonds. They own the Kimberly mine. They consistently and persistently held the price of diamonds low and they found more and more uses for diamonds. Maybe the European community would be an example of cooperation. When you work it out.

Three automotive companies in this country had together in 1960 a virtual monopoly. The management of the three companies spent their time worrying about shared market. There's our piece of the pie. Our piece is this big. How can we make the piece bigger? Worrying about share of market. All three of them worrying about share of market. What would have been better? While they were worrying about share of market there were a million families in need of smaller, lighter, more dependable, more economical automobiles. While the three automotive companies worried about each other, a million people needed automobiles. The automotive companies sat by and worried about share of market. Not expansion of the market. What they should have done is sat together and worked on expansion of the market. The Japanese came in and did it. And Americans squealed and squawked. The U.S. Postal Service is not a monopoly. We have the worst postal service in the world. It cannot be blamed on the postal people. They cannot do a thing without Congress. Can anything be worse?

A public school in the United States was not a component in the system. Optimization is obstructed by a city superintendent, a county superintendent, a school board, district board, local government, county government, state board of education, federal government, assessment by standardized tests of pupils, comparison between districts and states. Any wonder why we have trouble with our education? We deserve what we have. We ask for it, we get it. Can people learn? Maybe. What's to stop us from learning? Education is worse than you thought it was. This country invented, gave to the world, high volume, mass production. Through the work of Frederick Taylor and Henry Ford, gave to the world high volume mass production. Those days are over. Mass production, high volume has moved out to Mexico, Taiwan, Korea, and other places. We're going to have to live by brains. Our education system is not supporting those brains, not producing those brains. How could it, under the system that we have? We're worse off than we thought we were.

From a presentation at General Motors,
July 1992.

Deming believed that quality and productivity must come from management and be companywide before QC-Circles could be effective, and that they would evolve naturally under receptive management. In this article he states that if companies try to start their improvement efforts with QC-Circles, it will delay improvement.

Productivity, Management, and QC-Circles

Summary

The major portion of responsibility for improvement of quality and productivity, to capture the market, and to stay in business, rests with management. This is obvious in the comparison between growth of productivity in Japan and growth of productivity in America, over the past 32 years. Japan and America stood in 1950 very unequal. America had all the advantages: raw materials, oil, iron, wood, ore, coal, plus the reputation for good quality. American products were in demand the world over. Japan had no resources except lessons in good management. Today, Japanese products have taken over the market in many lines of product. Good management is obviously the winner.

The possible contribution to productivity that factory workers can make to improvement in quality and productivity is limited, being possibly only 1/5th or 1/7th of the contribution that good management can make. This small fraction puts a ceiling on the contribution that QC-Circles can make to quality and productivity.

Moreover, little contribution from QC-Circles is possible except where the management is ready to act on recommendations of a Circle. The fact is that, in America, management is not ready.

Quality and productivity start with management, and must be company-wide, nation-wide, as Deming taught Japanese management in 1950. QC-Circles are the last step, not the first step, in improvement of quality and productivity. A company that starts with QC-Circles will delay years any substantial improvement of quality and productivity.

The first step is therefore good management. QC-Circles will follow naturally after good management is established.

Summary of a speech at the opening address of the
International Convention on QC-Circles,
Seoul, South Korea,
November 1982.

2

Quality Is Made in the Boardroom

(Only Top Management Can Make the Decisions Necessary to Assure Quality)

━━━◆━━━

Hundreds of thousands of workers are made redundant every year because of mass layoffs, companies going out of business, some mismanaging funds, and others just not knowing how to stay in business. What percentage of these layoffs was because of poor management is unknown. I doubt very many were because the workers weren't doing their jobs.

Deming often said that quality is made in the boardroom. The important decisions are made there. All the workers can do is follow the instructions they are given. They cannot change decisions, designs, or systems. They can only do their jobs.

This chapter starts out with two statements of the need for change, then a letter to the president of a large manufacturer with specific recommendations. The bulk of this chapter is in the last two sections, extracted from four-day seminars that Deming conducted in 1992.

In a 1990 speech at Western Connecticut State University in Danbury, Deming said, "Anytime you say something, people will give you ten reasons why you can't do it. What I want to hear is the one reason you're going to do it."

What Must We Do?

Better quality is necessary for the survival of industry in the Western World. American industry dominated the world from 1920 through the two decades after World War II. Now it lies in a state of slumber.

The rest of the world waited in line after World War II to buy whatever North America could produce. Why? The rest of the industrialized world lay in ruins. Everyone in the U.S. expected the good times to continue. What happened? Why?

The answer is that the quality of most American products has been found wanting, not competitive. Emphasis in the U.S. is still on quantity, not on quality. Devaluation of the dollar against the yen is a disappointment, as anybody could predict. Lower prices against the yen will not produce a market for goods that nobody wishes to buy. Most American products are simply not salable at any price. Devaluation of the dollar is not the road to better business. Better quality is. We are in a completely different position than we were in up till around 1960.

What must we do? Better quality for international trade is the answer, not restrictions to trade, nor self-pity, nor the beggar's cup. The U.S. has already installed more restrictions to trade than any other country, second only to France. Costs go down and productivity goes up, as improvement of quality is accomplished by better management of design, engineering, testing, and by improvement of processes. Better quality at lower price has a chance to capture a market. Cutting costs without improvement of quality is futile.

Quality and innovation. Quality is improved in three ways: through innovation in design of a product or service, through innovation in processes, and through improvement of existing processes. [In later writings Deming added a fourth way: through improvement of existing product or service.] Hard work will not ensure quality. Best efforts will not ensure quality, and neither will gadgets, computers or investment in machinery. A necessary ingredient for improvement of quality is the application of profound knowledge. There is no substitute for knowledge. Knowledge we have in abundance. We must learn to use it.

Styles of management. Wrong styles of management, with concomitant bad practices have grown up and taken root in the western world. They become obvious under the theory that reduction in variation improves a product. Theory of variation (statistical theory) helps to identify practices of management that induce variation, high cost, and poor quality, with consequent loss of market. The same theory points to better practices.

I have for years noted appropriate practices for management; here I will list some of the faulty management practices.

The wrong style of management.

- *Management of failure* (too late). It is better to work on the causes of failure. Failures are not causes; they come from causes.
- *Tampering with a stable system.* For example, track down anything that goes wrong with a product or service. This policy does not improve the system. It is tampering, worsening the problem.
- *Compile a list or chart to show percentages right or percentages of product or service that went wrong last month.*
- *Annual appraisal of performance, the so-called merit system* – a destroyer of people.
- *Annual rating of divisions.* (A manager of a division is rewarded on the basis of this rating.)
- *Campaign to reduce costs*—as if costs were causes.
- *Incentive pay, commissions and bonuses.*
- *Top management failing to understand their responsibility for quality, for innovation of product and processes and for improvement of processes.* Quality starts in the boardroom.
- *Short-term planning and quick profit.*
- *Churning money.*

- *Competition without cooperation.* Getting a bigger slice of the pie, but not making the pie bigger.
- *Doing business by price tag.*
- *Short-term contracts.*
- *Management by objectives (MBO) or management by the numbers.*
- *Investment in gadgets, computers, automation and new machinery without guidance of profound knowledge.*
- *Posters and slogans for the workforce.*
- *Work standards—quotas.* They double the cost of production, rob people of pride of workmanship and are a barrier to improvement.

From "The Need for Change,"
Journal for Quality and Participation,
March 1987.

The Need for Change

Where are we? The answer is that the good economic times have leveled off. The problem is quality. The possibility to improve the future under the present system of management is slight. The present system runs by the economics of WIN, LOSE: I WIN, YOU LOSE. I CAN WIN ONLY IF YOU LOSE. There is no more free land. The sacred cow (WIN, LOSE) has run dry.

We need a transformation to a new kind of economics where everyone comes out better: COOPERATION, WIN, WIN. There will be inequalities and some people will win more than others, but everyone will gain. For instance, there is worldwide recognition of the color of traffic lights, the system of time derived from Greenwich Mean Time, and metric measurement. All these benefits are the result of COOPERATION, WIN,

WIN. Examples abound, but the new economics are not yet a way of life in North America.

What is at the heart of the transformation? It is the release of the power of intrinsic motivation. How? By creating joy, pride, happiness in work; joy and pride in learning. Two changes are required:

1. Change the system of reward. Everybody loses under the system that nourishes the WIN, LOSE philosophy and the race to be number one. We must abolish the merit system and systems of incentive, as they choke intrinsic motivation. We must develop leadership and participation.
2. Create leaders with attributes that work to help their people, who know how the work of the group fits in to the aims of the company, that focus on the internal and external customers, and who understand variation and use statistical calculation to determine if there are people outside the system in need of special help.

Management's new job is to accomplish the change required. Yet people fear change and ask "Where would change leave me?" When everyone has a part in the change, fear of change will vanish. It helps to paddle the canoe.

Management must not only transform the system of reward, but must also take responsibility for the transformation to the new economics.

There are four prongs of quality and four ways to improve quality of product and service:

1. Innovation in product and service
2. Innovation in process
3. Improvement of existing product and service
4. Improvement of existing process

The common mistake is the supposition that quality is ensured by No. 4, improvement of process, that operations going off without blemish on the factory floor, in the bank, in the hotel will ensure quality. Good operations are essential, yet they do not ensure quality. Quality is made in the boardroom.

A bank that failed last week may have had excellent operations—speed at the tellers' windows with few mistakes; few mistakes in bank statements; likewise in the calculation of interest and of penalties and loans. The cause of failure at the bank was bad management, not operations.

Here is an example of wrong management thinking: "Our people in the plants are responsible for their own product and quality. We expect them to act like owners."

WIN, LOSE is the wrong philosophy, and as a business strategy it often merely seeks to choke the competition. Although it was an efficient tactic in an ever-expanding market, the principle of I WIN ONLY IF YOU LOSE has run out of steam. The days of an ever-expanding market that we knew so well are over and will not be seen again until we change. We need to learn to live and work in the world that now envelops us.

Business survival in the western world is dependent on transformation to the new economics of COOPERATION, WIN, WIN. And once the transformation is made, the course of western industry will move forward and upward.

From "The Need to Change," TQC World,
Texas Instruments Semiconductor Group,
February 1989.

In this memorandum to the president of a large manufacturer, Deming lines up some agenda items for consideration at their next meeting.

Suggestions for discussion at our next meeting:

1. The whole world knows about Ford's success in quality. The big lesson to the world is that you yourself led the system of improvement. My fondest wish is for Ford to be a model to copy in every respect. Suggestions follow.

2. This memorandum is concerned with never ending and continual improvement of quality. Productivity is also important, but productivity follows inevitably from success in pursuit of quality in all its aspects.

    This chain reaction was on the blackboard of every meeting with top management in Japan from July 1950 onward.

    Improve quality → Costs decrease because of less rework, fewer mistakes, fewer delays, snags; better use of machine-time and materials → Productivity Improves → Capture the market with better quality and lower price? Stay in business → Provide jobs and more jobs

3. Quality can not be delegated. A company with a manager of quality by any name is stuck in the mire.

    Wrong way:

    An office of quality, by any name. For example, a Vice President in charge of quality.

    Manager of quality.

    Manager of quality control.

    It is important to note that your Office of Statistical Methodology is not an office of quality, nor of quality assurance.

4. Cut costs; cut waste. This sounds like good management. What is wrong? Anybody can cut costs, and multiply losses in other divisions. For example, purchase of materials on price tag, cut maintenance, use a cheaper polymer, cheaper inserts, omit an operation, discontinue guidance of profound knowledge. Results (and I can cite examples): sales drop. The

customer perceives the difference. A project or program to cut costs is management downstream, at the far end, too late, as if costs were causes. It is management of defects, an interesting pastime, tampering, tinkering, increasing costs overall.

It is better for management to work on causes of cost and waste, to work at sources. This means improvement of design, care and maintenance of equipment, materials, processes, care and maintenance of people, training and education. Costs will decrease with success in these endeavours; productivity will go up.

5. Hard work will not ensure quality, nor best efforts. Experience, noble intents, wishful thinking, do not ensure quality.

   The President of a company delegated quality to his plant managers. A plant manager, with all his duties, can not possibly know what quality is, nor do anything about it if he did know. The only thing that he can do without help and guidance of profound knowledge is to conform to specifications, to achieve zero defects: down the tube we go.

   Conformance to specifications is not quality. Certainly no one would deliberately violate specifications, but conformance to specifications will not ensure quality. Zero defects is not quality. Quality is much more complex than zero defects.

   How many heads of divisions are rated on conformance to specifications, and not at all on improvement of problems of management? Could anything be worse?

6. Investment in gadgets, high technology, automation, new machinery, are not by themselves the answer. Expenditures must be guided with profound knowledge. Money alone will not buy quality.

   It sometimes turns out, in fact, that when a recommendation for new equipment is studied with care and knowledge, no new investment is needed. It is better in any case to first learn to use the machinery and technology on hand.

7. Promise of increase in pay to be based on increase in productivity is beating the wrong horse. Incentive-pay ruined the

steel business in the U.S. It can ruin any company. As noted earlier, increase in productivity follows inevitably from successful pursuit of quality in all its aspects.

I realize that there are other problems, such as work rules.

8. Performance on the factory floor needs help of management. People on the factory floor can not penetrate the ceiling of performance that is defined and limited by the environment-design of product, equipment, its maintenance, processes, procedures, faults with incoming materials, training, education, etc.

All that the people on the factory floor (and in management, too) ask for is a chance to work with pride. How many people have this privilege? 2%? Production will go up

with better quality of design

with better incoming materials

with less variation in incoming materials

with better care and protection of machines and equipment
   (less down time, fewer emergencies, modification)

with improvement of processes

with expert attention to systems of measurement. (What proportion of gauges and instruments show statistical control? Someone estimated 1 in 30.)

with better care and protection of people

with training, retraining, and education.

9. Improvement of operations, however essential, can have only limited effect on quality, still less on innovation and new products. Quality is limited by the intent, instruction, and leadership of top management.

An example is the Continental-Illinois Bank of Chicago. It was the seventh largest bank in the country, continuance of which in some form was essential for the country. What happened?

Sailing was smooth for years. Winds gentle. Then the bank somehow moved into shallow water, rocky coast; heavy winds came up. The bank was in trouble.

Did the trouble come from operations? Sluggishness and mistakes at the tellers' windows? Mistakes in bank statements? Mistakes in calculation of interest and penalties on loans? No. Even had the operations in the bank been carried off without blemish, the trouble would have been the same. As a matter of fact, operations in this bank were excellent. The trouble came from the management.

10. Need for investment and improvement of people. Protection of investment in equipment is important, to be sure. Protection and investment in people is more important. It is pleasing to note that you are initiating a Center for Education and Training, the purpose of which will be to improve consistency of understanding and of effort throughout the company. People are saying different things, everyone trying to understand the new philosophy, but sometimes working at cross purposes. Your buyers sing one song, suppliers sing another, people in management of production still another. The Center will help to establish common understanding and consistency, yet be creative.

Consistency of understanding is especially essential amongst the people in top management.

11. For example, there is the matter of education in statistical thinking, a prime function of the Office of Statistical Methodology. It is too big to tackle in one memorandum, but here are a few points.

For top management, including finance, legal, personnel, education in the new Philosophy. Suggestion: my 4-day seminar. Alternate possibility: ten stretches, each of about two hours, under a master: a week or two apart. Better, eight half days, a week or two apart. Continuing education in monthly sessions.

For middle management, the same, supplemented by examples from your own company. Continuation with monthly sessions provided by people on the line, people that belong to the Office of Statistical Methodology and by others or by anybody.

For research, development, engineers, my 4-day seminar. Continuation.

Supervisory level, 20 hours, with continuation for refreshment.

As continuation of the above paragraphs, I may add that it has been a long time since I have had the pleasure to work directly with some of your top people. Meanwhile, much has been learned. I suggest that a way be found for regular contact.

From a memorandum to Donald E. Petersen,
Chairman of the Board and Chief Executive Officer of
Ford Motor Company,
September 22, 1987.

Present Practices and Better Practices

One time in one of my four-day seminars a man arose and asked, "Where's the crisis?" He was from the aircraft industry. "We and our competitors," he said, "have 70 percent of the world's business. Where's the crisis?" My answer was "You, in strong position, are in the best position to improve, and have the greatest obligation to improve."

Customer Expectations

People talk about customers' expectations. What do they mean by that? Seems to me that the customer has no expectations. The customer does not generate anything. The customer has only what you and your competitor have led him to expect.

No customer asked for electric lights. We have gas mantles, a good
   light. What need would there be for electric lights?
No customer asked for photography. No customer asked for the
   telegraph, or for a telephone. No customer asked for an automobile. No customer asked for pneumatic tires. No customer
   asked for facsimile.

All those come from the producer, not from the customer. And
the producer has to watch out for the customers. He cannot be
a producer unless he has customers. Customers keep him alive.
They give him purpose in life. The producer must think, "What
will help the customer? What would he be willing to buy?" The
customer again has only what you and your competitors have
led him to expect. Those are his expectations. What you have
taught him.

He's a rapid learner. An educated customer may have a firm
idea about his needs. What he may wish to purchase. He may
be able to specify these needs so that a supplier may understand
him. A wise customer, though, will listen to the supplier. Listen
to the suggestions of the supplier. In other words, they work
together as a system.

Is it sufficient to have happy customers? You certainly don't
want unhappy customers. But is it sufficient to have happy
customers? Loyal customers? The kind that come back, wait
in line? It's not enough.

Where today are the makers of carburetors? They are gone.
Maybe carburetors are used on motorcycles. I can't verify it.
Twenty-five years ago, automobiles had a carburetor. How could
it run without one? Not anymore. Not even on heavy trucks anymore. What happened? Came the fuel injector. It costs more
than a carburetor. But it does a lot more. The makers of carburetors went out of business, in the space of about a year. They were
flourishing one day and a year later, they were out of business.

They were in the business of making carburetors. That's where they failed. They did a good job making carburetors. Continual improvement in carburetors. Lower and lower cost. They had happy customers. What else could this world ask for? But now they're gone. You see the trouble is, the makers of carburetors were in the business of making carburetors. They didn't look into the future. What ought we to be making five years from now? Ten years from now?

The Business That We're in Must Include the Future

What ought we to be doing five years from now? Ten years from now? To do a good job today is not enough. The makers of carburetors should have considered themselves in business to put a stoichiometric mixture of fuel and air into a combustion chamber. What's the best way to do that? They didn't think that way. They thought in terms of carburetors. And went out of business. Where today are the makers of vacuum tubes? They're gone, too. They did not look ahead. The integrated circuit and pocket radio came along.

A good question to ask anybody in business is "What business are we in?" To do well what we are doing, to turn out a good product, good service, whatever it be. Yes, of course. But that's not enough. Let's keep asking it: "What product or service will help our customers more?" You must think about the future. If you have no defects, will that keep you in business? Something more is required.

Why does a plant close? Shoddy workmanship? Inefficiency? No, no, that's not the reason. Probably because there's not enough demand for that product. The plant's no longer profitable. Did the wrong thing, in other words. And nothing there to take its place. What else can you do but close the plant?

Why does a bank close? Ever heard of a bank that closed? Why did it close? Mistakes at the tellers' windows? Sluggishness at the tellers' windows? Mistakes in bank statements? Mistakes in calculations of interest on loans? Nonsense. All those operations could go off without blemish and the bank could close just the same. Bad loans. That's why it closed. Where's quality made? In the board room, at the top. There's where quality is made. Jobs are dependent on management's foresight to design products and services to entice customers, and build a market. To be ready ahead of the customer.

A Flow Diagram

I want to point out the advantage, the need, of a flow diagram. You can draw a flow diagram for your job. And that's the first step. See what your job is. I'll take, for an example, one in service, the Sacred Heart League of Memphis. One of their aims is to provide medical care and food to impoverished, indigent children in four counties adjacent to Memphis in the state of Mississippi. This purpose requires money. You can't provide medical care and food to those children without money. Where do you get money? The league appeals to people on mailing lists.

First of all, the zero stage. The idea is in somebody's head. The most important stage—the zero stage, generation of ideas. For a message, to go out, by mail, to the public. You may say that mail is not the only way to reach the public. Well, you're right. At this time it goes out by mail. The message will explain the purpose of the endeavor. And it will ask for donations. The purpose is to supply medical care and food to impoverished indigent children in those four counties in the state of Mississippi adjacent to Memphis.

Stage 1. Those ideas are put on paper. Sentences written out.

Stage 2. Then printed on sheets of paper. Make them one page, maybe two.

Stage 3. Machines fold the papers. Put them in envelopes. Address the envelopes. To the post office they go. The post office delivers them. At least some of them. And some people send money. Money's received by the Sacred Heart League. Acknowledged with thanks. And the money's used for food and medicine.

If the aim was to get money, how would you measure the quality of these operations? Well you could say by the amount of money that comes in. This time we could measure it. We shall learn that for most losses and gains there is no measure. But this time there is. The amount of money that comes in could be a measure of the quality of the operations. What's the main determinant of the money that comes in?

The message. The message on those sheets of paper. That's what determines the quality of the job. That's what determines the amount of money that comes in. Whose responsibility is that? The people who fold the sheets of paper? Don't be silly. The post office? Don't be silly. Who's responsibility is that message? Father Bob's. It's his responsibility. Can't blame it on anybody else. It's his job. And that message is the determinant. All else can go off without blemish.

There is another measure of quality you might be concerned with. How the league spends money. Do they find the most impoverished children? Do they provide medical care in the best way they can with the limited funds that they have? And food? How do they spend the money? That would be another measure of quality. But that you cannot measure. There's no way to measure it.

The most important losses cannot be measured.

The Heavy Losses

The present style of management is the biggest producer of waste, causing huge losses. The magnitude cannot be evaluated. It is these losses that must be managed. Let's identify the most important sources of loss—waste. And suggestions for better practice. Unnecessary paperwork is a serious loss. Have any unnecessary paperwork on your job?

Someone, with the name of Dr. Stewart Rice, observed forty years ago that reports in industry are easy to start. No one ever heard of a report being abolished. Unnecessary paperwork, a serious loss. A lot of it originates in management's supposition [for a need]. Is the cure for repetition of a mistake or fraud more audit, or more inspection? A letter to the London Times, dated July 7th, 1990, displayed the fact that 23 percent of the cost of running a hospital in the United States is for paperwork, against 5 percent in the United Kingdom. Which hospital would you rather be in? You'd rather not be in either one, of course.

Make this quarter look good. It may be that quarterly reports required by the Federal Trade Commission and the Securities and Exchange Commission build hot fires under these evil practices. Maybe you can blame it on the government.

By what method? Can you measure the losses from short-term thinking? No, of course not. But that's the kind of thing we must manage. Can you measure the loss from shipping everything on hand? Make this month look good, make this quarter look good? Defer maintenance till next quarter? Defer orders till next quarter? Can you measure the effect? No. But those are the losses we must manage. Short-term solutions have long-term effects.

Differences there will always be between any two people. The question is what do the differences mean? Maybe nothing. Statistical theory is required to answer these questions.

There's also the Pygmalion effect. Once somebody gets a high rating he'll always get it; once somebody gets a low rating he'll always get it. Ranking creates competition between people, salesmen, teams, divisions. The competition is demoralizing. Ranking comes from failure to understand variation.

Performance of the individual cannot be measured, except on a long-term basis, for which I mean 15, 18, 20 years. Are top salesmen causing serious loss? Do they do more harm to the company than anybody else? Maybe from overselling. For example, selling to the customer a bigger copier machine than the customer needs. The salesman gets more commission that way. Gets more sales dollars. The customer grumbles. Because the salesman tricked him. Sold him a bigger machine than he needed. The customer tells his friend about it, grumbles. The company loses eventually. The salesman may have sold to the customer a smaller copier machine than the customer needs under the excuse that the customer does not have enough money to buy the right one. So the salesman sells him a machine that is too small on the theory that it's better to get some sale than nothing at all. And the customer learns in due time he bought too small a machine. He's unhappy. He grumbles, tells his friends about it. You get all this reaction against the company. How much? Nobody knows. You cannot measure these types of losses. But they are the ones we must manage.

Tampering

Management by results. Take immediate action on any fault, mistake, defect, complaint, delay, accident, breakdown. Take immediate action, do something. Action on the last data point. Wrong. A great temptation but it's wrong. What we need to do is work on the process that produced that fault, defect, and complaint. Sure, take care of the complaint of a customer. Clear it away, never mind the cost of it. Take care of the customer, certainly. What's wrong? Management by results is not the way to get good results; it is the way to get worse results. Work on causes, not on results. This kind of management is tampering.

In the case of Management by Results, it is better to understand and improve the system.

> Example: Senior manager to a plant manager, eight o' clock every morning: "What was your production yesterday?" One thing's sure: it's either higher or lower than it was the day before. So what? That's not the way to get results. That kind of information is useless. Sure we need to have figures, and use them. But, yesterday's production compared to the day before is not going to tell you anything.
>
> Another example: Worker training worker in succession. A better way is to entrust the training to one person, preferably someone who knows the work and is a good teacher. It is true that he who is on the job knows more than anyone about it. But worker training worker in succession takes us off into the Milky Way. We're talking about a skill, we're not talking about education, self-improvement, learning.

Be careful about the use of figures. You could make a list of the companies that are doing well with bad business practices. They are plain lucky. Having products that sold, and great engineers, in spite of bad management. Turn out wonderful products in spite of bad practices.

Conversely, you could make a list of companies that are trying to do better. They've been to this seminar several times, have learned, and they're trying to do better. Trying to abolish bad practices, and NOT doing well.

Common sense tells us that if an item or service fails to meet requirements, take action, do something about it. And do it now.

Do what? Action will only produce more mistakes. It's important to work on the process that produces that fault. Not in him that delivered it. Common sense tells us to reward the salesman of the month, the one who sold the most. Actually, you may be doing great harm to the company.

A furniture store took its salesmen off commission and put them on salary. Results: sales ... up, up, up. Every month was better than the month before. Salesmen now will try to understand the customer. Older salesmen help the younger fellows. They work together. When they were on commission, no salesman would help another one. How could he? Don't be silly. The salesman now takes time to go to the warehouse and try to work with people in the warehouse. Diminish scratches and breakage and make sure the customer buys what he needs. Will his furniture fit into his home? Is it the right thing for him to buy? And sales go up. The salesmen now work for the customer. The company wins, everybody wins.

Numerical goals

A numerical goal is a number drawn out of the sky. A numerical goal outside the control limit cannot be accomplished without changing the system. A numerical goal accomplishes nothing. What counts is *by what method*. Three words. If you can accomplish a goal without a method, then why weren't you doing it last year? There's only one possible answer: you were goofing off. May the numerical goal be achieved? Yes. We can make almost anything happen. But what about the cost? What about the loss? Anybody can achieve almost anything by distortion and faking, redefinition of terms, running up costs.

An example: The manager of a grocery store has allowed 1 percent shrinkage. And he needs it. How'd he do it? Well, one way. A load of goods comes in the back of the store. You take two people off the cash registers at the front, take them to the back of the store to count cases, compare labels on the cases with contents, compare contents with invoices. Make sure we don't get charged for goods we did not receive. And what happens? Lines build up at the front of the store because of the two cashiers missing. People grumble. They swear they won't come back to this store because of the long wait at the cashier.

The manager of the store may discontinue certain fruits and vegetables that are slow movers. Danger of spoilage at the end of the day. So he doesn't put them in stock. A customer comes in to buy one of them. "No such thing on hand today." Customer grumbles. Declares he'll go to some other store next time. He won't come back to this one.

The manager can buy up fat. Fat is cheap. Now the meat is 1 percent shrinkage. Some customers become aware of it. They go elsewhere thereafter for their business. The store manager knows 55 other ways to help meet that 1 percent shrinkage, and every one of them loses customers. But he makes his 1 percent shrinkage. He had to be pretty smart to do it. Can you blame him? Can you blame him for doing his job? That's his job.

The worst example of numerical goals came out of our own Department of Education. We did it. On the 18th of April, 1991: Numerical goals. No method. No method suggested. Just numerical goals drawn out of the sky. Such nonsense in high places. Think of the harm done by those numerical goals put out by our Department of Education. Unwitting, innocent people read them and do not understand what is wrong. The harm done cannot be measured. The high school graduation rate will increase to 90 percent. Why stop at 90? If you don't have to have a method, why not make it 95? 98?

Every school free of drugs. We should hope so, but where's the method?

And we decided that American schools were expected to produce extraordinary gains in student learning. Performance standards. Could anything be worse? Individual schools that make notable progress deserve to be rewarded. Do they? What would happen?

From presentation at a seminar for CEOs,
"Quality, Productivity, and Competitive Position,"
1992.

A System of Profound Knowledge

The layout of profound knowledge appears in four parts, all related to each other, not separate:

i. Appreciation for a system.
ii. Some knowledge about variation.
iii. Theory of knowledge—vital.
iv. Psychology.

One need not be eminent in any part of profound knowledge in order to understand it and apply it. The 14 points of management—in my book, *Out of the Crisis*, chapter 2. In industry, education and government follow naturally the application of the system of profound knowledge. The transformation from the present style of Western management to one of optimization. The various segments of the system of profound knowledge interact with each other. Thus, knowledge of psychology is incomplete without knowledge of variation. The managers of people need to understand that all people are different. That's not ranking them. That's taking account of their differences: family background, education, special capabilities, their hopes.

I. A System

We've learned that a system must have an aim. Without an aim there's no system. The aim of a system must be clear to everybody. The system of schools—public schools, private schools, parochial schools, trade schools, universities, for example. They are not merely pupils, teachers, school boards, boards of regents and parents. It should be instead a system of education in which pupils, from toddlers on up, take joy in learning. Free from fear of grades and gold stars. A system in which teachers take joy in their work. Free from fear of ranking. It should be a system that recognizes the differences between pupils. Sure, the pupils are different. That's not ranking them. There are differences between teachers. Such a system of schools would be destroyed if some group of schools decided to ban together to lobby for their own special interest. The components of the system need not all be clearly defined. People need only do what needs to be done. Management of a system therefore requires knowledge of the interrelationships between all the components within the system. And of the people that work in it.

Optimization is orchestrating efforts of all components in the system to achievement of an aim. We've also learned the main job of management is to generate and enhance positive interactions between components. And to change the signs of negative interactions into positive ones. Again, why is your company not equal, not as good as the sum of the individual efforts of the people in it? It ought to be that, and better. Why is it less? Negative interactions. Competition between people, between groups, between platforms.

A system must be managed. A system will not manage itself. Time will bring changes. It must be managed. It must be predicted so far as possible. Growth in size and complexity of a system, change over time, external forces such as competition, new products, and new requirements will require ongoing management of efforts of components. Management and leaders have still another job: namely to govern their own future. Not to be merely victims of circumstances.

Instead of taking loss from spurts in production to meet spurts in demand, followed by lower demand, and so on, repeating peaks and valleys, it might be better to flatten production. Or to increase production at an economical rate. Another possibility is to become agile and efficient in meeting peaks and valleys of demand.

A flow diagram is actually an organization chart. It shows how the different components, each with its expert knowledge, work together for the gain of all. If the components become competitive, the system is destroyed. Everybody loses. National planning is not necessarily management of a system; it has so far been instead devoid of knowledge about a system. Or worse, aimed at welfare of isolated entities. In almost any system there is interdependence among components. The greater the interdependence between components, the greater be the need for communication and cooperation between them.

I held a meeting with 40 people in a company. Everybody there worked with or for somebody else there. In the room were customers and suppliers. People should have been working together. They never talked with each other. Nobody understood; nobody talked with anybody else to see how his work fit in. Why don't people talk to each other? What holds them back? Are they afraid? Why should that be? It doesn't make any sense. But when people don't talk to each other, they cannot understand what the job is.

Efforts of the various divisions in a company, each given a job, are not additive. Their efforts are interdependent. One division to achieve its goal may, left to itself, kill off another division.

An example of a system well-optimized is a good orchestra. The players are not there to play solos, like prima donnas, each one trying to catch the ear of the listener. Each of the 140 players in the Royal Philharmonic Orchestra, London, is there to support the other 139. An orchestra is judged by listeners, not so much by illustrious players, but by the way they work together. That's what counts.

The obligation of any component is to contribute its best to the system. It's not to maximize its own profit, production, sales, or savings. Some components may operate at a loss. For example, the travel department. Not send people at the cheapest rate, but to think of the company as a whole. What's the best way for that person to travel? What's best for the company as a whole?

What about basis for negotiation? Optimization for everyone. Concern should be the basis for negotiation between any two people, between divisions, between union and management, between competitors, between countries. Everybody would gain.

In summary, the obligation of any component is to contribute its best to the system. But it will not do that unless the system is managed. A system will not manage itself. Some components may operate at a loss to themselves in order to optimize the whole system.

II. Variation

There's more variation and more need for knowledge of variation than maybe you ever thought. For example, should a teacher know something about variation? Why does a teacher need to know anything about variation?

An example: Mr. Hero Hacquebord sent his six-year-old daughter to school. She came home in a few weeks with a note from the teacher. The teacher had thus far given two tests and this little girl was below average in both tests. Warning to the parents: trouble lies ahead. Other parents received the same note and were worried. They wished to believe Mr. Hacquebord's words of comfort, that such comparisons meant nothing, but they were afraid to believe him. Other parents received notes. For example, one little boy was above average in both tests. Prepare for genius coming up. One little girl was above average on the first test, sank below average on the second test—declining. The news affected Mr. Hacquebord's daughter adversely. Only six years old. She was humiliated. Think of it. Inferior. Below average in both tests. She recovered. What if she had not recovered? A life lost. How many children were affected and had not the benefit of remedial education? Nobody knows. Think of the harm that the teacher accomplished. Not understanding variation. With 32 in the class, some were going to be below average in both tests. Some would be above average in both tests. Some would go from below average to above. Some would sink from above average to below. Inevitable. Of course, inevitable.

Management of people requires knowledge of the effect of the system on the performance of people.

A company requires the help of profound knowledge. And as a good rule, profound knowledge comes from outside. And by invitation from someone eager to listen. A system cannot understand itself. A system cannot understand itself.

III. Theory of Knowledge

The course in the theory of knowledge is the most important course you ever took, I believe. Theory of knowledge helps us to understand that management in any form is prediction. The simplest plan: how may I get myself home tonight? requires prediction. Prediction that my automobile will start and run. Or that the bus will come, or the train. You see, any plan is prediction. Any assumption is prediction. Well you say, "I believe that," "I assume that," "I'm predicting." Management is prediction. And with the risk of being wrong, the theory of knowledge teaches us that a statement, if it conveys knowledge, predicts future outcome, with the risk of being wrong. What do our schools teach? Our schools teach information, not knowledge. Information is handy. But it is not knowledge. The dictionary has information in it and I use the dictionary. Frequently. Sometimes a French dictionary or a German dictionary.

The dictionary will not write a paragraph. It contains information. Very handy. But not knowledge. I'm afraid our schools teach information. How do you pass an examination? You cram your head full of information. Not knowledge. Rational prediction requires theory and builds knowledge through systematic revision and extension of theory based on comparison of prediction with varied short-term and long-term results. The barnyard rooster, Chanticleer [from French fable], had a theory. He crowed every morning, putting forth all his energy, flapped his wings, the sun came up. The connection was clear. Very obvious, wasn't it? His crowing caused the sun to come up. That was his conclusion. No question about his importance. Then came the snag: he forgot one morning to crow. The sun came up nonetheless. Crestfallen, he saw his theory was in need of revision. But without his theory he would not have learned. He would have had nothing to revise. He wouldn't have learned. With a theory he had a chance to learn. Break down of his theory taught him he had to revise his theory, come through with another theory.

Plane Euclidean geometry served the world well for a flat Earth. Every corollary, every theorem had been correct in that world. But use of a theory for a flat Earth fails when man extends his horizons to bigger buildings. Our distance from here over to the tech center. Theory for a flat Earth breaks down. Parallel lines north and south are no longer equidistant. Angles of a triangle no longer add up to 180 degrees. Add up to 180 plus spherical excess. We have to revise the geometry that we use. But the geometry of the flat Earth is nevertheless correct for a flat Earth.

The Earth *is* flat. Anyone with doubt about the Earth being flat should take a ride on a clear day from Chicago to Urbana. The Earth is flat.

Theory is a window into another world. Theory leads to prediction. Without prediction experience and examples teach nothing. Experience teaches nothing without theory. It's only by theory that you have experience. It's only with theory that experience teaches anything.

To copy an example of success, without understanding the success with the aid of theory may lead to disaster. Any rational plan, however simple, is prediction concerning conditions, behavior, performance of people, procedures, equipment, [and] materials. Prediction of the behavior of the customer. Interpretation of data from an experiment is prediction.

No number of examples establishes a theory. Yet a single unexplained failure of a theory requires modification, or even abandonment of a theory. Chanticleer had to revise his theory. The sun came up, even though he did not crow. He had to revise his theory.

There's no true value of any characteristic that's defined in terms of measurement or observation. There's no true value for the number of people in this room. There's a number that you get by carrying out a procedure. Change the procedure, you get a new number. The question is whom do you count? Do you count people on the stage? Do you count people working on the sound and visual equipment? Sure they're important. But do you count them? Do you count people who are not attending the seminar but are simply working here? Do you count somebody out there drinking coffee? Or somebody on the telephone? Do you count him or don't you? There's no true value for the number of people in this room? There's a number that you get by carrying out a procedure. Change the procedure, you get a new number. Any two people have different ideas about what is important to include in the count.

There is a true value for the number of prime numbers under 100: 1,2,3,5,7,11 … Any of us can do it. Anybody can count them. But that's information. Nothing but empirical observation. It predicts nothing.

On Wednesday night, after the date of the census, which is the first of April in our country, on the next Wednesday night at ten o'clock, an army of census workers descend on every mission, shelter and flophouse, to count the men there. Never any women. You know what that costs? 100 dollars for every one that you add. What about people sleeping in the street over the grate? In the park? In the subway? How do you count them? You can try. Costs you 200 dollars for every name that you add. The number of people in an area depends on how much money you want to spend. Spend more money, get more people. How much is it worth? But there are other ways to count people that will be used in the next census.

The Canadian government knows how many Canada geese there are. Now the geese don't line up when you count them, five, ten, fifteen. No, they're pretty smart. The way you used to count them is to snag 300 geese. Tag them, put a ring around his foot, with a place and date. Sometime later, when the geese are pretty well mixed up, you snag a few hundred, count the number that have rings on their feet. With a little multiplication you have an estimated number of Canada geese. I think it's far refined beyond that now. I think you count people the same way. Next census it will be done that way. Our last census would have been done that way, except for political reasons. Dr. Barbara Bailor left the Census. She would not have some politician dictate to her what she should do.

I was in Tokyo. Came a telegram from Bernise, on Madison Avenue, Young and Rubicam. They were carrying out a national survey that I had designed. They carried out this study three times every year. The telegram asked this question: "Please tell us what to do with Trailor Camps." I sent a telegram back, "Follow the Census procedures." Did I make it right? No, there's no right or wrong. But by following the Census procedures your figures will be comparable with the Census figures. Might be some advantage. The rules are simple. If the inhabitants of a trailer have been here 10 days or more they belong to this precinct. It doesn't matter if they move on tomorrow. As of today they belong to this precinct. If they've been here less than 10 days, the question is "Are you on your way to somewhere? Do you have a destination?" If yes, then they're allocated to that destination. If they have no destination in mind, then they belong to this precinct, even though they've only been here 2 days. Does that make it right? No, there's no right or wrong. Those are the Census procedures.

Operational definitions

Communication and negotiation between customer and supplier, management and union, and between countries, require operational definitions. An operational definition is a procedure agreed upon for translation of a concept into measurement.

We do business on operational definitions: buyer and seller must agree on the method of assay for example, for iron ore. What do you mean by the amount of iron ore on a shipload of iron ore? Buyer and seller have to agree on a procedure to measure the amount. And it isn't just words, it's an operation. Operational definition is a means of communication in terms of a procedure.

Information is not knowledge.

There never was a time when we had so much information. Anything can happen anywhere in this world, and it's known within a minute all over the world. Information. Does it help us to understand the future and obligation of management? Not a bit.

Many of us deceive ourselves into the supposition that we need constant updating to cope with the rapidly changing future. Not so. You cannot, by watching every moment of television or by reading every newspaper acquire a glimpse of what the future holds. To put it another way, information, no matter how complete and speedy, is not knowledge. Cramming your heads full of information for an examination. That's not knowledge, that's not learning. It has not temporal spread. Knowledge must involve the future, and have explanation of the past. Knowledge comes from theory. Without theory there's no way to use the information that comes to us on the instant.

IV. Psychology

Mr. Harold Dodge, in the Bell Telephone Laboratories, discovered by many tests that the results that an inspector gets depends on the workload that you hand over to him. The daily output may be the same, regardless of the way you present the work to him. You give him 25 at a time, he'll find every defect. Hardly miss one. Give him a hundred at a time, he'll miss 10 percent of them. Results depend on the size of the batch that you hand over to him.

An inspector may pass an item that is doubtful. In case of doubt, pass it in order not to penalize anybody. Pass it. Thus distort the figures.

An inspector trying to save jobs never lets the percent defective go as high as ten. Rumor had it that the plant manager had said that if the proportion defective any day ever goes as high as 10 percent he will close the place down and sweep it out. The inspector was trying to save the jobs of 300 people. She never let the proportion defective go to 10 percent. What you have here is entwinement of psychology with results desired. She was afraid to put down the right figures. Where-ever there's fear you get wrong figures. By trying to save their jobs she may be putting them on the street because some customers will get poor quality. She meant well. You may say, "Well she should not do that." This is what people do, whether they should or should not. This is what they do.

You may say you don't think the plant manager ever said any such thing. That's totally irrelevant whether he said it or not. The only thing that matters is what those 300 people thought. They thought that he had said that. Nothing else matters. You may say, "Well even if he said it I don't think that he would do it." That thought is totally irrelevant. All that matters is what those people thought. They're in fear of their jobs, and an inspector was trying to save them.

A committee appointed by the president of a company will come through with a report in line with what the president wants. They better. Their lives depend on it.

From a presentation at Fordham University,
September 1992.

3

By What Method?

(How Can We Bring About Improvement?)

———◆———

After listening to a corporate executive expound on all the ways in which he was going to improve his enterprise, Deming would ask, "By what method?" This disarmed most people. How is it that you plan to improve? Somehow, once executives had decided that they wanted to improve, the rest would fall into place, they thought. It never does. Zero-stage planning on how something is to be accomplished is the most important stage of improvement – without it you have only wishful thinking. Deming offered a number of methods by which one might go about improvement, ranging from his ground-breaking theory of management, to statistical methods, changes within the organizational structure, and international cooperation.

———

Deming's presentation on the foundation for management of quality, delivered at an Osaka conference in 1989, became the basis for his now-famous book The New Economics for Industry, Government, Education.

Foundation for Management of Quality

Where is quality made? The answer is, in the top management. The quality of the output of a company can not be better than the quality directed at the top.

The people in the plants and in service organizations can only produce at best the design of product and service prescribed and designed by management.

Job security and jobs are dependent on management's foresight to design product and service that will entice customers and build a market.

Profound knowledge. Hard work and best efforts, put forth without guidance of profound knowledge, leads to ruin in the world that we are in today. There is no substitute for knowledge. What is profound knowledge? An attempt to supply some answers follow.

The System of Profound Knowledge appears here in four parts, all related to each other:

A. Appreciation for a system
B. Theory of variation
C. Theory of knowledge
D. Psychology

One need not be eminent in any part of profound knowledge in order to understand it as a system, and to apply it. The 14 points for management in industry, education, and government follow naturally as application of the system of profound knowledge, for transformation from the prevailing style of Western management to one of optimization.

The various segments of the system of profound knowledge can not be separated. They interact with each other. Thus, knowledge of psychology is incomplete without knowledge of variation. If psychologists understood variation, as learned in the experiment on the Red Beads, they could no longer participate in continual refinements of instruments for rating people.

A manager, in the role of leader of people, must have some knowledge of variation and of psychology.

Management of a system is action based on prediction. Rational prediction requires systematic learning and comparison of predictions of short-term and long-term results from possible alternative courses of action.

Theory of variation can play a vital part in optimization of a system. Statistical theory is helpful for understanding differences between people and for understanding the interactions between people and the systems that they work in.

Assistance to systematic learning is a specialty of the statistician. Statisticians that understand a system and optimization thereof, along with some theory of knowledge and something about psychology, could apply their specialized knowledge of variation toward continual improvement of methods for better prediction, and hence for better management. They could help people to retain their intrinsic motivation to learn.

Statistical theory, used cautiously, with the theory of knowledge, can be useful in the interpretation of the results of tests and experiments, to understand cause and effect relationships. The interpretation of the results of tests and experiments is for future use: prediction.

If economists understood the theory of a system, and the role of cooperation in optimization, they would no longer teach and preach salvation through adversarial competition. They would, instead, lead us into optimization, in which everybody would come out ahead, including competitors.

Indeed, if a monopoly or any two or more companies or institutions that dominate a market were to put their heads together for uniform prices, they would be fools to set the price higher than what would optimize the whole system—they themselves, their customers, suppliers, employees, environment, and the communities that their people work in. Anybody that goes into negotiation without the avowed aim to defend his rights will defeat his avowed purpose. Loss of rights for anybody brings eventual loss to everybody.

The theory of knowledge helps us to understand that management in any form is prediction. The simplest plan—how may I go home tonight—requires prediction that my automobile will start and run, or that the bus will come, or the train. Management acts on a causal system, and on changes in the causes.

A. A System

1. What is a system? A system is a series of functions or activities (sub-processes, stages—hereafter, components) within an organization that work together for the aim of the organization. The mechanical and electrical parts that work together to make an automobile or a vacuum cleaner form a system. The schools of a city, including private schools, parochial schools, trade schools, and universities, provide an example of components that ought to work together as a system for education.

There is in almost any system interdependence between the components thereof. The greater the interdependence between components, the greater be the need for communication and cooperation between them.

The components need not all be clearly defined and documented: people may merely do what needs to be done. All the people that work within a system can contribute to improvement, and thus enhance their joy in work. Management of a system therefore requires knowledge of the inter-relationships between all the components within the system and of the people that work in it.

The aim of the system must be clear to everyone in the system. Without an aim, there is no system. The aim is a value-judgment.

The aim proposed here for any organization is for everybody to gain—stock-holders, employees, suppliers, customers, community, the environment—over the long term. For example, with respect to employees, the aim might be to provide for them good leadership, opportunities for training and education for further growth, plus other contributors to joy in work, and quality of life.

2. Optimization. Optimization means accomplishment of the aim: everybody gains. Failure to optimize, suboptimization, causes loss to everybody in the system.

For optimization, a system must be managed. Management's responsibility is to strive toward optimization of the system, and to keep it optimized over time. Growth in size and complexity of a system, and rapid changes with time require overall management of efforts of components. An additional responsibility of management is to be ready to change the boundary of the system to better serve the aim.

If the aim, size, or boundary of the organization changes, then the functions of the components will for optimization of the new system change. Time will bring changes that must be managed to achieve optimization.

The components of a system could in principle, under stable conditions, manage themselves to accomplish their aim. A possible example is a 4-piece string quartet. Each member supports the other three. None of them is there to attract individual attention. Four simultaneous solos do not make a string quartet. They practice singly and together, to accomplish their aim. Their aim is challenge for self-satisfaction, and to provide pleasure to listeners.

Any system needs guidance from outside. The 4-piece string quartet mentioned above may well study under a master. The master need not be present at a performance.

A large organization will require someone in the position of aid to the president to teach and facilitate profound knowledge.

A flow diagram is helpful toward understanding a system. By understanding a system, one may be able to trace the consequences of a proposed change.

An example of a system, well optimized, is a good orchestra. The players are not there to play solos as prima donnas, to catch the ear of the listener. They are there to support each other. They need not be the best players in the country.

A business is not merely an organization chart, all departments striving for individual goals (sales, profit, productivity). It is a network of people, materials, methods, equipment, all working in support of each other for the common aim.

A system of schools (public schools, private schools, parochial schools, trade schools, universities, for example) is not merely pupils, teachers, school boards, board of regents, and parents. It should be, instead, a component in a system of education in which pupils from toddlers on up take joy in learning, free from fear of grades and gold stars, and in which teachers take joy in their work, free from fear of ranking. It would be a system that recognizes differences between pupils and differences between teachers. The reader, after study of the rest of this paper, might wish to try to construct a system of medical care.

The performance of any component is to be judged in terms of its contribution to the aim of the system, not for its individual production or profit, nor for any other competitive measure. Some components may operate at a loss to themselves, for optimization of the whole system, including the components that take a loss.

It would be poor management to save money on traveling expenses without regard to the physical wellness of the travelers. For example, it would be bad management to save $138 on a night rate for transportation, which would force the traveler to be up most of the night to take advantage of the reduced rate, but unfit for duty next day (actual example). It might be better for the travel department to ensure, at whatever cost, that the traveler arrive alert and well.

Optimization for everyone concerned should be basis for negotiation between any two people, between divisions, between union and management, between competitors, between countries. Everybody would gain. The two greatest forces of failure to optimize are now described.

1. Failure to optimize through time. Failure to evaluate the consequences of demand for short-term performance.
   a. The quarterly dividend. Make it look good.
   b. Ship everything on hand before the quarter ends. Mark it shipped, and show it as accounts receivable.
   c. Defer till next quarter orders for material and repair.
   d. Quick return on investment. High dividends, now. Churning money.
   e. Pension funds must be invested for highest return. This requirement leads to rapid movement of large sums of money—out of this company, into another. Churning money.
2. Failure to optimize human resources. Failures in the management of people. Losses huge but unknowable, short-term and long-term.
   a. Ranking people, teams, divisions, with reward and punishment
   b. The fallacy is easy to understand. If two people be compared with each other on any measure whatever, one of them will inevitably be higher than the other—one above, one below. Likewise for two teams, two plants, two divisions. Of six people compared on any measure whatever,

one will be highest and one will be lowest. Likewise for six teams, six plants, six divisions. So what? What does the comparison mean? Does it predict performance in the future? Some knowledge of variation is necessary in order to draw a conclusion.

c. Sales are down. Rank salesmen. Punish the poor performer of the month.

d. Ticket sellers in an area are ranked by the arithmetic sum of the daily discrepancies between cash on hand and the sum of the prices printed on the tickets. The ticket seller with the highest score is rewarded with a day off without pay (from British Rail). Can the reader think of a better way to destroy morale?

e. A far worse result of ranking is that it induces conflict. The aim of anyone ranked is to get a high rank. Optimization of the system is destroyed. Morale and quality suffer.

f. Two divisions in an automobile company were ranked on sales. As a result, both divisions put out a full line of cars, from small to big: cover all bases. To do otherwise, either of the two divisions would lose position with respect to the other.

Examples

- The merit system (actually, destroyer of intrinsic motivation. Emphasis is on rank, not on the work).
- Grading in school, from toddlers on up through the university.
- M.B.O., M.B.I.R (management by imposition of results).
- Incentive pay.
- Business plans, each division with its own business plan, not coordinated toward an aim.
- Work standards for production; quotas for sales. Quotas for accidents and breakdowns.
- Competition for share of market.

- Barriers to trade.
- Anybody, team, division, establishment (management, union) gouging the other in negotiation.

Fortunately, precise optimization is not necessary. One need only to come close to optimization. As a matter of fact, precise optimum would be difficult to define.

B. Some Knowledge of Theory of Variation (Statistical Theory)

1. Some understanding of variation, including appreciation of a stable system, and some understanding of special causes and common causes of variation, is essential for management of a system, including leadership of people.
2. Variation there will always be, between people, in output, in service, in product. What is the variation trying to tell us about a process, and about the people that work in it?
3. Understanding of the capability of a process. When do data indicate that a process is stable? The distribution of the output of a stable system is predictable with a high degree of belief. A process that is stable, in the state of statistical control, has a definable capability.
4. The leadership of people (manager, leader, supervisor, teacher) is entirely different in the two states, stable and unstable. Confusion between the two states leads to calamity.
5. Knowledge about the different sources of uncertainty in the system of measurement. Is the system of measurement stable, in statistical control?
6. There are two mistakes in attempts to improve a process, both costly:

   Mistake 1. To treat as a special cause any outcome, any fault, complaint, mistake, breakdown, accident, shortage, when actually it came from common causes. (Tampering.)

Mistake 2. To attribute to common causes any outcome, any fault, complaint, mistake, breakdown, accident, shortage, when actually it came from a special cause.

7. Knowledge of procedures aimed at minimum economic loss from these two mistakes. (Shewhart control charts.)

8. Knowledge about interaction of forces. Interaction may reinforce efforts, or it may nullify efforts. Effect of the system on the performance of people. Knowledge of dependence and interdependence between people, groups, divisions, companies, countries.

9. Understanding of the distinction between enumerative studies and analytic problems. An enumerative study produces information about a frame. The theory of sampling and design of experiments are for enumerative studies. Our Census is an enumerative study. Another example is a shipload of iron ore. Buyer and seller need to know how much iron is in on board. The interpretation of results of a test or experiment is something else. It is prediction that a specific change in a process or procedure will be a wise choice, or that no change would be better. Either way the choice is prediction. This is known as an analytic problem.

10. Knowledge about the losses that come from unfortunate successive application of random forces or random changes that may individually be unimportant (exemplified in the experiment with the funnel). Examples:
Worker training worker in succession.
Committees in industry or in government, elected or Civil Service officials, working with best efforts on policy, but without guidance of profound knowledge.

11. Enlargement of a committee does not necessarily improve results. Enlargement of a committee is not a way to acquire profound knowledge.

Corollaries of this theorem are frightening. Will popular vote provide the right answer?

12. As a good rule, profound knowledge must come from the outside and by invitation.

C. Theory of Knowledge

1. Any rational plan, however simple, requires prediction concerning conditions, behavior, comparison of performance of each of two procedures or materials.

   For example, how will I go home this evening? I predict that my automobile will start up and run satisfactorily, and I plan accordingly. Or I predict that the bus will come, or the train.

   Or, I will continue to use Method A, and not change to Method B, because at this moment evidence that Method B will be dependably better in the future is not convincing.

2. Interpretation of data from a test or experiment is prediction—what will happen on application of the conclusions or recommendations that are drawn from a test or experiment? This prediction will depend largely on knowledge of the subject-matter. It is only in the state of statistical control that statistical theory aids prediction.

3. A statement devoid of prediction or explanation of past events is no help in management.

4. Theory leads to questions. Without questions, experience and examples teach nothing. Without questions, one can only have an example. To copy an example of success, without understanding it with the aid of theory, may lead to disaster.

5. Communication and negotiation (as between customer and supplier, between management and union, between countries) requires for optimization operational definitions.

6. No number of examples establishes a theory, yet a single unexplained failure of a theory requires modification or even abandonment of the theory.

7. There is no true value of any characteristic, state, or condition that is defined in terms of measurement or observation. Change of procedure for measurement or observation produces a new number.

   There is a true value of the number of prime numbers under 100. Just write them down, and count them—1, 3, 5 .... It is a fact that the reader is reading these lines.

   On the other hand, there is no true value of the number of people in a room. Whom do you count? Do I count someone that was here in this room, but is now outside on the telephone or drinking coffee? Change the rule for counting people; you come up with a new number. Whom do you except? There is no true value of the amount of iron in a shipload of iron ore. Why? Change of procedure for taking samples of the ore from the shipload produces a new number for the proportion of iron in iron ore.

8. There is no such thing as a fact concerning an empirical observation. Any two people may have different ideas about what is important to know about any event.

D. Knowledge of Psychology

1. Psychology helps us to understand people, interactions between people and circumstances, interaction between teacher and pupil, interactions between a leader and his people and any system of management.

2. People are different from one another. A leader must be aware of these differences, and use them for optimization

of everybody's abilities and inclinations. Management of industry, education, and government operate today under the supposition that all people are alike.

3. People learn in different ways, and at different speeds. Some learn best by reading, some by listening, some by watching pictures, still or moving, some by watching someone do it.

4. A leader, by virtue of his authority, has obligation to make changes in the system of management that will bring improvement.

5. There is intrinsic motivation, extrinsic motivation, over-justification.

   People are born with a need for relationships with other people, and with need to be loved and esteemed by others. There is innate need for self-esteem and respect.

   Circumstances provide some people with dignity and self-esteem. Circumstances deny other people these advantages.

   Management that denies their employees dignity and self-esteem will smother intrinsic motivation.

   Some extrinsic motivators rob employees of dignity and of self-esteem. If for higher pay, or for higher rating, I do what I know to be wrong, I am robbed of dignity and self-esteem.

   No one, child or other, can enjoy learning if he must constantly be concerned about grading and gold stars for his performance, or about rating on the job. Our educational system would be improved immeasurably by abolishment of grading.

   One is born with a natural inclination to learn and to be innovative. One inherits a right to enjoy his work. Psychology helps us to nurture and preserve these positive innate attributes of people.

Extrinsic motivation is submission to external forces that neutral-ize intrinsic motivation. Pay is not a motivator. Under extrinsic motivation, learning and joy in learning in school are submerged in order to capture top grade. On the job, joy in work, and inno-vation, becomes secondary to a good rating. Under extrinsic motivation, one is ruled by external forces. He tries to protect what he has. He tries to avoid punishment. He knows not joy in learning. Extrinsic motivation is a zero-defect mentality.

Removal of a demotivator does not create motivation.

Over-justification comes from faulty systems of reward. Over-justification is resignation to outside forces. It could be monetary reward to somebody, or a prize, for an act or achievement that he did for sheer pleasure and self-satisfaction. The result of reward under these conditions is to throttle repetition: he will lose inter-est in such pursuits.

Monetary reward under such conditions is a way out for manag-ers that do not understand how to manage intrinsic motivation.

Effects of the present system of management. [Manage-ment] squeeze out from an individual, over his life-time, his innate intrinsic motivation, self-esteem, dignity, and build into him fear, self-defense, extrinsic motivation. We have been destroying our people, from toddlers on through the university, and on the job.

Transformation is required in government, industry, educa-tion. Management is in a stable state. Transformation is required to move out of the present state, metamorphosis, not mere patch-work on the present system of management. We must of course solve problems and stamp out fires as they occur, but these activ-ities do not change the system.

The transformation will take us into a new system of reward. We must restore the individual, and do so in the complexities of interaction with the rest of the world. The transformation will release the power of human resource contained in intrinsic motivation. In place of competition for high rating, high grades, to be No. 1, there will be cooperation on problems of common interest between people, divisions, companies, government, countries. The result will in time be greater innovation, applied science, technology, expansion of market, greater service, greater material reward for everyone. There will be joy in work, joy in learning. Anyone that enjoys his work is a pleasure to work with. Everyone will win; no loser.

The most important figures for management are unknowable. It was Dr. Lloyd S. Nelson who years ago remarked that the most important figures for management are unknown and unknowable. We could add that the most important losses and gains are not even under suspicion.

Examples:

1. The merit system, putting people into slots, a lazy way out: actually, destroyer of people
2. Failure to understand leadership
3. Worker training worker
4. Executives working with best efforts, trying to improve quality, the market, and profit, but working without guidance of profound knowledge
5. Tampering
6. Failure to optimize efforts of people and divisions within the company, accepting, instead, suboptimization—everyone trying to maximize the profits of his own division—and the consequent losses
7. Failure of customers and suppliers to work together for ever greater and greater satisfaction of quality, lower costs, everybody wins
8. Gains in quality and productivity throughout the rest of the company from improvement in one stage. It is wrong to suppose that "If you can't measure it, you can't manage it." Again, the most important losses are unknown and unknowable.

Some faulty practices with suggestions on better practice

Faulty Practice	Better Practice
Reactive: Skills only required, not theory of management, M.B.R. (management by results). Mind not required.	Theory of management required.

Management of outcome, too late; tampering; failure to distinguish between special causes and common causes. Immediate action on
    Costs
    Complaints from customers
    Poor quality, in or out
    Accidents
    Emergency breakdowns
    Absenteeism
	Work on the system, to reduce failure at the source. Costs are not causes. Likewise for complaints from customers, poor quality, accidents, emergency breakdown, absence. Avoid tampering. Instead, distinguish by appropriate techniques between special causes and common causes.

The so-called merit system—actually, destroyer of people.	Institute leadership. Change the system of reward from rugged individualism—I win, you lose—to cooperation, everybody wins.
Incentive pay for the individual. Pay based on performance. The incentive is numbers, not quality. Result: back-fire, loss.	Put all people on regular systems of pay. Provide leadership.
PRR, problem report and resolution. Actually, this is a form of management by results, tampering, making things.	Study the system. Learn methods by which to minimize the net economic loss.

Faulty Practice	Better Practice
Work standards (quotas, time standards): 1. Double costs. 2. Rob people of pride of workmanship. 3. Shut off any possibility to obtain data to use for improvement of process and output. This is so because the figures on production are forced.	Provide leadership. Everyone is entitled to pride of workmanship. Wherever work standards have been replaced by competent leadership, quality and productivity have gone up, and people on the job "are happier."
M.B.O., management by the numbers. (Do it, I don't care how you do it. Just do it.) A company will of course have aims; likewise an individual will have aims. But the aim should be improvement of the system, not a number. There are of course facts of life. Example: if we don't decrease faulty product to 5% by the end of the year, we shall not be here. This is not M.B.O.	A better way is to improve the system to get better results in the future. One will only get what the system will deliver. Any attempt to beat the system will cause loss.

From a paper delivered at a meeting of
The Institute of Management Sciences,
Osaka, Japan,
July 24, 1989.

Deming proposed creation of an Office of Statistical Methodology to report directly to the president of a company, with the caveat:

We may note that the Office of Statistical Methodology is not a group charged with responsibility for quality. Quality is everybody's job. The function of the Office of Statistical Methodology is to help people throughout the company to achieve continual improvement of design of equipment, processes, protection of investment in equipment; also—most important—education and protection of investment in people.

From a memorandum to Donald E. Petersen,
then CEO of Ford Motor Company,
September 22, 1987.

Two years later he was still focused on leadership, and sent this letter:

Whence Will Come Leadership?

I. Prevailing practices of management and education have crushed the individual. Toddlers at the age of three are crushed by prizes for costumes, grades in school, gold stars for athletics. Forces of destruction continue onward through further schooling, and onward into the work place through life, robbing the individual of joy in learning and joy in work. Examples: the so-called merit system, actually destroyer of people, quotas, system of reward. (See Figure 3.1.)

It may be that rating people in four categories

Outside the system on the high side, due for recognition of some kind.
Outside the system on the low side, in need of special help.
All others
Above average
Below average

is no improvement over putting people into the usual slots.

Forces of Destruction

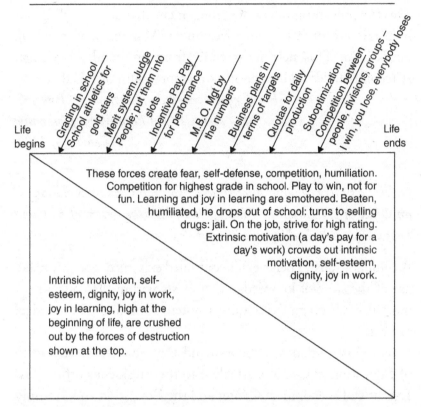

Life begins

Life ends

Grading in school
School athletics for gold stars
Merit system. Judge People; put them into slots
Incentive Pay. Pay for performance
M.B.O. Mgt by the numbers
Business plans in terms of targets
Quotas for daily production
Suboptimization.
Competition between people, divisions, groups – I win, you lose, everybody loses

These forces create fear, self-defense, competition, humiliation. Competition for highest grade in school. Play to win, not for fun. Learning and joy in learning are smothered. Beaten, humiliated, he drops out of school: turns to selling drugs: jail. On the job, strive for high rating. Extrinsic motivation (a day's pay for a day's work) crowds out intrinsic motivation, self-esteem, dignity, joy in work.

Intrinsic motivation, self-esteem, dignity, joy in work, joy in learning, high at the beginning of life, are crushed out by the forces of destruction shown at the top.

Figure 3.1 The forces along the top rob the company and the nation of innovation and applied science. We must replace them with leadership that understands the transformation to the new theory of management.

II. Everyone is crying for reduction in costs. I fear that most efforts are exerted on the easy exercises. The biggest losses go along unmanaged. These losses, though unknown and unknowable, some not even under suspicion, must nevertheless be managed. I refer to the rating of people, for rating teams and divisions, poor relationships with suppliers, system of reward for suggestions, failure to optimize the overall system, general lack of education in the new philosophy for transformation.

Whence will come the leadership to replace with better practices the prevailing forces of management that are humbling our industry, our education, our government? Management anywhere needs help. This help must come from profound knowledge. A recommendation is in another memorandum of this date.

From a memorandum to Donald E. Petersen,
then CEO of Ford Motor Company,
December 9, 1989.

On the same day he wrote another letter with this recommendation for an Office of Education in Quality, to include the system of profound knowledge, as he had begun calling it:

A company must, I believe, for continued existence, not only make use of the store of knowledge that exists within the company; it must also rely on guidance from a system of profound knowledge, as I call it.

For this guidance, I recommend that you create an Office of Education in Quality, attached to the President's office. The Executive Development Center and the Education and Training Center do not meet this need.

At the head would be a leader of education for quality, responsible to top management. This leader must be a man of unquestioned ability. He will have authority from top management to be a participant in any activity that in his judgment is worth his pursuit. He will be a regular participant in any major meeting of the president and staff. The choice of application for him to pursue must be left to his judgment, not to the judgment of others, though he will, of course, try to be helpful to anyone that seeks help.

From a memorandum to Donald E. Petersen,
then CEO of Ford Motor Company,
December 9, 1989.

Deming believed in cooperation between people, departments, divisions, companies, industries, nations. In this speech to fire chiefs he discusses the need for fire departments to form a system of cooperation and standardization if they are to serve society.

Cooperation and Standardization

Fire departments serve society. They live day by day a life of cooperation. Fire companies back each other up. Thus, if there be a huge fire on the south side of a city, occupying most of the resources on the south side, equipment comes from the other parts of the city to occupy the vacant fire stations, to be ready if there be another call.

Likewise there is widespread cooperation among fire departments from various cities and towns. It is not at all unusual for a large fire (or other emergency—chemical spill, plane crash, etc.) to receive service from fire departments from many communities. Competition between fire departments over which one will respond to a fire is unheard of because the cooperative arrangements have all been worked out in advance.

I could interject at this point that the dream of every youngster is to be a fireman. This address to the International Association of Fire Chiefs is as near as I shall ever come to this dream. As a youngster, I admired fire-horses – the greatest accomplishment for a horse. I imagined that the greatest achievement that a colt could aspire to was to be a fire-horse in later life. There were bucket-brigades, but I was too small to join one.

Despite the fact that fire departments are a model of cooperation, I shall nevertheless attempt to add a few words about cooperation and a system. My aim here is to show that we should all gain in many ways, material and spiritual, if all our activities followed the principles that govern fire departments.

First, let us talk about a system. A system could be fire departments, it could be a company, it could be a whole industry, or even (as I taught the Japanese) a whole country.

A system is a set of components. Examples of components in a city are fire departments, police, schools, and other services necessary to run a city, such as the judicial system, the office of motor vehicles, the traffic department, paving of streets, collection of garbage. All these components should work together toward a common aim.

And an aim there must be. Without an aim, there is no system. The various components of a system bend their efforts in cooperation toward the aim. For a city, the aim should be for the various components to work together to serve the citizens of the city, and to provide good quality of life for citizens and for all employees.

For example, there is never enough money to go around. Every city, every state, every province, is strapped for money, now more than ever. Optimum allocation of funds for accomplishment of the aim is necessary. Any component, such as the fire department, if it seeks a bigger slice of the funds than is optimum for the system, will only in the end impair itself, along with the other components. Any component is to be judged by its contribution to the system, not by some competitive measure.

We know how to optimize pieces, but optimization of a larger system is difficult. A system must be managed.

Without an aim, a fire department would only be firemen, fire trucks, equipment on these trucks, buildings, hydrants. They would be useless, singly and together, without an aim.

I remember a story about cooperation. It could have been in 1903. There was a big fire in Baltimore. Fire departments in New York put their equipment and men on 28 flat cars to rush themselves by train to Baltimore to help put out the fire.

When they arrived, they found their endeavor to be useless. The threads on the fire hoses brought from New York would not fit the hydrants in Baltimore.

There are two lessons here. The first lesson is cooperation: one fire department rushing to help another. The second lesson is cooperation in the form of standardization. We take standards for granted. The world was not made with standards. Standards must be made by man. Without standards, our life would be primitive. Examples are couplings for fire equipment. Other examples come readily to mind:

The time of day, based on Greenwich mean time, used the world over.

The date, fixed by the international date line, observed by everybody.

Red and green traffic lights, the red light above the green, the same the world over.

The metric system.

Sizes of batteries. If I need a AAA battery, I may buy it anywhere in this world, and it will fit.

The gauge of our railways. A car may move from Halifax to Montreal to Boston to Chicago to Miami to El Paso to Los Angeles to San Francisco, Portland, Seattle, Vancouver, Calgary, Saskatoon, Winnipeg, Duluth, Minneapolis, down to Chicago. All this is possible because of the standard English gauge ($56 \frac{1}{2}$ inches) between cities, same air brake system, same coupling between cars.

Meetings of professional people, such as this meeting of the Fire Chiefs for interchange of aims and knowledge.

Journals of professional and scientific people, for exchange of new knowledge with the rest of the world, competitors and all.

The best way to fight fires would be not to have any fires. This would be an impossible numerical goal, so we might settle for something less, namely, reduction in the number of fires. Fire departments could improve their efficiency by learning whether the number of fires per week in a city or in some section of city follows a stable system or an unstable system. Let us look at an example:

> The president of a company received a letter from his insurance company which stated that unless there be drastic reduction in the frequency of fires in this company's premises during the next few months, the insurance company would cancel the insurance.
>
> The president of the company, naturally worried, sent a letter to every one of the 8,500 employees of the company to plead with them not to set so many fires; we may lose our fire insurance. He treated his worries as if the people in the building were the source of the problem.

I obtained the data. It turns out that the number of fires in this company forms a stable system with an average of 1.2 fires per month. The upper limit calculated from the data was five fires per month.

Had someone in the insurance company, with knowledge of variation, plotted [the numbers], that letter would never have been written. He would have observed that the system of fires is stable, and that the insurance company has a good basis for the rate to set for protection of these premises, and to come off with some profit.

One could predict with of course some risk of being wrong, that the same system of fires will continue until the management takes action on the process to reduce the number of fires per month.

Reduction in the number of fires can be brought about by studying the process that produces the fires in this company. This is totally different from treating each fire as an accident, something special. Certainly we need to put out a fire, no matter what be the cause, but our aim should be to reduce the number of fires in the future. To go about reduction of fires, treating a fire as if it arose from a special cause, an accident, is totally different from regarding it as a product of a stable process. This supposition that every fire is an accident may well block the road to reduction in the number of fires.

A widespread problem in fire fighting is personal injuries to fire fighters. Inhalation of smoke also harms fire fighters. It is a dangerous job. Many injuries are injuries to the back and might very well exhibit a stable pattern of variation, indicating need for action on the system. Such action might include exercises for fire-fighters to strengthen back muscles, different methods of moving equipment at the scene of the fire, etc.

Does absenteeism in a company exhibit the characteristics of a stable process? If so, only action by management can reduce it. Is any division or group of the company outside the system of absenteeism, a special cause, requiring separate study?

Time of transit for deliveries to you, or to your customers: is it stable, or still afflicted with special causes of delays? If stable, how can the time of transit be reduced?

How about accidents on the job? How about beneficial days? Is their variation stable?

Fire departments spend considerable time and resources on training. When is training finished? The answer is that a man's training is finished when the number of mistakes that he makes per day, per week, or per lot, reaches a stable state. At this point further lessons will not help him with this skill. He that can learn a skill will come to a stable state. He that can not learn the skill will not come to a stable state.

If the work of someone who has reached a stable state is unacceptable, then he must be moved to some other work. Money and time spent in training him for this job is lost. It is accordingly extremely important that methods of training be improved year by year.

In this connexion it may be wise to mention the hazard of worker training worker in succession. The result is wild and unbelievable departure from the intent. It is better that training be placed in the hands of somebody competent to train.

Education and personal growth are different. Education and personal growth may go on forever. They need not come to a stable state.

Education of the public is a duty of fire departments. They have been successful, for example, in recommending installation of sprinkler systems in residences as well as in buildings.

It may be wise for fire departments to be aware of the possibility of outlandish extremes, such as a 100-year fire—the worst in 100 years, or in 200 years. There will be a flood not seen for centuries. There will be a drought not seen for centuries. Fire departments must be on the alert for a 100-year fire, and for a 100-year flood. This alert would require despatch of help from the surrounding regions.

Preparation for a 100-year fire requires resources. This means training of volunteers. It means extra equipment. This equipment must be kept ready for business. Such expenditures may seem unnecessary, excessive, in between 100-year fires. They bring criticism from well-meaning citizens that do not understand variation, in particular, the theory of extreme values. There is no substitute for knowledge. When the fire comes, criticism turns to thanksgiving for the wisdom of preparation.

In summary, I can only express admiration for the devotion of fire departments the world over for constant improvement, innovation, and cooperation. The only contribution that I could make is to suggest the possibility that knowledge of variation would assist innovation of fire departments the world over.

From an address to the
International Association of Fire Chiefs, Toronto,
September 22, 1991.

In a letter to the Dean of American University, Deming proposes formation of an international institute for study of management and productivity, so that different nations might learn from one another.

There is need in this country for a center that would bring together individuals from private industry and from government to learn from the Japanese principles of administration and trade that could help to improve the performance of American product both in quality and quantity. The miracle of quality and economic production in Japan could be adapted with modification in the U.S.

Unless productivity and innovation in the United States can compete with the Japanese, the fear looms up that the United States will push further toward protectionism through higher tariffs and quotas. As you have remarked, a more effective and constructive way to deal with this problem is to increase our own productivity, not to penalize the higher productivity of a foreign industry.

It will be difficult to dislodge from American minds some of the unfounded ideas that they have about the responsibilities of management and about Japanese industry, but it can be done to an effective degree, I believe, if the right effort and organization be put to the job.

It is vital to this end, in my judgment, to establish an institution that will bring together leaders in Japanese industry and leaders in our own industry and in our governmental agencies and in the legislative branch to establish a basis for better understanding of the role that efficiency, quality, and productivity have played in the success of the Japanese economy. I believe that American industrialists that participate will finally confront themselves with the obvious evidence that they have not been pursuing the proper paths toward productivity, but rather have been taking refuge in excuses, so wrapped up in industrial protocol and red tape (as bad as in government) that they have been in bondage, unable to face the difficult problems, and unable to adapt themselves to ideas from the outside.

The result could be great improvement in production in America, with a more favorable balance of international trade, especially with Japan.

An effective organization, as I envisage it, dedicated to the aims described, would eventually become an Institute for Advanced Study in the Management of Productivity, a focal point for people of all nations to exchange knowledge and experience to assist each other in the advancement of industrial productivity. It would of course cover evaluation of the immediate future need and demand for materials and product in various parts of the world. How to do business in other countries needs study. Our own legislative and judicial branches need to learn how to do business as much as American management needs it. Some of their interpretations of laws and regulations hinder very effectively the ability of American companies to do business abroad.

In a memorandum to the
Dean of the School of Business Administration,
American University,
August 23, 1978.

In this speech written for the 1955 Deming Prize Ceremonies in Japan, Deming focused on the importance of consumer research.

Statistical techniques have brought to industry during the past 15 years new possibilities in uniformity of quality and precision, and new levels of output of manufactured product. The same basic techniques have also produced new levels of reliability and economy in consumer research, where one learns about the preferences of consumers and of the *non*consumers of a product.

I wish to leave with you this afternoon four main thoughts. *First*, statistical techniques must be harnessed and put to work. They are like water-power in the mountains, which has existed for centuries but which does not work until man sends the water through turbines to produce electricity. Statisticians have created a vast international storehouse of power in the form of statistical theory, but this theory can not work for industry unless it has a chance. There must be a fusion of purpose (a) on the part of top management to learn the uses of statistical techniques, and (b) on the part of statisticians to learn to use their knowledge for the good of industry. It is not necessary that an executive in management know statistical theory: he only needs to know what this theory can do for him. He can do this, just as he has learned to use electricity and machine tools without becoming an expert in the theory of electrodynamics, metallurgy, and physical chemistry.

Second, there is the connexion between marketing research and design of product, which many executives in industry do not appreciate. The quality and the design of product that will sell in a domestic market and in an international commerce is not static, but depends upon the preferences of next year's customers. These preferences are variable: they change, and they can be guided by good advertising, with a good product to back it up.

It is not sufficient for the commercial research department of a company to learn about the preferences of the consumers and of the nonconsumers of the company's product and of the

competitive products. It is neither sufficient for the superintendent of a manufacturing plant to employ the best techniques,
statistical and otherwise, to achieve high uniformity and efficiency in production. He may be producing *very efficiently* the
wrong quality and the wrong design of product.

It is necessary to link studies of consumer preference with
the design and redesign of the product. This link is a responsibility of top management, to bring consumer research and
design together, in order that the product may enjoy the best
market.

Third, there is the inescapable fact that consumer research
and efficient production are the only safe and sure roads to more
goods at prices that people can pay, and the surest protection to
private enterprise. To Japan, they are the surest roads to a share
of the world's markets.

Japanese industry has proved to the world that statistical
techniques have their best application where raw materials
and machines are scarce. It is well to remember that a 10%
increase in production, with no increase in raw materials or
machines or floor space, is equivalent to the discovery of vast
new national resources, such as new veins of copper, new veins
of coal.

My *fourth* point is that the success of Japanese manufacturers and statisticians stems, I believe, largely from the unexcelled
educational facilities that the Union of Japanese Scientists and
Engineers has provided. I can say from first-hand knowledge
that the Union of Japanese Scientists and Engineers is unique;
no other country possesses such a vital instrument of dissemi-
nation of knowledge. The foresight and comprehension of its
leaders, my good friends Mr. Ishikawa and Mr. Koyanagi, and
many others who have helped to guide it can hardly be over-
estimated. Other countries possess the same knowledge but

they have not disseminated this knowledge as you have here in Japan to statisticians, engineers, and top management.

I believe that the fulfillment of these aims is a foundation of peace and the surest protection of private enterprise.

From a speech on the occasion of the
5th Annual Award of the Deming Prize, Japan,
November 25, 1955.

What Should a School of Business Teach?

What should a school of business teach? The answer is, I believe, that a school of business ought to teach profound knowledge as a system. A school of business has the obligation to prepare students for the future, not for the past. At present, most schools of business teach students how business is conducted, and how to perpetuate the present system of management—exactly what we don't need. Most of the time that students spend in a school of business today is to learn skills, not knowledge.

A school of business has an obligation to prepare students to lead the transformation that will help our balance of trade and our economy. A school of business has an obligation to teach profound knowledge as a system.

There would of course be elective courses in the curriculum for business, such as a language (two years or more), history, physics, chemistry, biology, geography, anthropology, economics. Some students might wish to take their elective courses in more statistical theory, such as the statistical theory of reliability or statistical theory of failure, or in psychology, or in the theory of knowledge.

What about a school of engineering; a department of statistics? Engineers need to understand a system and profound knowledge, so that they may use to the best advantage their knowledge of engineering. The same remarks apply to a department of statistics.

From a paper delivered at a meeting of
The Institute of Management Sciences in Osaka, Japan,
July 24, 1989.

Deming had a knack for recognizing important ideas and great thinkers. Under the auspices of the Graduate School of the Department of Agriculture in the 1930s, he invited a number of statistically minded people to come and give lectures there. Dr. Walter Shewhart was invited to present four lectures in 1938. Deming took copious notes, combined them with Shewhart's own lecture notes, and created a small book, Statistical Method from the Viewpoint of Quality Control, *which was originally published by the Graduate School of the Department of Agriculture in 1939. In the foreword to the republication of book in 1986 by Dover, Deming summarized some of the important principles explained therein:*

Any conclusion or statement, if it is to have use for science or industry, must add to the degree of belief for rational prediction. The reader may reflect on the fact that the only reason to carry out a test is to improve a process, to improve the quality and quantity of the next run or of next year's crop. Important questions in science and industry are how and under what conditions observations may contribute to a rational decision to change or not to change a process to accomplish improvements. A record of observations must accordingly contain all the information that anyone might need in order to make his own prediction.

This information will include not merely numerical data, but also, for example, the names of observers, the type of apparatus or measurement system used, a description of materials used, the temperature and humidity, a description of efforts taken to reduce error, the side effects and other external factors that in the judgment of the expert in the subject matter may be helpful for use of the results.

Omission from data (as of a test or a run of production) of information on the order of the observations may well bury, for purposes of prediction (i.e., for planning), nearly all the information that there is in the test. Any symmetric function loses the information that is contained in the order of observation. Thus, the mean, standard deviation—in fact any moment—is in most applications inefficient, as it causes the loss of all information that is contained in the order of observation. A distribution is another example of a symmetric function. Original data plotted in order of production may provide much more information than is contained in the distribution.

Dr. Shewhart was well aware that the statistician's levels of significance furnish no measure of belief in a prediction. Probability has use; tests of significance do not. There is no true value of anything. There is, instead, a figure that is produced by application of a master or ideal method of counting or of measurement. This figure may be accepted as a standard until the method of measurement is supplanted by experts in the subject matter with some other method and some other figure. There is no true value of the speed of light; no true value of the number of inhabitants within the boundaries of (e.g.) Detroit. A count of the number of inhabitants of Detroit is dependent upon the application of arbitrary rules for carrying out the count. Repetition of an experiment or of a count will exhibit variation. Change in the method of measuring the speed of light produces a new result.

All this has been known for generations. What Dr. Shewhart demonstrates in this book is the importance of these principles in science and industry, whether it be manufacturing or service, including government service. The requirements of industry are more exacting than the requirements of pure science.

As with many contributors to science, literature, and the arts, Dr. Shewhart is best known for the least of his contributions—control charts. Control charts alone would be sufficient for eternal fame (even though, because of poor understanding of teachers and books, many students' applications seen in practice are faulty and may be doing more harm than good). The fact is that some of the greatest contributions from control charts lie in areas that are only partially explored so far, such as applications to supervision, management, and systems of measurement, including the standardization and use of instruments, test panels, and standard samples of chemicals and compounds.

The great contribution of control charts is to separate variation by rational methods into two sources: (1) the system itself ("chance causes," Dr. Shewhart called them), the responsibility of management; and (2) assignable causes, called by Deming "special causes," specific to some ephemeral event that can usually be discovered to the satisfaction of the expert on the job, and removed. A process is in *statistical control* when it is no longer afflicted with special causes. The performance of a process that is in statistical control is predictable.

A process has no measurable capability unless it is in statistical control. An instrument has no ascertainable precision unless observations made with it show statistical control. Results obtained by two instruments cannot be usefully compared unless the two instruments are in statistical control. Statistical control is ephemeral; there must be a running record for judging whether the state of statistical control still exists.

Every observation, numerical or otherwise, is subject to variation. Moreover, there is useful information in variation. The closest approach possible to a numerical evaluation of any so-called physical content, to any count, or to any characteristics of a process is a result that emanates from a system of measurement that shows evidence that it is in statistical control.

The expert in the subject matter holds the responsibility for the use of the data from a test.

Another half-century may pass before the full spectrum of Dr. Shewhart's contributions has been revealed in liberal education, science, and industry.

From Deming's Foreword to the republication of
Walter Shewhart's Statistical Method
from the Viewpoint of Quality Control,
originally published in 1939,
June 1986.

4

There Is No Such Thing as Instant Pudding

(Deming's 14 Points for Management)

———◆———

Deming often remarked that when it came to changing how a company was managed, there was no such thing as instant pudding. Even in the best-run companies, he said, it would take five to ten years for transformation of the enterprise. Deming provided 14 specific ways in which a company might begin to move forward – none of them instant pudding.

Although Deming wrote the 14 points for management before he wrote about a system of knowledge, he later said the 14 points were outtakes from the System of Profound Knowledge. Many managers find the points useful because they are unambiguous actions they can take.

In this chapter, the 14 points are stated as they appear in Deming's 1986 book, Out of the Crisis, *where he also has an elaboration on them. You may find slightly different statements of the points in different articles Deming wrote over the years as he continually tried to clarify them, both before and after he wrote the book. I have interspersed comments about the 14 points excerpted from the many other places Deming talked about them. No attempt has been made to give "equal treatment" to each of the points. Deming himself wrote more on some points than others. Details on Point 4, ending the practice of awarding business on the basis of price tag, account for more than 25 percent of this chapter. I believe Deming received more questions about Point 4 from clients, academics, and seminar participants than all of the other points combined. Hence, Deming wrote considerably more on this topic than on the others.*

The 14 points are the basis for transformation of American business and industry. It will not suffice merely to solve problems, big or little. Adoption and action on the 14 points are a signal that the management intend to stay in business and aim to protect investors and jobs.

The 14 points apply anywhere, to small organizations as well as to large ones, to the service industry as well as to manufacturing. They apply to a division within a company. These 14 headings show top management what they must do."[1]

"We're here to learn what management must do. That's why we're here. This seminar is about the responsibility of management for improvement [of] quality, productivity, and competitive position. I summarized the obligation under fourteen points. And these fourteen points require action. A woman started to say something to me not long ago. She said "we have the support of top management." I said, wait a minute, don't finish your sentence. You've got to have more than support. Support isn't going to do it. You need action under a top management.[2]

The 14 points come from experience, just trying to be useful, trying to perceive problems that other people cannot be expected to perceive. It seems obvious to me that the cost of living, or what you have to spend to live, depends inversely on how much a given amount of money will buy. People could learn that in school. What money will buy depends on quality, the quality available as well as on price.[3]

And here they are [the 14 steps management must take]: *The italicized questions are mine. The answers are Deming's.*

Point 1

Create constancy of purpose toward improvement of product and service, with the aim to become competitive and to stay in business, and to provide jobs.

It is a mistake to suppose that efficient production of product or service, or both, can with certainty keep an organization in business. You have to make something that has a market, and you may have to develop that market. That takes resources.[3]

Companies that adopt constancy of purpose, establish it as an institution for quality and productivity and service, and go about it with intelligence and perseverance, have a chance to survive. Some others will [also survive]; yes, I know. Charles Darwin's law of the survival of the fittest, and that the unfit do not survive, holds in free enterprise, as it does in nature's selections. In free enterprise, you have a right to make a mistake. The penalty, thereof, is to get beat up a little, a lot, or maybe pretty severely. We come to the problem of obstacles. What's holding it up? Why not move? Well, what is holding it up? What are some of the obstacles?[4]

Well, the main obstacle is failure of constancy of purpose, isn't it? Don't you think so? Establish constancy of purpose. People ask me, "How?" Well, I don't know how. That's up to the company. If it isn't done, the company will be under handicap, and that handicap may have severe consequences. So much of American industry is run on the quarterly dividend. [The] President is brought in by the board of directors for this very purpose. He accomplishes the purpose, moves to another company to do the same thing. What he does is ruin both of them. Even when top management has announced constancy of purpose, it takes a little while for credibility to seep and soak around.[4]

How do we implement this point? Allocate resources for long-term planning, plans for the future, all for consideration. Look ahead for new services and new product that may help people to live better materially and which will have a market. You can't always tell that something will have a market. I have no secrets. New materials will be required, have to be tested, tried in production and in service. The cost has to be considered. Methods of production will change. Equipment may change. There will be new skills required day by day. Training and retraining of personnel comes up. Training of supervisors. Cost of marketing, plans for service, cost of service, and of course it takes capital and the capital has to live through the introduction of a new service, a new product.[3]

Take into consideration performance in the hands of the user, satisfaction of the user, how he'll use the product, how he'll use the service, whether he will use it, how he'll misuse the product and the service. One requirement for innovation is faith that there will be a future. Well, there will be one. Only problem is, who's going to live through it? But until this policy of constancy of purpose can be enthroned as an institution to worship, middle management, top management and everyone in the company will be skeptical. It's necessary to put resources into research, into education. It's not cheap.[3]

The consumer is the most important end of the production line. If you don't have a consumer, someone who will buy your product or use your service, you might as well shut down, close up.[3] Allocate resources to fulfill long-range needs of the company and of the customer.[5]

Why? The next quarterly dividend is not as important as existence of the company 5, 10, or 20 years from now. One requirement for innovation is faith that there will be a future.[5]

What are some ways to do this?

A. Put resources into plans for product and service for the future, taking into account
   - Possible materials, adaptability, probable cost
   - Method of production; possible changes in equipment
   - New skills required, and in what number
   - Training and re-training of personnel
   - Training of supervisors
   - Cost of production
   - Performance in the hands of the user
   - Satisfaction of the user

B. Put resources into education

C. Put resources into maintenance of equipment, furniture and fixtures, new aids to production in the office and in the plant.

D. Intensify attention to future needs of the consumer. Learn how the consumer uses the product, and how to improve tests thereof in service.

E. It is a mistake to suppose that statistical quality technology applied to products and services offered at present can with certainty keep an organization solvent and ahead of competition.

F. It is possible and in fact fairly easy for an organization to go broke making the wrong product or offering the wrong type of service, even though everyone in the organization performs with devotion, employing statistical methods and every other aid that can boost efficiency.[5]

G. Innovation generates new and improved services.
   Some examples:[5]
   - New and different kinds of plans for savings in banks
   - Financial service offered by brokers, insurance companies, and credit agencies

- Meals on Wheels
- Day care in out-patient clinics
- Leasing of automobiles is an example of service that did not exist years ago.
- Express Mail is a new service of the U.S. post office.
- Intercity and intra-city messenger service is a growth industry, thriving on the failure of the U.S. post office.
- Mailgram by Western Union is another.[5]

Aim proposed here for any organization is for everybody to gain. This is simply my idea. I'm not going to force it on anybody. Everybody gains: stockholders, employees, suppliers, customers, community, the environment, over the long run. For example, with respect to employees, the aim might be to provide for them good management, opportunities for training and education, for further growth, plus other contributors to joy in work and quality in life.[2]

Point 2

Adopt the new philosophy. We are in a new economic age. Western management must awaken to the challenge, must learn their responsibilities, and take on leadership for a change.

A new theorem: I'm afraid that it's new in a lot of American industry. Dependability of service is an important quality characteristic. Reliable service reduces cost. Delays and mistakes raise cost. Alternate plans are necessary in expectation of delays. In a lot of American industry a production line in place has parallel to it, one similar to it for re-work. Look at the cost. I think of the economy that would come from dependable product, dependable parts coming in, dependable service and transportation, for example, not having to lay out for yourself alternative plans in case one does not work.[3]

What's wrong? We can no longer live with commonly accepted levels of mistakes, defects, material not suited to the job, equipment out of order, people on the job that do not know what the job is and are afraid to ask; handling damage; failure of management to understand the problems of the product in use, antiquated methods of training on the job, inadequate and ineffective supervision.[5]

Acceptance of defective materials and poor workmanship as a way of life is one of the most effective roadblocks to better quality and productivity. The Japanese faced it in 1950.[5]

We can no longer accept the common level of mistakes, defects, everything late, nothing right, just as an accepted way of life.[3]

Dependability of service is an important quality characteristic. Reliable service reduces cost. Delays and mistakes raise cost. Alternate plans are necessary in expectation of delays. A lot of American industry have a production line in a spot and then parallel to it, one just similar to it for re-work. Look at the cost. Think of the economy that would come from dependable product, dependable parts coming in, dependable service and transportation, for example, not having to lay out for yourself alternative plans in case one does not work.[3]

Think of the cost of living with waste and how much you could get with the same dollar if there were not waste imbedded in it. My friend, Dr. Higgenbaum, published a paper not long ago in which he estimated by a considerable amount of experience, that from 10 to 40 percent of the manufacturer's cost in anything made American is payment for waste that need not be there.[3]

Example of imbedded waste: [A friend] told me about his lawn mower. He said, I actually bought it last week, started it up, the motor caught on fire. Well, I put out the fire, took it back to Sears Roebuck. The manager looked at it. Somebody put in the wrong motor. Just one of those things. Nothing unusual about it. Gave him a whole new outfit, no problem. Wiped out the profit for I don't know how long.[3]

Example from service industry: When I was to travel in Japan,

17:25: leave Taku City
19:23: arrive Hakata, change trains
19:24: leave Hakata
21:20: arrive Osaka

One minute to change trains. No problem, no alternate plan. Why would you need an alternate plan? Think of being able to plan, with one plan, not two or three.[3]

Example of defective deliveries: Two weeks ago I was in a manufacturing plant. It was a large one, and it was a fine company. I was listening to some of their problems with incoming materials. Stuff comes in not just defective, but as a matter of fact, some of it might be 100 percent conforming, not that it was, but it comes in showing carelessness. [They received a panel] to be screwed onto something that needs four holes; it has three holes. Where is the fourth hole? The count is right, a hundred to the package. Some had only three holes.

You can believe that anything could happen. Here stuff can come to a manufacturer who needs it. It comes in and it was intended for another company. He can't use it. It isn't quite right for him. Or he would not use it since the stuff was meant for a competitor. Suppose that his competitor and he, himself, needed that shipment. They might both have to shut down for, what, a day? A day won't do it. First place, you've got to work through the vendor, let him take care of the problem, and if he galloped all the way, it would still take him at least a day to make that switch. Meanwhile, what are these people going to do?

If they needed inventory—thank goodness they didn't need it—they could live a day or two without it because of backlog which, of course, is one of the curses inflicting American industry. They require huge inventories because so much of the stuff is defective, or wrong. You've got to lay in a big stock, hoping that you can use some of it.[3]

Example on an airplane: I've often wondered on board an airplane, finding that the seat is rigid, won't move, or it drifts backward no matter what, and will not stay fixed in any position—goes back right into the lap of somebody sitting behind you. It must be very uncomfortable. Well, I had that experience not long ago. I have it any day, maybe every other trip, maybe one trip in four. The seat wouldn't budge. As we arrived at the destination, I asked the flight attendant who had pushed and shoved and tried to move the thing, "Do you have any system by which to report little things like that out of order?" "Oh, yes, the mechanic fills out a report on all those things and at the next layover, the men take care of it. Oh, thank you very much for reminding me about that seat."

I might not have thought of [telling the flight attendant]. You call that a system for reporting? That girl has other duties. Reporting a seat out of order or a light blinked out, were the least of her problems.[3]

Point 3

Cease dependence on inspection to achieve quality. Eliminate the need for inspection on a mass basis by building quality into the product in the first place.

Why? Inspection does not improve quality.[3]

Why not? The quality is already there. Inspection raises the cost. Necessity for inspection only indicates that somebody doesn't know how to do the job. You have to inspect it. Two hundred percent inspection means that nobody has a job. A hundred percent inspection is about the same way. I make some stuff. Jim over here inspects it and I have a lot of confidence in him, so if I make a mistake, I expect him to pick it up. That's his job, so I'm not totally responsible. Jim thinks that I'm pretty good, so he can go on now and then about inspecting something. Chances are pretty good that it's all right, need not look very carefully because most of it's right. He thinks there's a slim chance that I could make it defective and he could miss it. So neither of us has a job.[3]

Dependence on final inspection to produce quality: curse all over the world. Not everywhere. The Japanese know better; I taught them in 1950 and all 19 trips after that. Inspection does not improve quality; the quality is already there.[4]

I was talking with one of the companies I work with. They own a number of plants. One of them makes men's suits. Every suit goes through 200 percent inspection. 100 is not enough. They have to be sure of the quality. Dealer was putting suits on the rack, and behold it was a nice looking suit, but no buttons. No buttons. Well, there's no calamity. Everybody laughed.[4]

Some accidents are not so funny. Well, you'd expect things like that with 200 percent inspection. Nobody has a job. Inspectors fail to agree with each other. Machines fail to agree.[4]

Should we never inspect? There will always have to be some inspection. Even to make a control chart, we require tests. You need to know what tests to make, and how many to make. Some testing will always be necessary, on maintenance of instruments, certainly. Dependence on mass inspection is an epoch that is over. [Good] quality has to be built in.[3]

What should we do? Make it clear to vendors of critical parts that they must learn and use process control. Purchasing managers must learn the statistical control of quality. They must proceed under the new philosophy: the right quality characteristics must be built in, without dependence on inspection. Statistical control of the process provides the only way for the supplier to build quality in, and the only way to provide to the purchaser evidence of uniform repeatable quality and of cost of production.[5]

Another example: I was in a plant watching these wonderful people working so rapidly. A group gathered around me and one of the women asked me, "why is it that we have to spend so much time straightening out these plastic plates that we work on"? She said, they come in warped and we have to straighten them out before we can work on them. [Deming], "Well, can't you straighten them out?" Yes, but it takes our time. That interferes with our work. She said she thinks that they were made in perfect condition and jammed into a box, tossed around, and by the time this group gets them, they're warped. The others nodded approval.

I said to her, what is the problem? You get paid for straightening them out. We're spending so much time, they said, that necessity for straightening them interferes with our work. [Pay had nothing to do with it.] And the management had inspections. I never saw so much inspection, nowhere, never in my life.[3]

How much does unnecessary inspection cost?

In capital equipment? I asked [management], how much of your capital equipment is invested in gages, recording machines, computing machines and for printing out reports? Eighty percent of their capital equipment was invested for gages, measuring instruments and computers in which to store the information.[3]

In payroll? I said, how much of your payroll goes for inspection? Answer: Between 55% and 60%. I said, those are large figures. Well, yes, but we have to be sure of our quality.

That is confession that they don't know what quality is. They're trying to build it in by inspection, and they did not know that those plates were coming in warped. The woman that complained about it, she and the group, were way ahead of the management and they knew about problems the management should have known, should have corrected. There's all the capital investment and labor that they were putting into inspections and recording figures, knew not what was happening in the plant.[3]

Point 4

End the practice of awarding business on the basis of price tag. Instead, minimize total cost. Move toward a single supplier for any one item, on a long-term relationship of loyalty and trust.

How much does it cost to have a policy of awarding business to the lowest bidder? How much education does it take to award business to the lowest bidder? Here are two figures:

$778 per 1,000 (Bidder A)
$762 per 1,000 (Bidder B)

How much education does it take to make that wonderful statement that the bid from Bidder B is the lower of the two? You know, you don't even need to subtract to observe that B is lower than A, and that's all the education that you need to find out who is the lowest bidder.

The days are over when purchases are made on that basis. Quality has to come into consideration. There is no such thing as price without knowledge of quality. That is not new. Everybody knows it.[3]

What's the problem? Most purchasing managers do not know at present which of their suppliers are qualified.[5]

What should we do? Purchasing managers must learn enough about the statistical control of quality to be able to assess the qualifications of a supplier, to be able to talk to him in statistical language.[5]

Some suppliers are already qualified and are conforming to this recommendation. Some follow their product through the purchaser's production lines to learn what problems turn up, and to take action, so far as possible, to avoid problems in the future.[5]

You have to learn about process control. It is only by statistical evidence that we can know what a vendor is able to produce. Every company has a booklet of rules for their vendors and have teams around to inspect the vendors, make sure they can produce quality. Two weeks ago I said to a company, ["H]ere's this booklet, so thick..."

"How long have you been using it?"

"Thirteen years."

"How effective has it been?"

"It's totally ineffective; we have to do something different."

Well, of course, there wasn't anything in there by which to measure quality, totally ineffective. The managers of purchasing, the whole group, have a new job. They won't learn in three weeks. They have to learn about process control—statistical methods. They'll have to learn to buy materials whose quality is demonstrable before it left the door of the vendor. That demonstration can come only by statistical charts to be furnished by the vendor. Yes, the purchaser will be there, of course, helping, keeping instruments in line with his own, and working as a team.

When the vendor is able to [furnish statistical charts] then he knows what his quality will be tomorrow, and the day after that. You know that he knows his costs and that those costs are at a minimum under that system. Can you do business otherwise? Well, you could say, well, we are. Those days are over.

There's no better way to get rooked. American industry is getting rooked; the government is getting rooked by buying at the lowest price without consideration of quality. Consideration of quality requires education, a program, with experience. You have to learn to talk French; it takes a while to do it. [5]

What about a company that hasn't started yet? You have to allow five years for managers of purchasing, to learn enough about statistical control of quality, to stop dealing with vendors that depend on inspection, to find vendors, and to persuade them to learn, so that they can produce evidence of quality along with the goods. That's a five-year job, and then, of course, you start all over again. Take five years to reduce the number of vendors to those that can furnish evidence of quality. You can't just halt right now production, and start up again when everything is all ready, five or six years from now. You have to keep running, keep moving, make these changes, and how long will it take? Five years.[4]

One company that I work with is reducing their number of vendors from 4,000 to 800, and they are allowing themselves five years. I think that's about right. I don't see the possibility of accomplishing so much in less than five years. There's a lot of teaching; a lot of learning has to be done within that company, and in the houses of their vendors. A long, thorny road lies ahead of American industry. How long? Ten to thirty years, to settle down to what? An acknowledged, competitive position.[4]

Example of an award of a contract. I copied this from a proposal. The contract will be awarded to the responsible offer [whose] offering conforming to the solicitation will be most advantageous to the government, price, and other factors considered. That's Paragraph A. I'll skip down to Paragraph B: The right is reserved to accept other than the lowest offer and to reject any/or all offers.[3]

It sounds great. There's only one little trouble. Someone that puts this into effect has to know something about quality, how to measure it. He has to understand process control and its relationship to cost, the relationship to stability for tomorrow, the next week, the next week, and to know that the quality and the cost will stay there until the management of the vendor improves the system and makes it still better.

Companies that I work with, are putting their managers of purchasing, sometimes twenty, sometimes fifty, sometimes more than a hundred, not all at once, ten at a time, twenty at a time, into courses and then into more courses and then they require experience.

Another thing: Materials and components may all be excellent. A component, all by itself, may be excellent yet not work well in production, or in a finished product. It is thus necessary to follow samples of materials through a whole production process into sub-assembly, assembly, and into the customer's use. A theorem seems to be unknown, certainly ignored, in government regulatory agencies. So many of them suppose that all you need is good components, put them together and you'll have a system. That's not so. They have to have parts that work together. This is so simple, it seems, today.

For example, to make a toll call to Chicago, nothing to it. How many people know that in completing that connection, they may be using millions of parts working together, made to work together so that that system is not just made up of good parts. It's made up of parts that were made well; yes, they were good, but they were made to work together. And they do. There are so many ways to improve incoming materials. What this means is they're going to have to do business with vendors that can furnish evidence of quality which only means evidence that they know what they're doing, that they know their costs, that they can produce the same stuff tomorrow and next week, but at the same cost.

We hope that they will continually improve, yes, but that would mean intervention by management with a system, with the aim of improvement. This will mean, in many instances, maybe most instances, the companies will find only one vendor that is qualified, just one. The problem is to find one. You don't talk about two until you find one. I don't know whose theorem it is, but in order to find two, you have to find one first. The problem is to find one good vendor that can furnish the evidence, along with the goods. Why should you buy goods without knowing what you're buying, and there's only one way to know, and that is by evidence that comes along with the goods, physical evidence, for example, in the form of X-bar and R charts.

Never mind if you don't know what they are. You can learn. It's important to know that they exist and that they must be used. That's the important thing. I ask again: Why should you buy goods without knowing what you're buying and you do not know without that evidence. Hardware? Oh, yes, maybe half of what companies buy is just hardware or materials of standard quality or put up by ASTM specifications, maybe 50 percent, maybe 55 percent of what you buy for your company is simply hardware. No problem. Actually, so much of what you buy is for sale day by day and the price fixed in the Chicago market. Well, don't make problems where there aren't any.

Hardware is hardware, but when it comes to parts that have to be right, you're talking now about the problems that I'm trying to explain, the problems of purchasing materials that are not hardware. The company that adopts this policy will work with a vendor. The vendor will find his own teacher. Don't ask me where. His people will learn. It's a chain reaction and the vendor that you buy from sells to your competitor. He sells to other people. As you help your vendor to improve, you help all American industry to improve. Everybody will come out ahead as a result of anybody's effort to improve.[3]

What should we expect? This requirement will inevitably lead to drastic reduction in the number of vendors that a company deals with. A company will be lucky to find one vendor that can supply statistical evidence of quality. The theory that competition automatically regulates quality and price does not work in today's requirements for uniformity and reliability. Price has no meaning without a measure of the quality being purchased. Without adequate measures of quality, business drifts to the lowest bidder, low quality and high cost being the inevitable result. American industry and the U.S. Government are being rooked by rules that award business to the lowest bidder.[5]

Whose fault is it? The purchasing managers of a company are not at fault for giving business to the lowest bidder, nor for seeking more bids in the hope of getting a still better price. That is their mandate. Only the top management can change their direction.[5]

Example 1: An American manufacturer of automobiles may today have 2,500 vendors. A Japanese automobile company may have 380. Rapid and determined reduction of the number of vendors in American manufacturing is already under way. A request for bids usually contains a clause to say that quality may be considered along with price. That is, the award will not necessarily be given to the lowest bidder. Such a clause is meaningless without a yardstick by which to measure quality. The buyer and his purchasing manager usually lack such a yardstick. They are candidates for plunder by the lowest bidder.[5]

Example 2: A flagrant example is a request for professional help, to be awarded to the lowest bidder. Example (actual, from a government agency): For delivery and evaluation of a course on management for quality control for supervisors. An order will be issued on the basis of price.[5]

Consider Several Different Worlds[8]

We consider here a number of worlds. Any theorem is true in its own world. But which world are we in? Which of several worlds makes contact with ours? That is the question.

World 1

1. The customer knows what he wants, and can convey to a supplier his needs in terms of specifications or other description.
2. The price paid is the only cost to consider: no other cost is involved.
3. Several suppliers can without question meet the specifications right down the middle, all equal.
4. The only difference between the suppliers is the prices quoted. One is lowest, including transportation and the cost of doing business with him.
5. The customer has no scruples nor prejudice against any of them.

In this world, anyone would be a fool not to do business with the lowest bidder.

We sometimes find ourselves in this kind of world. A homely example is food in a package. Of three grocers handy, one sells it at lowest price. He will get our business.

World 2

1. The customer knows what he wants, and can convey to a supplier his needs in terms of specifications or other description.
2. Several suppliers or jobbers can without question supply the material as specified.
3. They all quote identical prices.
4. One of them, however, provides better service than the others. He has inventory, or has access to inventory. His delivery is

dependable. When he says that he will deliver the material at 1500 h this Thursday, he means this Thursday, not just some Thursday. The material will come in the right kind of car, and the car will be clean. He will have a man on the customer's receiving platform to give advice to the customer on how to unload the material, and how to store it, if there be risk of handling damage, risk of warp or of aging from wrong temperature, wrong humidity, wrong way to stack the pieces.

In World 2, the customer will do business with the jobber that provides the best service.

A possible example is sugar. No one could care less what company made the sugar. Sugar is sugar, no matter who made it, no matter who sells it; 998 parts in 1,000 are sucrose; the other 2 parts are other kinds of sugar. All six jobbers will quote the same price, the price posted this hour on the Commodities Exchange.

World 3

1. As in World 1. However, the customer will listen to advice from a supplier. Some changes in his specifications might be worthy of thought.
2. The price paid is not the only cost. There is also the cost of use, predictions of how the material will work in manufacturing, along with consideration of the final quality that will go out the door.
3. Several suppliers tender their proposals, all at different prices, all different in other ways. One or more of them will be concerned about quantities at each delivery, fluctuations of demand, and about the number of days allowed from order to delivery. One or more of them will propose a long-term arrangement, with the aim to follow the customer's use of

the material (which might of course be a sub-assembly) in his various stages of manufacture and onward, with the possibility that small changes from time to time, arrived at by joint effort, might turn out to improve performance and decrease overall costs for the customer.

The customer's ultimate aim is continual improvement of quality along with lower costs. Judicious reduction in the number of suppliers, with long-term contracts, for any one item, may seem to offer tempting advantages.

The choice may be difficult. The customer might be wise to divide the business at the outset between two or three suppliers, for further study.

We pause here to recall a few facts of life. Any supplier worthy of consideration possesses specialized knowledge about his products—more than the customer can hope to have, even though the customer will be the user of the supplier's product.

It is good to perceive that customer and suppliers form a system, and that everybody will win on optimization. But cooperation is a two-way street. Can the customer uphold his obligations? The customer has barely enough knowledge to work with one supplier. He will stretch himself too thin to try to work with two suppliers for any one item. Neither of them owes allegiance to the customer. Each of them has his own interests at heart. A customer with several suppliers for any one item is accordingly at a disadvantage.

Another point is that a supplier must be assured of a long-term relationship with the customer in order to make his contribution toward optimization of the system. A one-year contract barely gives the supplier time to get his house in order by the end of the year, at which time the business may go to a competitor.

Optimization of a system with several suppliers for any one item makes good talk, but as a practical matter it is only talk, even under long-term contracts.

Selection of the single supplier. Prime consideration. Has the suitor of choice sufficient capacity? If not, then he can not entertain any thought of being a single supplier. Two or more suppliers all pushed to capacity is not unusual. I have seen six.

Sudden expansion of a supplier to produce the required volume may turn out to be annoying for both people, customer and supplier, because of variable quality and uncertain delivery, temporary though these may be.

Sudden jump to a single supplier is inadvisable. There are risks. Go slow. It is not a relationship to enter into lightly. The wise customer will take into account a number of characteristics of a candidate, for example:

His record of past performance
Capacity and ability to meet demands
Has his management adopted the new philosophy?
Labor-management relations
Turnover in management
How much money does he spend for training? for education?
Turnover on the factory floor
Has he borrowed money from his pension fund?
What rate of interest does he pay his bank? That is, does his
    banker consider this supplier to be a good risk?
How about relationships between this supplier and his suppliers?
    Are they happy, or do they indicate external friction?
Does he depend on inspection for quality? Does he have a system
    of continual improvement of processes?
How important is the customer to the supplier? Will the customer
    provide but a small fraction of the supplier's business?
How important is the supplier to the customer?

An over-riding criterion is the supplier's burning desire to work with the customer on a long-term relationship backed up by a demonstrable store of specialized knowledge, with management that is trying to adopt the new philosophy.

If the relationship goes sour, whose fault is it? The customer's, mostly, and he is the one that will suffer most.

Advantages of having a single supplier for any one item. A long-term relationship with a single supplier may be a wise decision if customer and supplier play their parts for optimization of the system. Advantages:

1. Constant improvement of quality, design, and service
2. Lower and lower costs
3. Improved profit for both parties
4. Happiness and satisfaction

Obligations of customer and supplier. There is a strong movement toward the single supplier, maybe too strong. It is feared that many people fail to understand their obligations before they enter into this relationship. The customer has distinct obligations to the single supplier. He must concentrate efforts to cooperate with the supplier to optimize the relationship. It may be a new kind of relationship to both customer and supplier.

Heretofore, under the system of business on price tag, and with several suppliers on short-term contracts, such as a year, competitors watched each other. The single supplier faces a new kind of life; he has no competitor to watch. He is alone with his customer.

The customer has obligation to work with the single supplier, to keep in touch with problems and with help. The days are over when the supplier's obligations end with delivery and acceptance.

It is now common practice for hourly workers of the supplier to see how their product works when somebody tries to use it. What could we do to decrease some of the problems encountered? Conversely, hourly workers of the customer visit the supplier to try to understand his problems, and try to help.

Some of the usual fears about a single supplier:

1. When he gets a chance, he will choke you, raise his prices. Actually, this has never happened. For sure, a supplier can make an honest mistake in prediction of costs—he can underestimate his costs. Embarrassed, he asks the customer to help him out—either that or he (supplier) may go out of business.

    If a supplier were to try to choke his customer, whose fault is it? The customer made his choice of supplier. Is this the kind of man to choose for a life-long relationship of trust and happiness?

2. What about a catastrophe? – fire, strike, frozen water mains – somebody bought out the supplier and will discontinue this business. The answer is that we can rely on Murphy's law. There will be trouble. He that hopes for none is living in some other world. Unfortunately, having two suppliers for every item will only ensure twice as many fires in a year, twice as many strikes, twice as many suppliers that discontinue this business. For more trouble, have more suppliers.

A customer is concerned that his single supplier may suffer a catastrophe. There have been in the past two solutions: (1) Have two suppliers for the same item. Perhaps allot only a small amount of business to the second supplier; (2) Arrange with some other supplier to come in suddenly and fill in, in case the one and only supplier suffers a catastrophe. This is for most materials a wild idea. In the first place, the catastrophe would for most materials be over and business restored before the alternate supplier could get started. An exception may exist when the alternate supplier is already in the business making materials very similar to that which was cut off.

A better plan would be for the customer to express to his single supplier his concern about a catastrophe, and ask him to arrange for a competitor to take over the business if needed.

A suggestion offered by Dr. Joyce Orsini is for a customer to ask the sole supplier, in the event of a catastrophe, to make an arrangement with a competitor, to step in and try to provide (unfortunately on short notice) the material or service required.

This makes good sense because the single supplier, if he is good enough to be chosen as single supplier, knows far better than the customer could know his competitors and what they can do; also how a competitor's product will differ from what is currently being supplied. Contributed by Dr. Joyce Orsini.

Engineering changes. What about engineering changes, or other changes that the customer makes? These may raise the supplier's costs.

The supplier may have laid in a heavy inventory of material. The customer has a moral obligation to come through with help to the supplier. The customer should either buy it, or help the supplier to sell it.

A forging company laid in a heavy inventory of a special type of bar steel, only to learn after a few weeks that because the customer will make a change, this bar steel will be excess inventory. The customer should buy it, or help the forging company to sell it. The supplier will call by telephone a number of competitors—maybe one of them is looking for just this kind of bar steel. Trade magazines play a helpful part in disposition of excess inventories.

Point 5

Improve constantly and forever the system of production and service, to improve quality and productivity, and thus constantly decrease costs.

How? Use statistical methods to find out, in any trouble spot, what are the sources of waste, low productivity, and poor quality. Which are local faults? Which faults belong to the system, the responsibility of management to correct? Do not rely on judgment.[5]

Why? Judgment always gives the wrong answer on the question of where the fault lies. Statistical methods make use of knowledge of the subject matter where it can be effective, but supplant it where it is a hazard.[5]

What about training? How many people doing training know when training is finished? You can only know by use of statistical methods when training is finished.[3] You can only know by statistical methods when training is not yet finished and when further training by these same methods will be helpful. When someone is trained and in statistical control of his work, further training by this method of training will be totally ineffective. How many people doing training know when they've finished the job and when they've not finished the job?

How many people doing training know they have only one chance? Train a man wrong, in the wrong way, so that he produces defectives or does not realize his potential, get him into statistical control, he'll make defectives for you and there isn't anything they can do about it. They've got one chance. Why not do it right? Supervision must be totally reconstructed.

Management must constantly improve the system. This obligation never ceases.[5]

Point 6

Institute training on the job.

Use effective methods by which you can improve the system. People are part of the system. Management could improve the system by making it possible for people to understand better what is acceptable and what is not. Improvement of the system could be improving the machines, procedures, design of the product, but you don't have to take the engine out, the air conditioner, and half dozen other items that I wouldn't be able to describe in order to repair a water pump. If that happens during manufacture they've got a terrific expense. Part of management's job is to improve design, not just of new product, but design of present product as well.[2]

What should we do? Institute modern aids to training on the job. Training must be totally reconstructed. Statistical methods must be used to learn when training is finished, and when further training would be beneficial.[5]

Why? It is demoralizing and costly to call to the attention of a production-worker a defective item that he has made, when he is in a state of statistical control with respect to the cause of that defect. He is in effect drawing random samples from a bowl. He can not govern the random appearance of black beads in his samples. He is handicapped by the proportion of black beads in the system. Only the management can change the proportion of black beads in the bowl.[6]

A man, once hired and trained, and in statistical control of his own work, whether it be satisfactory or not, can do no better. Further training can not help him.[5]

What if a person's work is not satisfactory? It is better to shift to a totally different job a worker that has developed statistical control of his work in his present job, but whose output in quality or in quantity is unsatisfactory.[6]

Point 7

Institute leadership. The aim of supervision should be to help people and machines and gadgets to do a better job. Supervision of management is in need of overhaul, as well as supervision of production-workers.

There was a supervisor devoted to the company, seven people working for her. They all loved her. She would lay out on a table every day the defective items that her seven people made. At the end of the day she'd spend the last half hour talking with them, explain this defect and that, turning it over, getting out a microscope, everybody watching, learning, resolving never to do such a thing again, devoted to the company. Everybody thought that she was a good supervisor. Do you know what she was doing? Making problems and guaranteeing them forever. Intentionally, no, only doing her best. She needs help.[2]

She needs to know how to supervise. She can learn. Do you see what I mean? Supervision has to be improved. Finding those defects and studying them doesn't reduce the number of defects. A little later we'll perform an experiment with red and white beads, trying to draw out random samples of fifty beads at a time, all white. The problem is that there are red beads and white ones in the bowl and when we pull out our day's work, we have red beads along with white ones, sometimes three, sometimes thirteen, sometimes sixteen, sometimes nine. As long as those red beads are in the system, the people that work there will produce defectives.

See, the problem is that her seven people did not make the defectives; the system did it. She supposed that they could, by manipulating their fingers differently, eliminate defects. These seven workers did not make the defectives. They delivered them, yes, but they did not make them; the system made them. The supervisor, only doing her best, with compassion and patience and the respect of everybody in the company, was trying to help them and in doing that, was only making things worse for them, leading them to suppose that by changing their work habits, they could do better. Instead of that the only possible effect was they could only make things worse and she was guaranteeing this problem forever.[2]

What should we do? Improve supervision. Supervision belongs to the system, and is the responsibility of management.[5]

- Foremen must have more time to help people on the job.
- Statistical methods are vital as aid to the foreman and to the production manager to indicate causes of waste, low productivity, and poor quality. Is the fault local, or is it in the system?
- The usual procedure by which the foreman calls the worker's attention to every defect is wrong. It creates trouble and defeats the purpose of supervision.[5]

Point 8

Drive out fear, so that everyone may work effectively for the company.

Why are people afraid? Most workers, and even people in management positions, do not understand what the job is, nor what is right or wrong. Moreover, it is not clear to them how to find out. Many of them are afraid to ask questions or to report trouble.[5]

People are afraid to talk to one another because someone talked with somebody else, getting advice from somebody else, would indicate that he knows not all that there is to know. Must not let that rumor get around.[4]

What happens when people are afraid? The economic loss from fear is appalling. It is necessary, for better quality and productivity, that people feel secure. *Se* comes from Latin, meaning without, *cure* means fear or care. Secure means without fear, not afraid to express ideas, not afraid to ask questions, not afraid to ask for further instructions, nor afraid to report equipment out of order, nor material that is unsuited to the purpose, poor light, or other working conditions that impair quality and production.[5]

People don't report anything out of order. We might have to halt our production in order to take care of it, and we dare not halt.[2]

No use to report again about equipment out of order because nobody is interested. How could the foreman be interested? He has no time. Second place, he has to get his quota out. He can't stop to take care of anything.[4]

People don't ask too many times about the job. It may become obvious that he cannot learn the job. The foreman may have to tell him, "We may have to let you go if you can't learn the job. It's the same as what I told you yesterday, don't you know?" That doesn't help him any. I have already mentioned several times the matter of supervision needs overhauling badly. People are required to follow certain rules to get out a quota of production, to just go ahead and use material, no matter what, just get it out. It's closely associated with work standards. Get it out. Never mind the quality. Get it out.[4]

Another aspect of fear is seen in inspection. An inspector may record incorrectly results of inspection for fear that the result will show up somebody. It might show up a whole group doing very badly, so she records fictitious figures. Must not let things look too bad, you know.[4]

An example: The inspector didn't dare to put down the right figures. She had heard what would happen to that plant, if her figures ever showed as much as 10 percent defective going out the door. She never notified anybody in the plant. She didn't care about herself, but looked at all the other people in the plant. She heard the plant manager would close the place down and sweep it out if the proportion defective went [up] to 10 percent per month. She made sure it didn't happen. Producing useless figures, of course. Eliminate numerical goals (e.g., 10% defective). They don't help anybody to do a better job—they're counterproductive. They only indicate that management has resigned, knowing not what to do.[2]

Only the top management can reduce fear.[4]

Point 9

Break down barriers between departments. People in research, design, sales, and production must work as a team, to foresee problems of production and in use that may be encountered with the product or service.

Why can't people talk with each other? Engineering, engineering design, marketing, sales, and production have common problems. Why don't they learn from each other and work together? Why have departments? Everybody should be working toward the same end. Sure, you have different kinds of expert knowledge devoted to the company, but why not pool that knowledge?[4]

A student took her doctor's degree under my direction at NYU some years ago. The title of her dissertation was, "How Companies Use the Results of Consumer Research in the Redesign of Present Product and the Design of New Product." She conducted four interviews in four companies. I wrote some letters for her on NYU letterhead, and they talked to her with great kindness. She came back to me and said, "The title ought to be changed. The question is not how companies use the results of consumer research, but whether they do." They apparently do not.[4]

Do you think that's good management? People talk about QC-Circles. Where you need one is in the management.[4]

Only the top management can bring people together. Distances between departments are so common in America, hobbling production, raising costs. This cannot happen in Japan. People go to Japan trying to copy quality control. I'm afraid most of them have no idea what to look for. I hope they enjoy the ride.[4]

What should we do? People in research, design, and sales, must learn methods of production, and learn about problems encountered with various materials and specifications. Otherwise, there will be losses in production from necessity for rework and from attempts to use materials unsuited to the purpose. Why not spend time in the factory, see the problems, and hear about them?[5]

Some examples where communication between departments would have helped:

(a) A flood of waivers of specifications for the components of a product is clear indication of failure to test prototypes, and failure to understand the problems of production. In a recent experience, a company approved 352 waivers in one product.[5]

(b) Here are two pieces from two different suppliers, same item number, both beautifully made, yet sufficiently different for one to be usable, the other usable only with costly rework, a heavy loss to the plant. Both pieces satisfied the specifications. Both suppliers had fulfilled their contracts. The explanation lay in specifications that were incomplete and unsuited to the requirements of manufacture, approved by the man that had no problems. There was no provision for a report on material used in desperation.[5]

Point 10

Eliminate slogans, exhortations, and targets for the work force asking for zero defects and new levels of productivity. Such exhortations only create adversarial relationships, as the bulk of the causes of low quality and low productivity belong to the system and thus lie beyond the power of the work force.

Sure, the company has goals, maybe lots of goals.[4] One is to improve our economic position, our competitive position. Let us try to be a better service. Try to be in business 10 years from now. Let's improve our market position. Those are all wonderful goals. Let's try to make everybody happier. Sure, the company has goals. Individuals have goals. I'm going to finish this chapter before morning. I'm going to spend more time studying a lot of things. Everybody has goals and the company has goals, but what I'm speaking about is numerical goals and slogans posted around in plants for hourly workers and other people. They do no good. They need a route. How do you do it?[4]

Someone told me one time that the Postmaster General was going to improve productivity 3 percent next year. I said, "Does he have any idea how to do it?" "Oh, no, we're just going to do it." Sounds great. Numerical goals for the other fellow without any explanation of how. The question is how do you do it? People need to know how. Here I was one time in a plant, in a part of a factory, on route to a conference room where we were going to have a conference about something. Here on the walls of the cafeteria, plastered six feet high for everybody to see week by week, for the past six months, proportion defective.

There was a chart, proportion defective. It was running around 4.5 percent defective, and there was a red line, about halfway up, labeled "Goal." Yes, but how? Not a word said. That doesn't do any good. If it did no harm, well, that would be all right. Only trouble is it's counterproductive. People need to know how. Can't just let it stand that way without explaining how. That indicates that the management has abandoned the job. They know not what to do, so they put these posters on the wall. Along with it, was another one, production week by week, for the last six months, and it went along pretty steady.

All this showed statistical control, which showed, incidentally, again the only remedy was action by management. There wasn't any. I didn't see any posters lying around telling what the management was doing. Now, that would make some sense. Put posters around with what the management is doing about number 1. What's the management doing about number 2? What's the management doing about number 3? What's the management doing about number 7, number 6, and so on? Change posters every once in a while. Tell people what the management is doing. That might do some good.

Nobody can help without a way.[2] Best efforts don't do it. Best efforts need help. Where is the help? Zero defects is another one plastered around. Four words, same effect. Sounds great.

Some company asked everybody, all 2,000 people in the company, to sign a pledge, "I will hereafter make no defects," and sign my name. Out of the 2,000 people, 3 people refused. I won't say they were the only smart ones. They're probably all smart enough to know that that's not the way to do it. Signing a pledge won't do it. "How" is the question. That's what people are asking. How? And what is the management doing about it? Plaster that around on the walls. It would help. I won't try to draw a picture: A man hotfooting it upstairs increasing productivity. How?

The purpose of these lectures is to find out how. It starts at the top with the 14 points. If management doesn't carry those out, it won't happen. What do you get from goals without any help? zero defects, increased productivity? What you get out of it is failure to accomplish the goals. Well, of course. There's nothing there to help anybody. Disrespect of the management could be the worst thing. [You get an] increase in variability because people that are already in statistical control will try to meddle with what they're doing, and make it worse. Therefore, you get increases in proportion defective.

It will be bigger than you're entitled to. You'll increase costs and demoralize the workforce. You can't fool the people on the job. They know better than that. Well, as I said, I was going into a conference room when I saw these. We went into the conference room. There were maybe twelve people there, around a table, and I gave a little speech about the nonsense of numerical goals, Point 10. Maybe eight minutes, maybe nine. When I got through, or when I was about finished, some man rose and made this wonderful statement, "A goal never helped anybody to do a better job." How many words? You can sum it all up that way. Why say anymore? A goal can never help anybody to do a better job." Eleven words.

The president of the corporation happened to be present at that meeting. It was an important product. He was deeply interested in it. He heard my speech, and when I finished, he gave it over again in shorter time and did a better job than I did. There are no more goals there. Goals and I don't work together. Wherever there are goals, either they come down or I do, one or the other. Why doesn't management advertise that they're out of business? They don't need to advertise it. Eliminate work standards.

Again, I ask you, did a work standard, so many per day, with a 10 percent allowance for defectives, 20 percent allowance for scrap, ever help anybody to do a better job? Sure, you need work standards for budgeting or estimating costs in advance. Estimates are always in advance. Sure, you need to have some idea of what something is going to cost, but to use them on the job is taking an incalculable economic toll from American industry. We obviously cannot afford it. People don't like it. Oh, some people do.

Take a man who's been on the job a number of years, 15 or 16 years, outlived five generations of people in and out from the same job. He learns to live with it. He finishes his goal, his quota, for the day, and he and some of his friends then play cards for two hours. Other people, not having adapted themselves to this, finish and just have to stand around. They can't go home, can't do any more work, but some of the men learn to live with the situation. You can always learn to live with anything, I think, if you live long enough. They look forward to finishing their quota, so they can finish up that card game, that tournament that they had started yesterday.

I sat alongside a man by accident, but we won't go into this. He was in a large company, in the service end of it, taking care of items that this company makes. He said that the repairman, technician, that pays no attention to the quota of five calls per day, or four calls per day, is doing more for the company than the one that meets the quota, day after day, always makes it. He says the technician that stays on the job until he has made that repair to his satisfaction is doing more for the company, even in dollars and cents, than the men that meet their quotas. This man stays on the job until he's sure that that machine will run, that nobody will have to call him back the next day.

He says that sometimes it's two years before that same trouble reappears. Others that make their quota cause trouble.

Sure, they meet the quota. I can meet one myself. I could make nine calls a day, drive 80 miles an hour and take things apart. Never mind putting them back right. Anybody can do that. The man that does a professional job to suit himself, to suit his standards of workmanship, is doing more for the company, earning more for the company, than people that meet their quotas.

So, in summary, what's wrong with slogans, exhortations, and targets? Posters and slogans in the factory try to push people into new levels of productivity without showing them how.

Some examples of targets seen on signs, without a method on how to reach them:

- Zero defects
- Increase productivity (with a picture of a man running upstairs)
- Reduce waste
- Reduce the proportion of defects

Another useless sign:

"Your work is your self-portrait. Would you sign it?"

No. Not when you give me defective canvas to work on, paint not suited to the job, brushes worn out.[5]

Posters and slogans like these do not help anyone to do a better job. Of course, the company has goals, such as to put out a better product, to reduce waste, to advance into better competitive position. Anybody has goals, such as to get a better education, to reduce his weight, to study music, to be less of a grouch. But a numerical goal for the rank and file is wrong, as it does not tell anyone how to achieve it. They even have a negative effect through frustration. They are management's lazy way out. They indicate desperation and incompetence of management.[5]

Point 11

(a) Eliminate work standards (quotas) on the factory floor. Substitute leadership.
(b) Eliminate management by objective. Eliminate management by numbers, numerical goals. Substitute leadership.

A bank that I worked with had engaged a consulting firm to come and set work standards. A beautiful, bound book it was. A girl should be able to process so many checks per hour. Another one should be able to compute interest on so many checks per hour, and penalties. A teller should handle so many customers in an hour. Not one word in there about quality or how many mistakes. Not one word about how to reduce mistakes. Is that good? The bank paid for it, and they thought that it was wonderful. They found out what I thought about it.[4]

Think of paying out money for something like that. Can you imagine somebody taking money for something like that? I can. Somebody did. He didn't know any better.[4]

What should we do? Look carefully at work standards. Do they improve quality, or only ask for numbers? Do they help anyone to do a better job? Work standards are costing the country as much loss as poor materials and mistakes. There is a better way.[5]

Example of incompatible hopes: A corporation published this:

GOALS AND OBJECTIVES

1. Provide systems of reward that recognize superior performance, innovation, extraordinary care and commitment.

2. Create and maintain stimulating and enjoyable work—environment, with the aim to attract, develop, and retain self-directed, talented people.

Comment. These two goals are incompatible. The first one will induce conflict and competition between people. This is the road to demoralization. Goal 1 will take the joy out of work, and will thus defeat Goal 2, however noble it be.[7]

Point 12

(a) Remove barriers that rob the hourly worker of his right to pride of workmanship. The responsibility of supervisors must be changed from sheer numbers to quality.
(b) Remove barriers that rob people in management and in engineering of their right to pride of workmanship. This means, inter alia, abolishment of the annual or merit rating and of management by objective.

What should we do? Institute a massive training program for employees in simple but powerful statistical methods, to be accomplished over a period of several years. Thousands of people must learn rudimentary statistical methods. One in 500 must spend the necessary 10 years to become a statistician. This training will be a costly affair.[5]

The first training program is for management. They're going to have to learn what the 14 points are and why, and they're going to have to train, depending on the size of the company, maybe 6 people, maybe 16, maybe 50. Two companies that I work with are each training 50,000 people. Difficult. Where are you going to get the teachers? They're finding some. Good teachers are teaching others. Everybody has to scrape.[4] (See The Merit System: The Annual Appraisal: Destroyer of People, in Chapter 1.)

Point 13

Institute a vigorous program of education and self-improvement.

What type of training? Institute a vigorous program for retraining people in new skills, to keep up with changes in model, style, materials, methods, and—at times, if advantageous—new machinery.[5]

Make maximum use of statistical knowledge and talent in your company. Engage counsel from a competent, experienced statistician.[5]

Nobody in management or any other position need ever ask again what top management must do. No school of business never need ask, "What must we do?" But how? I could offer a word.[4]

A plan that seems to work well, you can think of a better plan, but one that seems to work pretty well is for a vice president, empowered to act, to report to top management and to report to the consulting statistician at every visit, to review the accomplishments of top management to date. A vice president came to see me Christmas Eve; we had no other time. It was the day before Christmas, but we did it. It wasn't always convenient, but he did it. I admire him. That's his job, and he's doing it. To review on a regular basis the accomplishments of top management to date. On each of these 14 points, what are you doing?[4]

Every time I go to one of my companies, that's the program, that's the question, what are you doing? What are your plans for the next three weeks?[4]

It's a long road. How long? A company that sets off today, full steam on the 14 points, will take a long time. Oh yes, you'll see brilliant accomplishments, some in three weeks, some more in another three weeks, and maybe every week some. There will be brilliant fires, yes, but that's not quality control. Quality control is not a bag of techniques or a bag of tricks, nor few accomplishments. Those are merely manifestations of what happens when the management goes to work. It is easy to be misled by quick games.[4]

Supposing we're doing pretty well, that must be it. This is what happened in America in 1942, [19]43, [19]44, and up to 1950. There were techniques. Ten thousand people learned simple, but powerful techniques, and not one man in management learned them. Maybe one. There were brilliant fires. By 1950, they had all died out. Oh, you're asking, "How long is this going to take?" Well, in five years, a company should see some effect, and will. The bigger the company, and some are empires, it's simply too colossal, too complex. It would take a long time. There should be visible results in five years. Some will show results in three.[4]

Management must learn the new economics. Economists have to learn the new economics. Regulatory agencies, the government, have to learn. Unable, they are, to predict consequences of economic theory. They may meanwhile wreck a lot of institutions that we have been very happy with and proud of, which have set standards for the world. They will have to learn. The number of parts, say, in a communication system, going to pick up the telephone and use it, you use millions of parts that have to work together.[4]

They have to be made with a purpose of working together, not just that they are good. Throwing everything open to competition could wreck one of our finest institutions. The history of recent years is replete with examples of government regulation, born of the best of intentions, but which would end up deadlier than the disease that they were supposed to conquer.[4]

Point 14

Put everybody in the company to work to accomplish the transformation. The transformation is everybody's job.

How soon? When? How rapidly will improvement of quality and productivity be achieved in America? The answer depends on the vigor with which top management carries out responsibilities that are clearly theirs. Quality and productivity are everybody's job, but top management must take the lead.[5]

The following letter illustrates the problem. "I am manager of one of our plants. There are five plants in this region. The manager is only interested in the bottom line. Quality, no. Get the stuff out. I will be with this company another two years. At the end of that time, I will either be promoted or I will move to another company." See his loyalty? And his question to me was, "What can I do that will live on after me?"

Another obstacle came in a letter received only a week ago. "The quandary is whether we, as one division in our corporation, can be successful in improving our quality and productivity without active involvement of our top management." My answer is, "No."

"As I was reading your notes, which I picked up in your seminar, I took the eerie feeling into my head that most of the examples in your book had come from our company, and that you were never there. I don't know how you look through the walls and see all that's wrong with our company, but your examples fit perfectly."

What did I tell him? Without the top management, forget it.

What's the problem here? The mobility of top management. A Japanese friend [remarked] "America can't make it because of the mobility of top management. In and out. No loyalty to the company. Not there long enough to make impact."

Average term, I don't know what it is, three and a half, four, four and a half years. In Japan, it's forever. How can top management be committed when their tenure is only a few years? I don't know. I don't have the answers. I'm stating problems. You might say, well, a problem is no good if you don't have a solution.

[The problem] could be insulation. It surrounds top management. [Management doesn't] understand production, sales, marketing, and are not doing anything to bring themselves and everybody together on Point 9. Aloofness of top management from the problems of production. Only yesterday, Mr. Charles Bicking, far better consultant than I am, told me that he abandoned, temporarily at least, some seminars with top management that he was giving in a fine company for the simple reason that they seemed to understand nothing about the problems of materials coming in, purchase, production, instrumentation.

They understood none of those problems. Their job is finance, accounting. He had to abandon the seminars. He was giving them six months to get acquainted with the company, after which he may resume the seminars.

What about looking at other companies? Another obstacle. People ask for examples of success. Well, that doesn't make any sense. I could show somebody six examples of wonderful success making the same thing, making pencils, making paper, making shares, which will have absolutely nothing to do with his success or failure. Not at all. His success or failure depends on what he puts into it and nothing else. Examples don't help at all.

A man called me up last week and wanted to know if I couldn't arrange for his top management to go visit some of the companies that I work with. I said, "Well, in the first place, I do not mention names of clients, but I will talk to some of them about it. Why is it that you want to do this?" "I might be able to persuade my top management to go and see some examples." I said, "I'm not going to do that. I'm not going to waste the time of any of my clients for such foolishness. Their success or their failure is their problem, and had nothing to do with the success or failure of your top management. What they would get out of it is what they put into it, and your top management doesn't even know what to do. They don't even know that they're in trouble. You told me that. Have they ever heard of these 14 points? How could they know what their job is? They don't and examples won't help them.

What if we're different? Another excuse, "Our problems are different." Well, every problem is different, but nothing to do with the case. There are many obstacles. One of them is the supposition that our problems all lie with the workforce. I've disposed of that one. Most of the problems lie in the system.

What if we're having problems? When some people find themselves in trouble, the figures don't look right on the bottom line, what do they do? Tighten up on work standards, cut down on travel, cut down on first class travel, cut out some research because we don't need all that.

Some company or some division that's in such desperate circumstances, things are so bad, that they don't have time to do anything about it. They don't have time to listen, don't have time to learn. They have to get this stuff out defects and all. Yes, they are on the way toward non-profit.

The 14 Points[5]

When shall I see results? Tangible results from each of the 14 points will not all be visible at the same time. Perhaps the best candidate for quickest results is to supplant work-standards (No. 11) with statistical aids to the worker and to supervision. No one knows what productivity can be achieved with statistical methods that help people to accomplish more by working smarter, not harder.

A close second for quick results would be to start to drive out fear (No. 8), to help people to feel secure to find out about the job and about the product, and unafraid to report trouble with equipment and with incoming materials. Once top management takes hold in earnest, this goal might be achieved with 50% success, and with powerful economic results, within two or three years. Continuation of effort will bring further success.

A close third, and a winner, would be to break down barriers between departments (No. 9). Small gains will be visible within a few weeks after a company mobilizes for quality, but sweeping improvement over the whole company will take a long time, and will continue forever.[2]

Tangible results from all the 14 points won't all come at once. Some will come quicker than others. The situation will take care of itself in nature's way, which is cruel.[4]

Unmistakable advances will be obvious within 5 years, more in 10. Twenty years may elapse before it is clear that American industry will in time (another decade?) recapture the position that it once held. But American industry may by then have a totally different composition than it has today. Products that have been the backbone of American industry may by then be of secondary importance. New products and new technology may ascend to top place. Agriculture may move up further in foreign trade.

Notes

1. From "Transformation of American Management," *Executive Excellence*, January 1987.
2. Presentation to CEOs, "Why Productivity Increases as Quality Improves," 1981.
3. Presentation of "The 14 Steps Management Must Take" at MIT/CAES, March 1981.
4. From a presentation at a CEO seminar, "Quality, Productivity, and Competitive Position," 1992.

5. From *Obligations of Management in the New Economic Age*, ca 1981.
6. From "New Principles in Administration for Quality and Efficiency," presented in Manila, July 2, 1979.
7. A note dated November 2, 1991.
8. Some Notes on Continuing Purchase of Supplies and Service, July 14, 1990.

A System Must Be Managed

(People Are Part of the System)

Deming said that an organization needs to operate as a system. The system includes the company, its customers, and its suppliers. And the system must be managed. He often added with emphasis that people are part of the system—as if it were a revelation. Many managers find it far simpler to deal with machinery, budgets, and financial issues than to deal with people, he believed. Deming held that knowing how to manage people is the single most important part of management, and the part that management is most ill-equipped to deal with.

To help management better understand what was required, Deming wrote numerous papers and gave many speeches detailing specific actions management could take when working with people issues, be they employees, customers, or suppliers. Here is a sampling.

Introduction to a System

A system is an interconnected complex of functionally related components, divisions, teams, platforms, whatever you call them, that work together to try to accomplish the aim of the system.

A system must have an aim. Without an aim there is no system. The aim of the system must be clear to everyone in the system. The aim includes plans for the future. An aim is a value judgment, not a theorem. Is your company a system? In other words, is there an aim? To some companies, because of short-term thinking, the only aim is survival for the day, with no thought about the future.

The spark that turned Japan around. I displayed to top management and engineers a system of production. The Japanese had knowledge. They had great knowledge. But it was in bits and pieces. Not organized. Uncoordinated. [A flow diagram of an organization that I showed them] directed their knowledge into a system of production, including prediction of the needs of the customers. The whole world knows about the results. A simple flow diagram, I believe, is what did it. Action began to take place as top management and engineers saw how to use their knowledge. And Dr. [Sigeiti] Moriguti of Tokyo pointed out to me a few months ago that when I talked to the 21 top management of Japan, I was talking to 80 percent of the capital.

The flow diagram starts with ideas about a possible product or service. The job is prediction. What might the customer need and buy? The Zero Stage is prediction. This prediction needs to design a product or service. Will the market be sufficient to keep us in business?

We study the results in the hands of the customer. How does he use our product or service? Do we lead him to expect too much? Do we need to modify our advertising or our claim? How do we improve our service or product? How can we help the customer? It may lead to redesign of the product. The cycle repeats and goes on and on. The consumer is the most important part of the production-line. Without the consumer there is not a production-line.

You need to work with your vender on a long-term basis. There needs to be a relationship of loyalty and trust to improve the quality of incoming material and to decrease cost on a long-term basis. Working on continual improvement. Each working for the other as a system. Better and better quality, lower and lower cost.

Some Americans have trouble with this. They tell us they go to Japan with their product and can't sell it. Remember this: supplier and customer in Japan have been working together for 20, 25, or 30 years, with continual improvement to both. Do you think they are going to break that up? Of course they are not going to break that up. You have to go over there with something new that the Japanese don't have, in order to sell it. You can't go over there expecting to break up a relationship. The Japanese are too smart for that.

The aim of the flow diagram is for raw material to come in at the front and to emerge at the end as a useable product. There is a flow of information needed to manage the system. A flow diagram also assists us to predict what components of the system will be affected, and by how much, as a result as a proposed change in one or more components.

A flow diagram is actually an organization chart. It shows people what their jobs are. How they should interact with each other as part of a system. Anybody can see from such a chart what his job is. Take the chart, put names on it. You belong here. Somebody else belongs over here. Then anybody can see from the chart what his job is. And how his work fits in with the work of others in the system.

An organization chart is far more meaningful than the usual pyramid. The pyramid only shows who reports to whom. Information flows from the top. Instructions flow from the top. A pyramid does not describe a system of production. It doesn't tell anybody what his job is. It does not tell anybody how his work fits in with the work of other people in the system. If the pyramid conveys a message, it is that anybody should, first and foremost, try to satisfy his boss (get a good rating). A pyramid, as an organization chart, thus destroys the system [as everyone is looking to get a good rating for himself]. The pyramid contributes to fragmentation of the organization. In fragmentation each component becomes an individual profit center, destroying the system.

Now, we learn that a system must have an aim. Without an aim, there is no system. A system must be managed. Otherwise the teams, divisions, people within it become competitive. And become individual profit centers. The management should try to achieve optimization, that is, maximum benefit toward the aim of the system. This means the components, instead of being individual profit centers, now make a contribution to the whole system. Optimization is a process of orchestrating the efforts of all components toward achievement of the stated aim. And again the system must have an aim. Without an aim there is no system. Optimization means accomplishment of the aim.

May I remind you the aim must also include the future. What will we be making five years from now? Any group should have as its aim optimization over time of the larger system that the group operates in. That is not for individual profit, but for contribution to the whole system. And in the end, that pays off. Everybody gets more. Purely a matter of being selfish enough. If people could only be selfish enough, they would understand the system and operate as a system, not as individual profit centers. Preparation [for the future] includes creation of a process for lifelong learning of employees. It includes constant scanning of the environment—technical, social, and economic. To perceive need or innovation. New product. New service. Or innovation of method. A company can thus, to some extent, govern its own future, not be a victim of everything that happens.

There's almost in any system interdependence of components. The greater the interdependence within the components, the greater be the need for communication and cooperation between them. Also, the greater will be the need for overall management.

Negative interactions between components, often from competition, [harm the system]. The main job of management is
to generate enhanced, positive interactions between people,
between teams, between platforms. Is a company hampering
itself by mismanagement of people? Let $A + B + C + D$ equal
the sum of the efforts of individual people. Is the company as
good as the sum of those individual abilities? It ought to be better. Why is it not? Because of interactions. Interactions between
platforms, chimneys, divisions, departments, whatever you call
them, two at a time, three at a time, and so on, may be positive
or negative. As negative interactions they subtract from the benefit of the individual people in it. Why is a company not as good
as the sum of all the people in it? With positive interactions it
ought to be more than the sum of all the individual efforts.

What is the cause of negative interactions? What causes positive interactions? Positive interactions between you, your team
and others? By working *with* them, not in conflict with them,
but in working with them you get positive interactions. Take a
look at the flow diagram. Who depends on you? Whom do you
depend on? Look at the people that you depend on. Look at the
people that depend on you.

Take four platforms, each to work on a different kind of
car. What do they do? First thing, they compete for resources.
Each of the four managers tries to garner for himself, for his
own platform, the best talent in the company. He needs money.
He competes against the others for money, and for brains in
the company. They try to destroy each other. They don't put it
down in those words. By competing with each other they help
to destroy each other and destroy the company. Their interaction is negative, not positive. But can you blame them? They're
only doing their jobs.

The system must be managed. And unless it is managed,
people, teams, platforms become competitive. We cannot afford

competition. It's destructive. Can we ever learn? Sure we can learn. That's what we're here for.

What may be the aim of a system? I have a suggestion. As I said the aim of a system is a value judgment; it is not a theorem. It's for your own self. The aim that I suggest [relates to] interaction between components of the system. Specifically, cooperation and competition must be evaluated in light of the aim, by competitors, acting jointly or together, aimed at expanding the market, instead of worrying about sharing a market. How many man years are lost worrying about sharing a market, trying to get a bigger piece of the pie? Take it away from the other fellow. Far better it would be to expand the market. Competitors should work together to expand the market. So more people could enjoy our product or our service. The bigger be the coverage the bigger be the system, the bigger be the possible benefits, but they're more difficult to manage. And they must include plans for the future.

Destruction of a System

A job description won't do more than prescribe motions. Do this. Do that. Do it this way. Do it that way. It must tell me what the work is used for. How this work contributes to the aim of the system.

Suppose that you teach me how to wash tables. How to use brushes, how to use rags, hot water, soap. I should rub this way and that way and round and round. I'm good at it. Now, you ask me to wash this table (one in front of him) and I could not do it. With all the teaching that you gave me, ask me to wash this table and I cannot do it. Not until you tell me what you're going to use the table for. What's the next stage? What happens to my work? Somebody's going to use it. Until I know my customer, who's going to use the table, I cannot wash the table. I'm helpless when asked to wash the table. I have no idea what you mean. Want to eat off it? Lickity split, good enough. Going to pile books up on it. Lickity split, good enough. But suppose you tell me you're going to use it as an operating table. Now what do I do? I scrub it. Top, bottom, sides, legs, inside, upside, I wash the floor over a wide radius. Totally different from a table you're going to eat off of. You see, unless I know what you're going to use the table for, unless I understand the next stage, I cannot do my work. That flow diagram tells people what the next stage is. Who depends on me? On whom do I depend? Then by communication, people may work together, improve their work. And *then* there may be joy in work.

Joy in Work

Joy in work comes from understanding why your work is important. Not from the work, but from knowledge of who's going to use it. Whom are we working for, who is our customer? Who depends on us? Whom do we depend on? That'll provide motivation. All that people need to understand is why the work is important. Motivation—nonsense. All that people need to know is why their work is important.

What about destruction of a system? How do you destroy a system? Very simple. Take the flow diagram [and isolate the different activities]. Each activity now is an individual profit center. Not working for the company as a whole but as an individual profit center. Every component now becomes competitive with the others. Each of them now does his best to make a mark for himself. Can you blame him? It's his only hope for survival under that system. Result—the system is destroyed. Causing loss of unknown magnitude.

An example from an automotive company: An automotive company divided itself into two groups. The pay of the top people in those groups depended on sales. They became competitive.

Results were destructive. Each group tried to outdo the other on sales. Can you blame them? That was the life dictated to them. And what happened? One group had been traditionally noted for small, dependable cars. The other group, the larger, made luxurious cars. What'd they do? The group that had been in the habit of making relatively small, dependable, lightweight cars, striving toward low running costs, extended their line. Put out a battleship. The group that had been in the habit of making luxurious cars put out light ones. Can you blame them? Their life depended on sales. They're competitive. Management made them competitive. They dang near ruined the company.

An example from a government: There is pressure on a congressman for a federal project to go to his state, regardless of what would be best for the country as a whole. Any federal money, get it for my state, get it for my district. My re-election depends on getting that money. Is it good for the country as a whole? Maybe yes and maybe no. How could it be best for the country as a whole? What's the congressman going to do? If he does not try to get federal money for his district, he may not get reelected. What about reduction in the number of naval bases? Some naval bases could be abandoned. Anywhere but in my state. Is that best for the country? The congressman and the senator forced into destruction of the system. What can you do about it? A solution, you might say, would be to limit the term of office. Election of the congressman or senator limited to 10 years, 12 years, 14, whatever you like. Second term—barred, no such thing. Then he could work for the country as a whole. He wouldn't have to work for reelection. He could understand the country as a system. It might do the job until the whole public understands the system. It might be better for the country as a whole to close the naval base in my state. It would be for everybody. Everybody would win.

Everything best is not enough. As Russell Ackoff pointed out years ago (1971), if anyone were to assemble the best parts [for an] automobile, never mind the price tag, never mind where it's made. Get the best of everything, disregarding for every part its price tag and source. The parts do not make an automobile, but everything is the best. They do not form a system.

Dr. H. R. Carabelli, of the Michigan Bell Telephone Company, wish he were here, remarked to me, "The company could have the best product engineer, the best manufacturing engineer, the best man in the country in marketing, have the best of everything throughout the company. Yet if their men do not work together as a system, the company could be swallowed whole by the competition. By people far less qualified but with good management. If the various components of an organization are all optimized, each for individual profit, each a prima donna, the organization will not be. If the whole is optimized, the different parts will not be optimized."

Who would wish to do business with a loser?

This letter came to me weeks ago, "My marriage went from rough to rocky. Rougher to rockier. Eternal trouble. Win. Lose. Each one jockeying to be the winner. I took your four day seminar. I learned about a system, win-win. I explained it to him. We thereupon worked together on every detail. Seeking win-win. Both of us win. We both won." Who would wish to be married to a loser? If one of them won, you'd be married to a loser. Who would wish to be married to a loser? This letter raises a good question. Who would wish to do business with a loser? Would anyone wish for a supplier to be a loser? Would you wish for the customer to be a loser? Would you wish for you employers to be losers? Would you wish the employees of your supplier to be losers? Or your customers to be losers? Of course not. Nobody would want it that way.

Optimization of a System

Under the prevailing style of management, [each division, department, area] naturally adopts an option that is beneficial to itself without consideration of any other [division, department, area]. He knows not and cares not about any other division, any other area. Thinks only of himself. Nobody knows, nobody cares, about any other division. The effect on the other divisions and on the company as a whole are unknown. Options that are locally beneficial to one area, [may] effect the opposite to another area. [Another area may lose because of our decision.]

[Instead of individual profit centers, what if] each area acts for maximum benefit for the whole company. Everybody now wins, including areas that take a loss for the benefit of the whole company. People seeing that their choices may affect the whole company now find other options. Improved environment options that previously never saw the light of day are now considered. These are options that may be locally disadvantageous to the areas that would adopt them. But might be a benefit to other areas. Amongst this greater range of options, you see a greater range—far more options. You've become inventive. The ones to be adopted are now chosen according to whether they are a net benefit to the whole company. The results on the bottom line speak for themselves.

Cooperation

What about cooperation? Have you ever thought of it? Does it rain on competition? You'd have to unlearn a lot. Think of cooperation. The benefits of cooperation.

The time of day. One twenty. Based on what? The time signals at the observatory at Greenwich. You, your competitor, and your enemy use the same time of day. Cooperation and didn't even think of it as cooperation. So natural.

The date. The International Date Line. Used the world over. By friend and foe, you and your competitor. International Date Line. Cooperation.

Red and green traffic lights. The red above the green. So that somebody who has difficulty to distinguish the red from the green need not distinguish red from green. The red light is above the green the world over. The world is not made that way. Man made the world that way. It was their effort. Public service citizens. Their work on established committees for international standards.

The metric system, used the world over.

Batteries. Here's a little magnifying glass, has a light in it. I press a button, I get illumination. If the batteries get low, I buy two AAA batteries, and I may buy them anywhere in this world. And they will fit. I don't have to get tailor-made batteries. Think of the economy. Think of the benefit we get from cooperation. We didn't even think about it. We are so in the habit of receiving these benefits we don't even think about them. We just accept them. Licensing of a product. Our product to some other company. Cooperation.

Companies make parts and products for each other. Almost any chemical company is dependent on competitors for intermediate products. Automotive companies make parts or even whole engines or transmissions for each other. A large data processing company does work for small companies that are not equipped for some jobs. Both companies win. And the customer wins. Meetings of scientists and other professional people as speakers and participants contribute to other members' theory and methods. An exchange of theory and experience.

A railway car, you don't even think about it. They move from Halifax to Montreal. Down from Boston, over to Toronto, down through Buffalo, to Kansas City, Miami, Houston, and so forth .... Same gauge. Matching systems of breaks and drawbars. Results— lower costs of transportation. More dependable performance. Was the world always that way? Was the world made that way? No. A hundred years ago there were three gauges in North America. [Cooperation brought a single gauge.] Think of the advantage. We would not be here except for the standard gauge all over North America. Our economy would suffer so much we could not afford to have a meeting like this. You'd be out digging carrots out of the ground. Cooperation between professional men. Ready to help each other. The world was not made that way. The rest of the world is not that way. Until recently, if you buy a vacuum cleaner or curling iron in London you wouldn't get a plug. It was just two wires dangling. Why? Because what fits in your house may not be what fits in your neighbor's house. Different plugs. That's being remedied. Just how far it's gone I just don't know.

These are examples of cooperation. We're so accustomed to cooperation we don't even think about it. And every one is a benefit to all of us.

One of my automobiles, sitting in front of my house would not start. I couldn't even get a cough out of it. I called up Bill at the Exxon station ... not far away, maybe a third of a mile. When one of his men came, named Richard, I noted he came in a tow truck owned by his competitor across the street. He explained it to me. Each station owns one tow truck. If a call comes in as mine did, and his tow truck is out, he uses his competitor's tow truck. Each of them, by owning one truck, and by cooperation, using the other fellow's truck, if it's idle, give the service to customers almost equal to ownership of two trucks each. Consider the savings from cooperation. And who wins?

Everybody. Customer wins, and those stations win. Why not? And they retain business at that end of town. Even further cooperation: One station stays open till midnight, every other night, and the other station stays open till midnight on the intervening nights. Why? Keep customers at that end of town. Need gasoline 11:30 at night, you know where you can get it. You don't have to start driving for some other town or some other part of the city. Everybody wins. They win, the customers win. Why not?

From a presentation at General Motors,
1992.

Leadership

A manager understands and conveys to his people the meaning of a system, everybody wins. He teaches his people to understand how the work of the group supports the aims of the system.

He helps his people to see themselves as components in a system, to work in cooperation with preceding stages and with following stages toward optimization of the efforts of all stages toward achievement of the aim.

A manager of people understands that all people are different from each other. He tries to create for everybody interest and challenge, and joy in work. He tries to optimize the education, skills, abilities, family backgrounds, education, of everyone. This is not ranking people. This is a recognition of differences. And where can he place people to their own best advantage?

He himself is an unceasing learner and encourages people to study.

He is coach and counsel, not a judge. Judging people does not help them.

He understands the interaction between people and the circumstances that they work in. He understands that the performance of anyone that can learn a skill will come to a stable system. A manager of people knows that in this stable state it is distracting to tell a worker about a mistake.

He has three sources of power:

Authority of office
Knowledge
Personality, persuasive power, tact

A successful manager of people develops knowledge and persuasive power; he does not rely on his authority of office. He has nevertheless obligation to use authority of office, as this source of power enables him to change the process and methods, to bring improvement.

He will try to discover who if anybody is outside the system, in need of special help.

He creates trust. He creates an environment that encourages freedom and cooperation.

He does not expect perfection.

He listens and learns without passing judgment on him that he listens to.

He will hold an interview, informal, unhurried conversation with every one of his people at least once a year. Several hours long, not for judgment, but merely to listen to their aims, hopes, fears.

From presentation at seminar
"Quality, Productivity, and Competitive Position,"
1992.

Innovation and Improvement

An overall prerequisite for innovation and improvement is to create an environment in which everybody takes joy in his work. One may confidently expect under these prerequisites innovation of product, innovation of service, improvement and innovation of process, improvement of existing product, improvement of existing service. Improvement of process.

The Plan-Do-Study-Act (PDSA) Cycle will help. The PDSA Cycle is a flow diagram for learning.

The first step is plan: ideas in people's heads about improvement or innovation, new method or comparison of methods. Those ideas go down on paper, become plans. Your first step. Ideas lead to a plan or test. Comparison—experiment. Step one is the foundation of the whole cycle. A hasty start may be wrong. I learned this in 1939. People can't wait to get started. They wanted to look busy, do something. They think that standing around, talking, generating ideas is not doing anything. Actually that's the most important part of the cycle. We'll learn more about this later.

A hasty start may be wrong, costly, frustrating. People have a weakness to short-circuit this step. They cannot wait to get into motion, to be active, to look busy. Move into step two.

Carrying out step one may lead to a whole new idea, more mature. Your backtracking will be less if you spend more time in that initial stage. The planning stage may start with a choice between several suggestions. Which one can we test? Another question, make it plural: which *ones* can we test? We can test several against each other all with the same experiment. What might be the result? Compare the possible outcomes of the possible choices. Of the several suggestions, which ones appear to be most promising in terms of new knowledge or profit? Plan accordingly.

Step two. Do it, carry out the test, comparison, or experiment, preferably on a small scale, according to the layout decided in step one.

Step three. Study the results. Do they correspond with hopes and expectations? If not, what went wrong? Maybe we didn't understand in the first place what we were doing. Maybe the layout for the test or experiment did not produce the information that we need. What went wrong? Maybe we tricked ourselves in the first place and should make a fresh start, backtrack, with a new plan. And finally:

Step four. Act, if we get that far. And what do we mean by act? We mean adopt a change, or abandon it, or run through the cycle again, possibly under different environmental conditions. I'd say certainly under different environmental conditions. Different materials, different people. See if we get anything like the same result. Maybe make some small changes in the rules.

Let's apply it. Planning for a new engine. Engineers were at work on plans for a new engine. They had worked on most of the pieces of the development, but had not put the pieces in sequence. A flow diagram, put on the screen, put the pieces in sequence and showed relationships between them. Results of the last stage may present reconsideration of earlier stages. With the flow diagram in view, everyone may understand the relationship between stages.

The process starts with the creation of need, ideas in people's heads. Those go into soft line proposals. Just rough drawings, free-hand. And then backtrack, take another look, more thoughts. Finally move into development of design, the actual drawings. Then you move into procurement of hardware, cylinder heads, engine blocks, crankshafts, castings, all unfinished, all one of a kind. The next step goes into machining, assembly, inspection, all to be done by skilled tradesmen. Then, finally, test the pieces and assemblies. Test the engine in the vehicle.

You can work on all the pieces but if you don't see how they fit together you get nowhere. There's much talk about shortening the time of development. Need to speed up development of a new product. The reasons given flirt around the alleged need to put a product into the hands of customers while they still have the same preferences as they say they have today. Another reason expressed or implied is to beat the competitor to the goalpost. The effort is noble but for the wrong reason. The customer will name a preference today, and buy something else tomorrow. The drive for reduction in time for development of a new product is important simply for reduction of costs. Cut the time to half, you save a lot of money, save a lot of costs of development. The usual method is to rush through the development of a new product, only to find at the end that the pieces do not fit together, or that new and brilliant ideas for design have meanwhile emerged. Have to start all over again. The whole play then starts afresh with act one. Time is lost; costs go up; the end product falls short of expectations. Short of their abilities.

The secret of reduction in time is to put more effort into the early stages. And to study the interaction between stages. Each stage should have more effort, more time, more expense, than the following stage. The Zero Stage, the most important of all, the costliest, if you want to get ahead. One could in simple terms say that any stage should cost some specified percentage more than the following stage. This percentage could be tailored stage-by-stage. Could be. But such refinement is a long way off.

The Zero Stage is the foundation of the whole project. The Zero Stage is the place for ideas and brainstorming. To avoid so far as possible changes in direction and backtracking. But there oughtn't be backtracking. Changes in direction cost more and more with each stage. We know that. It is impossible to eliminate backtracking entirely, but under the scheme proposed here backtracking would be reduced, and it would be more effective. The whole development speedier, with reduction of total cost. Reduction in time. Very important I should say. Reduction in time, I failed to note. Not just reduction in cost but reduction in time. At the end of the proposal submitted here a better chance to realize expectations in the end product.

The job of the program manager is to manage all the interfaces, to manage the system as a whole, not to optimize any stage.

Each stage may have a leader, but everyone involved might well work in all stages. A marketing man might well be a member of the team, especially at the Zero Stage. Suppliers and toolmakers should be chosen at the Zero Stage. In Japan they're right there at the beginning, at the Zero Stage, even though they might not have the business, they're there, made members of the team. They'll be ready and waiting with supplies and tools when development of the product reaches the last stage. Everybody ready—away we go.

The manager of the whole vehicle must be a member of the team for development of an engine.

It will be necessary for top management to block the privilege of anybody in top management or in any other level to come along at the end of the line with a bright idea. He belongs in the Zero Stage, now, not later.

The system of development must be managed. It will not manage itself.

From a presentation at Fordham University,
1992.

Knowing How to Manage People Is the Single Most Important Part of Management

Management is failing in many ways. One problem is that most managers would rather deal with rising costs or slipping sales than with the problems of their people. Knowing how to manage people is the single most important part of management—and the part that management knows least about. People can make managers very nervous. With people problems, managers often become immobilized—they cannot act—other than to turn the job over to somebody else.

A bigger problem, in my mind, is that many top managers, and I am speaking generally here, don't understand they are the ones who must do most of the work—they have no idea of the sheer magnitude of their own jobs. How can they "Do it right the first time," when they don't really know what it is they are meant to be doing? On-the-job experience doesn't tell them what to do either. Nor is it a matter of working harder—people already are working hard.

What's necessary is for management to understand the theory *behind* the changes that are needed. Knowing how your organization runs just isn't enough. You really do need outside help, preferably from knowledgeable consultants who can work with you on a long-term basis. Consultants understand all of the new management methods and statistical tools. They bring in fresh ideas and perspectives. And, of course, they are not encumbered by internal politics, so their ideas have a chance of getting heard. Of course, a lot of managers are looking for "instant pudding," and don't want to be bothered by someone who will actually make them think things through.

When I say "instant pudding," I am talking about people who ask me to spend a day with them to "Do for us what you did for Japan." A company on the West Coast called me a few years ago, begging me to spend a day with their top 300 managers. I declined—they would have learned nothing in 1 day. They would have only come away confused, I feared. It takes time to learn what the job is and then time to put into action what has been learned, and with help. It's a big job. Management has no idea how big the job is, or how long it will take.

Not enough education is taking place at the management level—and I mean *top management*. Management must learn a new kind of managing—one that is totally different from what they have been accustomed to.

American management is directly responsible for the decline of American industry. The most severe threat that any company in the western world faces is not from its competitors, or the Japanese. Its biggest threats are self-inflicted, created right at home by management styles that are off course. If factory workers are unemployed—or anyone, for that matter—it is because of bad management, and not because unemployment is inevitable.

In my mind, if you run your company on visible figures alone, you will have neither company nor figures, given a little time. The most important figures are unknown and *unknowable*. That opinion comes from my good friend, Dr. Lloyd Nelson. One unknowable figure, for example, is the multiplying effect of a happy customer who brings repeat or new business into the company. Another one is the multiplying effect of an unhappy customer who warns his friends, and even some of his enemies, about his experience. Another unknowable figure is the multiplying effect that comes from an employee group that is able to make a contribution to the company as a team. They see their jobs as important. They are helping the company to improve. They take pride in their work. Their lives change—I have seen it happen. These are all small increments, but they quickly add up. You need teamwork and good management—not reams of figures—to bring that about.

Managers are not faced with a deluge of information; they are faced with a deluge of figures. The challenge is to know when it is appropriate to respond to certain figures and when not to. Management must understand the theory of variation: If you don't understand variation and how it comes from the system itself, you can only react to every figure. The result is you often overcompensate, when it would have been better to just leave things alone.

Understanding variation is critical to good management. Take the idea of continual improvement, which says that the only way you can improve a process is to continuously shrink the variation. As you shrink the variation—in other words, improve the dependability of the product and improve its quality—your costs go down. It becomes a chain reaction; something the Japanese have understood for years. I taught them that in 1950.

Of course, when you talk about improvement of processes, you must include improvement of people. If management truly understood the concept of continual improvement, they would give their people every opportunity to learn and improve—and a chance to make contributions to the company. Organizations can no longer afford to just have good people—today, they need people who are improving continually.

To learn about factory floor problems, for example, you have to talk to people—and I don't mean by just walking around. Somebody once described good management as management by walking around. Well, it helps to walk around a bit, but you do not learn about the real problems that way. When you are just wandering around, everything looks rosy. The only way to find out about problems is by talking to workers in a group setting. Just ask questions. Start off by asking, "What robs you of your pride of workmanship?" They will tell you.

Workers the world over tell me that they are the only ones who are truly interested in quality. All they ask for, they say, is a chance to take pride in their work. Today, I dare say that only 10 workers in a hundred take pride in their work.

There are several barriers at work here, one of which is continued emphasis on quantity. Talk to any worker and he will say that, although management talks about quality, they are still looking at the numbers. The truth is, if you don't make the numbers, you are out of a job. Perception and rumor are what run the company.

Defective raw materials represent another major barrier. When you have to work with defective goods, nothing you do will produce a product that you can take pride in. Workers are also hampered by cheap tools. They are afraid to complain to the boss because, they say, they will be marked. Why? Because bosses fear for their jobs, too. The boss is just as helpless as they are.

Hourly workers are also stymied by uncertainty. How can people possibly devote themselves to a company when their future with the organization is uncertain? I once met with 40 skilled tradesmen who did not know until each Thursday if they would be needed the following week. One of them remarked, "We are a commodity" and I saw the connection. On the commodities exchange, you don't have to buy anything today. You can defer it until tomorrow. They were bought and sold like a commodity.

Fear takes a terrible toll. Where are the comptroller's figures on the losses from fear? They are enormous. Nobody knows their magnitude. Getting people to express their ideas without fear of retribution requires fundamental change, starting with the abolishment of the annual rating system and, in its place, major emphasis on teamwork. You see fear on the factory floor when the foreman won't stop a machine that is getting dangerously warm, for fear of missing the day's quota. There are hourly workers who are afraid to complain about tools that don't work or defective materials. Complain three times and you are a marked man at some firms.

Service industries face the same management issues as manufacturing, and the greatest chance of improvement. I think anybody who ever registered in a hotel or ate in a restaurant can understand very well what I am talking about. The service industries, including education, government, and health care, are in need of improvement. Everlasting improvement belongs in the service industries just as it does in manufacturing.

People in service industries do not understand that they too have a product. I find that, when people take an interest in improving their services, their jobs become more meaningful. No matter what business you are in, if you understand what your job is, and care about it, you will have more fun.

Managers don't dare produce work to their own satisfaction. They feel that if they present an idea that in any way varies from "the policy," they are marked. If you cannot disagree with the policy—if you have no voice, no way to present and defend your ideas—then how can you possibly put your heart and soul into your job? You can't. In other words, there is no teamwork. If you fear for your job, you will not speak up.

Annual individual performance ratings, as I've said time and time again, represent a major obstacle. In most rating systems, somebody has to get a low rating. No account is taken of the fact that most of the differences between people come from the system itself. Getting a low rating can make you feel despondent, especially if you had a good rating the year before. If people understood that it's all just a lottery, they would merely feel unlucky.

The idea of a merit rating is alluring. The sound of the words captivates the imagination: pay for what you get; get what you pay for; motivate people to do their best, for their own good. The effect is exactly the opposite of what the words promise. Everyone propels himself forward, or tries to, for his own good, on his own life preservers. In the end, the organization is the loser. Why? Because if someone gets a low rating, what do they do? They look for another job. And in my mind, job hopping in and out of an organization is destroying American management. Let me put it another way: Every man I work with is at the top of his organization because he came out on top in annual ratings, at the ruination of the lives of a score of other men. There is a better way.

From "An Interview with Dr. W. Edwards Deming,"
Forum Issues 13,
Fall 1991.

When Deming traveled in the 1970s and early 1980s, he liked to leave behind a paper that contained important ideas about understanding and treatment of employees. He wanted management to know that appropriate handling of employees led to improvement of the organization. He developed his ideas in a format he called "Principles." The principles would vary somewhat in number and detail, depending on the audience. Some papers were more statistical than others. But, they had a common core: if you understand how people work in a system, and treat people as part of that system, quality of your products and services will improve.

Below are two samples of these articles, sufficiently different, I believe, to give a good flavor of these papers.

New Principles in Administration for Quality and Efficiency

Principle 1. Statistical methods cover every step in the production-line, from specifications and tests of incoming materials to tests of product in service, to consumer research, design and re-design of product, design of new product, and of new processes. (See Figure 5.1.) Measurements are a product. Statistical control of the measurement-process is necessary. The need for consumer research and innovation of product received special emphasis in the teaching of statistical methods.

Principle 2. It is demoralizing and costly to call to the attention of a production-worker a defective item that he has made, when he is in a state of statistical control with respect to the cause of that defect. He is in effect drawing random samples from a bowl. He can not govern the random appearance of black beads in his samples. He is handicapped by the proportion of black beads in the system. Only the management can change the proportion of black beads in the bowl.

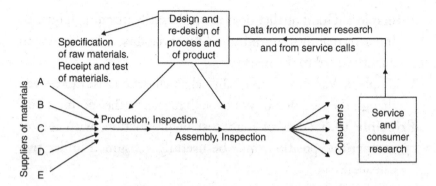

Figure 5.1 The production-line, from design, raw material to the consumer. Data from consumer-research and from service-requirements provide a basis for re-design of the product and for changes in the requirements for raw materials and in production

Principle 3. It is better to shift to a totally different job a worker that has developed statistical control of his work in his present job, but whose output in quality or in quantity is unsatisfactory.

Principle 4. It is possible to train and to re-train a worker who has not yet achieved statistical control of his work.

Principle 5. In a state of chaos (poor supervision, bad management, nothing in statistical control), it is impossible for a production-worker to develop his potential ability and capacity for uniformity or for quantity.

Principle 6. Maximum and minimum limits for the specification of a product are by themselves a costly and unsatisfactory guide to the production-worker. Training that merely teaches a production-worker to make no defects is deficient. Training should include use of a chart to get statistical control as well.

Principle 7. A job description should therefore, for best economy, require achievement of statistical control, with a distribution of individual items that meet specifications without the high cost of detailed inspection. Workers that are in statistical control but whose output is unsatisfactory can be transferred and trained in other work.

Principle 8. Good quality does not necessarily mean high quality. It means mainly uniformity and dependability, at low cost, with quality suited to the market.

Principle 9. Variation in a quality characteristic causes loss, even though the variation be not enough to exceed the specifications.

Principle 10. Causes of high cost of production, with loss of competitive position, may be usefully subsumed under two categories:

Faults of the System (common or environmental causes) 85%	Special Causes 15%
These faults stay in the system until reduced by management. Their combined effect is usually easy to measure by the same statistical techniques that detect special causes.	These causes are specific to a certain worker or to a machine. A statistical signal detects the existence of a special cause, which the worker can usually identify and correct.

Principle 11. Confusion between the two types of cause leads to frustration at all levels, and leads to greater variability and to higher costs—exactly contrary to what is needed.

Fortunately, this confusion can be eliminated with almost unerring accuracy. Simple statistical techniques, such as distributions, run-charts, Shewhart control-charts, all explained in books, provide signals that detect the existence of a special cause.

The fault behind the recall of automobiles for correction, wherever something was admittedly wrong, is not chargeable to workmanship, but to design, the system, hence the fault of management.

Principle 12. The first step in any process of manufacture, or of measurement, is to achieve statistical control of one of the main characteristics of the product; then another, and another. Once statistical control of the main quality-characteristics of a process is achieved, the process is ready for the next step—improvement, the responsibility of management.

Principle 13. A process has an identity and a predictable capability only if it is in a state of statistical control. In this state, the main quality characteristics of the product will dependably fail tomorrow within predictable limits. Output can be predicted; likewise cost of production.

Principle 14. A mechanical governor that merely holds a quality characteristic within specifications does not achieve better uniformity for tomorrow and the economic benefits thereof. It does not improve the system.

Principle 15. Measurement, simple or complex, visual or with instruments, is a production process, and must be in statistical control for profitable relations between vendor and purchaser. This is also necessary for inspection, for otherwise a production-worker will be frustrated with see-saw results of inspection.

Principle 16. The consumer is the most important point on the production-line. Consumer research and testing in service are statistical problems.

Principle 17. No one can measure the loss of business that may arise from a defective item that goes out to a customer.

Principle 18. Quality of product is difficult to define. Quality of product is determined by the opinion of the consumer.

Performance of a product is the result of interaction between three participants: (1) the product itself; (2) the user and how he used the product; how the customer installs it; how he takes care of it; the conditions of use (example: customer permitted dirt to fall into roller bearing); (3) instructions for use, training of customer, service provided for repairs; training of repair-men; availability of spare parts.

Principle 19. No system, whatever be the effort put into it, will be free of accidents. Human beings, their training, supervision, and drilling, are part of the system. The usual reaction of almost everyone, when an accident occurs, is to attribute it to some specific person or set of conditions (defect in design, malfunction, carelessness). This is almost always the wrong answer, and a sure road to continued trouble. Improvement of the system will reduce accidents.

From New Principles in Administration for Quality
and Efficiency, Manila,
July 2, 1971.

Overjustification

Is your company suffering from overjustification? Of course you don't have the figures. There are not any figures for the most important losses. Somebody asked a question this morning: "If one performs very well, how would you reward him?" Why should you reward him? It would be demoralizing to reward him. Overjustification was first explained to me by Dr. Joyce Orsini. A little boy took it into his head for reasons unknown to wash the dishes after supper every evening. His mother was pleased with such a fine boy. One evening, to show her appreciation, she handed him a quarter. He never washed another dish. Her payment to him changed their relationship. She hurt his dignity. He was washing dishes for the sheer pleasure of washing dishes for his mother. Once she paid him, he became a slave. An employee. Totally different. Never washed another dish.

That's so easy to do. I've done it so many times I can't count them. Sometimes I've not been aware of it. I came in late to a hotel in Detroit. Hungry, exhausted. Hoped to get into the dining room before it would close at eleven. I knew I could pound on the door, the manager of the dining room would let me in. He'd find some food somehow. I don't like to be a nuisance. I tried to get there on time. Worried about making it. A man picked up my bag—it was heavy. He walked rapidly. Had a hard time keeping up with him. Carried my bag to my room, set it down. Saved me some time. I was very grateful. You would be grateful, wouldn't you? What did I do? I fished in my pocket, found two dollars. Handed it to him. I wounded him. He carried the bag for me, not for money. What a horrible thing to do. I thought I learned a lesson.

I thought I learned a lesson. But I did it again. Two weeks later, landed in National Airport, Washington, from Minneapolis, on U.S. Airlines; there's no other way. How else would you go? There's only one way. I go up to check my bag. A woman in uniform picked up my bag. It was too heavy for her to carry, I know; but she picked it up and carried it with one hand, escorted me with her other arm, off the airplane, through the airport, down the lift, outside to my driver waiting. I was very grateful. I fished out of my pocket a five dollar bill. "Oh, no," she said. I had done it again. So easy to do. I hurt her feelings. I had done it again.

Does that mean we don't recognize favors, or good work? No. It means we better do it the right way because the wrong way hurts people. What are the losses in your company from overjustification? Paying for suggestions, maybe? Rewarding extraordinary performance? Is that costing you? Of course you don't know, nobody knows.

I was in the hospital. My right hind leg took on an infection. My physician, Dr. Davis, immunologist, prescribed a vaccine. He made it up, and it worked. A bill came from him. I did not just sign the check. I wrote, three or four lines. The words—I do not remember. Words of appreciation of his knowledge of medicine. And for him taking good care of me. Weeks later, I encountered him. He was going one way. I was going the other way.

We stopped and chatted for a while. The check he had forgotten about, the letter he had in his pocket. Think of what that letter meant to him. I did it right that time! A little note of appreciation. The words are not important. The spirit behind the words is what counted. He had the letter in his pocket. Think of what that meant to him. That somebody cared. It may have affected his whole practice of medicine. Two years later, I went to see a Dr. Short in Washington. As I was about to leave, he said to me, "You know what? I ran across a Dr. Davis yesterday. He asked about you." Wasn't that nice? I did the right thing. Just a little note of appreciation. What if I had added five dollars to the check in appreciation? I would have wounded him. He would have torn the check up. Fifty dollars. He would have seen to it that I got into the psychiatric ward. I did the right thing. Just a kind word.

If you want to give money, there's a way to do it. Give it to the hospital to be spent under his direction. He could buy some equipment, or he could help patients who have no way to pay for their services.

Many managers of people understand that the current methods of rating people do not distinguish the contribution of the individual from the rest of the system. They hold onto the belief that an appraisal system could be developed that could do so. So easy to miss the point. And even if a method were developed to rank people with precision and certainty, distinct from the system that they work in, why would anyone suppose that this would improve people or the system? One would have to believe that people must first be demoralized before they can be motivated to improve. This is faulty thinking. Once demoralized, those people stay demoralized.

From a presentation at a CEO seminar, Quality,
Productivity, and Competitive Position,
1992.

Leadership and Management of People

What is a leader? As I use the term here, the job of a leader is to accomplish transformation of his organization. He possesses knowledge; he himself has been transformed. He has personality and persuasive power. How may he accomplish transformation? First he has theory. He understands why the transformation would bring gain to his organization and to all the people that his organization deals with, the customers, suppliers, environment. Second, he feels compelled to accomplish the transformation as an obligation to himself and to his organization. Third, he is a practical man. He has a plan, step by step.

As an example of a leader, I will take Morris H. Hansen, he was eleven years younger than I. He died on the 9th of October, 1990, at the age of 79. He was a leader. A leader in the sense of the word. Out in front. How did it happen. The country in the 1930s was in a deep depression. Set off by the crash of the stock market, 1929, the country was in a deep depression. I mean it was a humdinger. Unemployment in the 1930s was pitiful. Though no definition of unemployment and employment had yet been formulated, the term used was gainful worker. One was a gainful worker if he earned money. Meanwhile, each of a number of experts made his own estimate of the number of people in the country not gainfully employed. These estimates were so wild, so far apart, that they were all discarded. Congress, frustrated with these wild estimates, ordered a census of people not gainfully employed. It sounded very simple, nothing to it. The Post Office Department had a complete list of postal routes. And the post office boxes where there is no route. It will all be very simple, so they thought. Simply have the postal carriers and postmasters make estimates, get figures for the number of people of their routes, and the number not gainfully employed. Total number of people on the route, and the number not gainfully employed.

All very simple. It was a very difficult thing to do. The FERA, Federal Emergency Relief Administration, you've forgotten about it, let us hope, was charged with the responsibility to carry this out, carry out this census. They recruited Mr. John B. Biggers, then President of Libby-Owens-Ford Glass Company, a great man he was. He took charge, and the study became the Biggers study. And it was a complete flop. Complete flop. Was too big a job, could not be done, not that way.

It so happened that Morris Hansen, then at age twenty-four, in the year 1924. He had just gotten out of college, the University of Wyoming, he studied under Professor Forrest Hall. He was a student, getting his master's degree at American University in Washington. He had some knowledge of the theory of probability and how to make it work and knowledge of errors in surveys. He contrived a plan for selection of 52 postal routes. Those 52 postal routes were selected by random numbers, and they list of thousands of postal routes. And those 52 postal routes would be worked very thoroughly, very carefully. The Biggers study was afflicted with too many errors, omissions and wrong responses. The mail carrier's job was mail, not collection of information. Whereas Morris Hansen could explain his plan. Fifty-two postal routes selected by random numbers. Why not 53? Fifty-three would be too big a number. The workload would be too great. Fifty-one would not provide the precision required. I make it sound very critical, it's actually so critical. But 52 was the right number. It would provide the precision required.

The point I wish to make is that Morris Hansen was a leader. He had in his head some theory of probability along with the practical sense for design of a sample of postal routes to acquire the necessary information. Further, he could explain his plan.

He could not by himself make it happen. He convinced enough men in power that were willing and able to understand his theory. Those men in power were Dr. Samuel Stouffer, who was Professor of Sociology at the University of Wisconsin, a great man. Philip M. Hauser, his student. And Frederick F. Stephan, his student. Dr. Stouffer and those two students, Philip Hauser and Frederick Stephan, could understand Morris Hansen. They had knowledge and could understand his theory. Morris came through with a practical plan—simple, small enough—and he reached the ears of these men in power. They were willing to listen, eager to listen. He made it happen. His study was carried out and those figures were regarded as useful and sufficiently reliable. And that was the beginning of probability sampling in this country.

He was a leader. And now again, what did it take? Knowledge, a practical plan, simple, one he could explain to other people. And he reached the ears of men in power—he made it happen. I receive several letters every week from people that are frustrated. Some from General Motors, some from your competitors. Some from other kinds of industries, not automotive at all. From people that have wonderful plans. Just wonderful plans. Only there's one little trouble—it's so wonderful I cannot understand it. Too complicated. I mean, not explained so that I cannot understand it. And the people are frustrated because nobody will listen. But the trouble is their plan is not simple enough, or they don't explain it in the words that other people can understand. You may have a brilliant idea in your head but if you can't tell somebody about it, it just lodges there—it never gets out of your head. The ability to construct a practical plan and explain it is pretty necessary. The frustration in this country is touching, appalling. The people that mean well have brilliant ideas, yet they can get no action. I'm afraid the main trouble is that they don't explain their plans in a way that other people can understand. I think there are some lessons in this chapter on leadership.

Statistical methods took hold. The Works Progress Administration commenced a quarterly survey of unemployment, later became a monthly survey of unemployment. We still have it. You see the figures on unemployment announced every month. Was helped by Mr. J.C. Capt, who in 1940 became Director of the Census. He was a political appointment. People shuddered, people in the Census shuddered. Think of it, a political appointment. What do you know about the Census? Nothing. People thought this was the end of the Census. A political appointment as head of the Census. Turned out he was a great manager. I've known in my life, two or three good managers. J.C. Capt was one of them. A political appointment. He said to me one time, that he himself had authority: "Only the President can remove me." He had himself to satisfy, and he was hard to satisfy. He set for himself a hard life. He was responsible only to himself. Was able to do a good job, and he did. Had uncanny ability to recognize ability in other people, and to put them to work at it.

Again, what's the requirement? Knowledge. And a plan that will work, a practical plan. Ability to explain the plan in terms other people can understand and somehow reach the ears of people in power. You may say, well I cannot reach the ears of people in power. Well you can, if you can write, if you can write a memorandum, a plan on half a page of paper. Simple enough so your boss can understand it. Ask him to give it to his boss and so on. There are ways. But if you describe a plan in complicated terms that nobody can understand, it dies right there. I'm afraid that's the trouble with a lot of plans that I see.

From a presentation
at Ford Motor Company,
1992.

While making a presentation at Fordham's Deming Scholars MBA Program, Deming talked about the tyranny of the prevailing style of management:

We're living in prison. Under the tyranny of the prevailing style of management. A style of interaction between people, between teams, between divisions, between competitors. We need to throw overboard our theories and practices of the present, and build afresh. We must throw overboard the idea that competition is a necessary way of life. In place of competition, we need cooperation. We need to examine the effects of ideas that govern us today and to learn better ways.

Transformation is required in government, industry and education. Management is in a stable state. Transformation is required to move out of the present state. Not mere patchwork on the present system. Throw overboard what we have. Of course we have to stamp out fires where they occur but stamping out fires is not improvement. If there were a fire here, somebody shouts "Fire!" runs for the fire extinguisher, pulls a lever for the fire department. We all get out, thankful to get out. Then the management restores the place where the fire was. Come in six months later you'd never know there had been a fire. Everything restored, in tip-top condition. That is not improvement. That's just putting it back to where you were in the first place. Stamping out fires is not improvement.

The transformation will take us into a new system of reward. They must restore the individual, and do so in the complexities of interaction with the rest of the world. The transformation will release the power of human resource contained within, intrinsic motivation in place of competition for high rating, high grades. There needs to be cooperation on problems of common interest between people, between divisions, companies, governments, countries. The result will in time be greater innovation, greater applied science, better technology, expansion of market, greater service, greater material reward for everyone. There will be joy in work because people will understand what their jobs are. Who depends on me? Whom do I depend on? There will be joy in learning. Anyone who enjoys their work is a pleasure to work with. Everyone will win, no losers. The function of government should be to assist business, not to harass business. Will we ever get that into our heads?

Presentation at Fordham University,
1992.

Visiting Fordham about a year later, Deming gave two examples to illustrate how divided responsibility means nobody's responsible and how this differs from joint responsibility.

Example of payroll cards: I was working with a client, came two people from the payroll department of a division in which they paid 900 people, hourly workers. They just had to talk to me. They horned in. They must talk to me.

"So what's the problem?" I asked them. "Well, those payroll cards. We try to pay our people on Thursday after the close of the preceding week. And we are working so hard to get those cards right." "What's the matter with the cards?" I asked. "Oh, omissions, wrong entries, inconsistent entries, and we have to get a card right before we can pay the worker. And in order to pay our people on Thursday after the close of the preceding week we have to work overtime, sometimes at night, Saturdays, and Doctor, it's getting worse, not better." "Let me see the card." They gave me the card. The problem was obvious. Two signatures required, nobody responsible. There was the problem. The worker signs it, and the foreman signs it. Who's responsible? Nobody. The foreman thinks the worker should know what he did so he signs it. The worker leaves it up to the foreman. Between the two of them, mistakes and omissions.

Divided responsibility means nobody is responsible. "I'll tell you what to do. You take the 900 cards that you'll use next week, take a heavy crayon and X out the foreman's name. I don't care which of the two names you take off, but, I suggest you take off the foreman. Do the same for the 900 cards that you use the following week. By that time you can have a new printing, with the foreman's name omitted. The problem will dry up in three weeks," I told them.

Another provision. If the worker could have filled the card out correctly, or if the foreman could have filled the card out correctly, give the card back to him. Do not work on it yourself. Just give it back to him. You need not print on it a message, "Your pay may be delayed," just give the card back to him. And all it took to dry up was one week. What happened? By Monday afternoon, a dozen people got their cards back. By Tuesday afternoon, another dozen people got their cards back. By Tuesday all 900 people knew that if you don't get your card right it will come back to you and your pay may be delayed. "What do you know, I got my card back. Never heard of such a thing. Got my card back." All 900 people knew about it by Tuesday afternoon. They got the cards right. The problem dried up in one week.

The secret: no secret. You just need to know what the job is. Divided, nobody has a job. Who's job is it? That's a guaranteed way to get mistakes.

Example of proofreading: David Chambers told me about a printing company that proofread everything eleven times. No matter where Mr. Chambers was, the manager of the printing company would get a hold of him on the telephone, would beg him to come. Well finally Mr. Chambers made it down to the printing company. The problem was mistakes being made in spite of the eleven proofreaders. I said, "Dave, maybe eleven is the right number. You need one proofreader for spelling, maybe two. You need one proofreader for hyphenated words, you need another one for hyphens at the end of a line, you need another one for sentences omitted, you need another one for flow from one paragraph to another, the bottom of one column to the top of another. If it's a catalogue, you need a proofreader for prices, you need another one for captions. So Dave, you're already up to nine proofreaders, maybe eleven is the right number." "Oh no, that wasn't it at all. Every one of the eleven proofreaders read everything." In other words, every proofreader had ten others to do his job. Nobody had a job. Result: mistakes.

Joint responsibility: Now there's such a thing as joint responsibility. Joint responsibility is totally different from divided responsibility. Many people's activities include joint responsibility. An example is teacher and pupil. Learning under a teacher is a joint responsibility, a joint effort between teacher and pupil. Anyone that works in an organization works jointly, or should, with his suppliers and customers. Two people that sign a note are jointly responsible for payment: either or both together are liable for payment. Marriage creates joint responsibility. Membership on a committee is joint responsibility with the other members: each member is responsible for the recommendations of the committee. We can't duck out of it and say, "Well that was the work of the committee." And for that reason I will not be a member of a committee unless I have the privilege to issue a contrary opinion. When I cannot go along with the rest of the committee, I feel a responsibility to say so. I must have the privilege of a minority report to be published right along with the report of the committee. Because if you're on a committee you're jointly responsible with the other members, you get the blame, unless you set forth your minority opinion.

Presentation at Fordham University,
1993.

Deming believed most of us, including himself, were too hasty in mak-ing the decision of whom to promote to the next level in a company. Here are some comments he made at a seminar in General Motors.

Promotion is movement into a new job. Movement from one job into a different job. There is no way to predict with a high degree of belief that someone selected for promotion will do well in the new job.

We have known that for twenty years. The usual method for selection of someone for promotion is by recommendation. Is there a better way? One's chance for promotion depends on who knows him—or put another way, who knows you? Is that a good way? I do not know of a better one.

If you recommend someone for promotion you are on your honor. You would not dare to recommend him unless you were positive that he would do well. You're entitled to make a mistake. That in your highest belief you think he would do well. You rec-ommend him for promotion. You would not do it unless you were pretty positive about it. And you could be wrong, of course.

Performance on the job held at present, even if we could eval-uate it, would not be a basis for promotion. That would not be a basis for prediction for performance in a new job. Promotion is into a new job. I realize in the Navy and the Army all it means is just another stripe—promotion—but I'm not using the word promotion in that sense. I'm using promotion here into a new job. Maybe to be head of the same organization that he works in. A new job.

No question in anybody's mind, that a certain man would be the one to head up the division of tabulation. There's nobody better. No question about it – he'd be a wonderful head. He was made head of the tabulation department. And within three months he tried to take his own life. Failed. He was a total failure in his new job. Performance at his present job in the tabulation division was famous. Everybody thought he'd be a wonderful head. He was not; had all kinds of trouble. Seemed to me the best thing that we could do would be to persuade him to stay as head of tabulation and let us all help. The psychiatrist in charge agreed with me. We all helped him. He learned his job and became a magnificent head. It had a happy ending, almost had a fatal ending.

One case, I was positive in my own mind, never could be more sure of anything, that a certain man ought to be elevated to head of that division. I was a consultant there. In my mind, no question about it. Magnificent man. Brilliant. Snowing me under in mathematics. A doctor of medicine. After about three years, no head had been appointed yet. I wrote a memorandum to the top man, urging him to close this gap. Put this man in as head. Why was he dragging his feet all these years and doing nothing about it? He finally did make this man head. Twenty-two years went by till he retired. And not one single thing happened in those 22 years. Nothing. Absolutely nothing. He didn't do anything. I was as wrong as could be.

What would it take? How would you know if somebody would do well on promotion? Certainly not short notice. Maybe you should know somebody for years. Are we too hasty in our judgments. Eminence comes after many years. Anyone eminent in any field took years to get there. If we didn't get any supper till we could think of 12 people in history that achieved eminence at an early age, we'd go mighty hungry. All of us together. Could we come up with 12 names through all history that had achieved eminence at an early age? I think we'd go hungry. I can start it. Alexander the Great. Isaac Newton, at age 22, had written down Newton's Laws of Motion, in Latin, of course, so that they would not be misunderstood. And had invented the infinitesimal calculus. At age 22, some people would say Mozart could be. Mozart died at age 33. But in life, 20, 22 years old he tore up or rewrote what he wrote as a youngster. Put down Mozart, that's three. Can you think of some more? Madame Curie, I don't know her age when she discovered polonium. I think she was a youngster. Could we build it up to twelve? I doubt it. Are we too hasty in judging people? Anyone eminent took years to get there. In any line.

A doctor of medicine, a surgeon, a lawyer, a chemist, a physicist, a psychologist, whatever it be, it took him years to get there. And what makes him eminent? Knowledge of his own limitations is what makes him eminent. He's trustworthy. He will not attempt what he cannot do. Are we too hasty in our judgments?

From a presentation at General Motors,
1992.

6

There Is No Substitute
for Knowledge

(Information Is Not Knowledge)

———◆———

In a speech at Dowling College in May 1990, Deming said that you "cannot force knowledge on anybody. They have to ask for it."

Everywhere he went, Deming saw tables of data, computer printouts, and information of all types, but little knowledge. People didn't know how to get knowledge, he said. Deming would point at tables of data and say, "Tons of figures—no knowledge."

Students in school at all levels memorize information rather than learn how to think. Throughout the 1970s and 1980s, Deming wrote and spoke about the need to improve education. He wrote many memoranda to deans and colleagues at schools where he taught. "Typed and printed at my expense" appeared at the top of these memoranda. No matter that he had tenure at the university; he wanted to be sure he was not falsely accused of spending university funds on an issue that he knew would be controversial.

This chapter includes a few of Deming's many letters and speeches on what to do to improve education.

———

In this speech Deming explains the difference between information and knowledge. He states that students need to be taught how to construct, use, and modify theory to explain and predict. Further, they should be taught how to collect and use information and data to modify their theories. He believed education should prepare people to make better predictions and to understand better the past.

Information Is Not Knowledge

What is more important than education of children? We know about material coming into factories, raw, semi-finished, or finished. We know how devastating it is to have shoddy material and faulty equipment. It is a difficult life for a baker if the stuff that comes in is of poor quality or greatly different from the usual run of flour or fat. We know about mistakes in banks, retailing, wholesaling, foul-ups in transportation.

Children are raw material. They will manage our country, our industry, our agriculture, our services, our government. They will do the work of the future. I wonder if anything is more important than children and their education. I have some appreciation of the importance of education at all levels, especially in the beginning.

I talk with management and in seminars about the importance of a good start, the intent of the management. That intent has to be carried out by people that put intent into motion, into design, into production, into action. What is the intent of education?

I understand that there is a builder here in the audience, and I think that he would agree with me that once the plans for a piece of construction (e.g., a house, a building) are 15% on the way, it is too late to make alterations, except to detour around a catastrophe. Changes are costly and time-consuming. It is important to think of education in the same way. You should think also of the intent and how to carry out the intent. The start—the first years of school—is very important.

There were many articles years ago in magazines and in letters to the editor to explain why Johnny can't read. I read about three years ago in the *Atlantic Monthly* another article on the same subject. There is not much of anything interesting for him to read today. The good stories that I read in school, which I knew, were interesting. We don't have stories like that today, so this article says. Now I have not gone back to school, to first, second, and third grades to find out, but the writer explained that the books that the children learn to read from today put the children to sleep.

Everybody at work in any pursuit, any endeavor, be it building, education, post office, transportation, manufacturing, service of any kind, has a customer. Somebody takes his work and does something with it. There is a chain of production.

The customer for people that select books for children to study is the children that are going to read them. The people that select the books are the school boards, not the teacher or the superintendent, and certainly not the children. The children merely use the books selected for them. The school board selects the books, the children read them, except that there is nothing to read any more. No such thing as race or color any more, nor religion, not even gender any more, no such thing. What is there left? Stories are bland. Children go to sleep reading them.

I think that children have as much intelligence today as they did when I was one of them. Yet according to what the figures say, 33 million adults in this country are functionally illiterate. They may be able to pronounce words but they can't read.

Maybe we ought to think about the end-product that we are trying to produce, and the means of making it. Who are the customers? Who are the school boards working for? Whom are the superintendents and the teachers working for?

If you take a look where your taxes go for public education, remember that half the people on the payroll don't teach at all. No wonder teachers are overworked. Half the people on the payroll don't teach, they are the so-called service part of the school system. I wonder if we need all that service. I don't know. It might be something to think about.

There was an article in *Harper's* for April 1985 under the title, "Why Johnny can't think." Johnny never had a chance to think. Children don't get a chance to think any more. Examinations are check-block systems. Children fill their heads with answers. Some children, by knowing the right answer, or by luck, mark off the right box. Some by luck mark the wrong box. In case of doubt, let it be heads or tails. That is not thinking. That is not education.

If you have enough information in your head, you can mark the right answers, very simple. It is a labor saver, because the teacher can tabulate in a flash the results of fifty pupils, bar diagram and comparisons. Neither the teacher or pupil need to think. All so simple. The Educational Testing Service grades applicants the same way; am I right?

Are we victims of great achievements in electronics? Do such tabulations test education? I raised that question with the Educational Testing Service, and I don't think that they liked it.

I would rather have a pupil present to me a paper in which he gave reasons why a certain answer to a certain question could be right, and under what condition it could be wrong, and why another answer could be right or could be wrong. That would require him to think. It would give him a chance to think. I would not care whether he gave the right answers or not, if he learns to think. He would develop some understanding of the world, why something is right or wrong. That would require him to think, and it would require the teacher to read the papers. What are we trying to create? Children that can think, or children that can carry in their heads a pile of information?

You know from your courses in the theory of knowledge that there is no meaning in any statement, no meaning in any conclusion, nor in any sentence, unless it has temporal spread, to enhance your degree of belief in something for the future or something in the past. Johnny with his head full of answers, like a dictionary, is not thinking. A dictionary is pretty important, of course. I use one frequently. But the dictionary can't think for me. Johnny will have his head full of information, be able to pass the course by being able to mark off the right blocks, but that is not education. Marking the right blocks does not explain anything. They don't help Johnny to predict or explain what happened in the past.

Science has advanced by explaining what happened in the past, as in geology, geometry, anthropology, geography, chemistry. Science is not a dictionary full of words, but is knowledge of the world, and this means temporal spread to explain what happened in the past, and what to predict in the future. We modify theory, and thus learn. We are thankful for the dictionary, but it does not lay out a course of action for us. It does not contain knowledge. It contains words. What is thinking? Construction, use, and modification of theory to explain what will happen. Nobody knows what will happen, but we can subject theory to experiment or observation. Education should prepare somebody to make a better prediction and to understand better the past. One enhances his degree of belief as he learns, but degree of belief can not be measured. It is not .8, .9, or anything else.

From an address by W. Edwards Deming
at the dedication of Cedar Crest Academy,
October 12, 1985.

What Ought a School of Business Teach?

A school of business has an obligation to prepare students to lead the transformation. to halt our decline and turn it upward. They ought to teach the theory of a system and the theory of profound knowledge for transformation. They ought to teach the damage, immeasurable, that comes from the evils of short-term thinking, ranking people, demoralization, and losses from incentive pay, pay for performance. Profound knowledge tells us why these practices cause loss and damage to people.

But who in the school of business is competent to prepare students for the future? What ought the schools of business to teach to prepare students for the future? What do ·they teach now? They teach how business is conducted. Exactly what we don't want. They teach students to perpetuate the present style of management. Exactly what we don't want.

In desperation on what to teach, two schools of business, namely the Stern School of Business of New York University and the Graduate School of Business of Columbia University [and many other schools as well], ask for suggestions from students. How could a student know what should be taught? They asked students toward the end of the semester, "Which readings and texts did you find to be of most value to you personally? Of the least value?" How could a student know, he could not possibly know. How could he? Maybe fifteen years from now. Then, well yes, he'd have some perspective.

I carried out a study at New York University School of Business. The Dean of the school, at that time, came to me about 1972 and suggested we carry out a study of students that had been here and graduated ten or more years ago. How are they doing? How might we have helped them more? A wonderful idea. I kicked myself that I had not thought of it myself. Right in my line.

We carried out the study and found only six teachers were mentioned as the "great teacher of my life." Only six of the scores of teachers that had been in that school all those years. Only six were mentioned. At the time when the students were there, they did not know it, they did not know that these were great teachers. Not one of the six teachers had received an award from the students "Teacher of the Year." Not one! The Dean made no special effort to keep any of the six. Nobody knew that they were great. Not till years later. Then the students knew.

The policy to ask students which topics were important enough to warrant more time next year. How would a student know? How would a teacher know? Wish I had answers to all these things.

Let's talk about education for a minute. There is deep concern in the United States today about education. No notable improvement will come until our schools abolish grades (A, B, C, D) in schools from toddlers, on up through the university. Grades are often a forced ranking. Only 20 percent permitted to get As. Thirty percent may get Bs, 30 percent may get Cs, 20 percent may get Ds. Forced ranking. You mean there's a shortage of good pupils? Well, I don't think so. Why should there be a shortage? I don't believe there is a shortage. Only 20 percent? That's nonsense. Maybe there aren't any; maybe everybody should get As. Forced ranking is wrong, I believe.

Abolish merit ratings for teachers. Who knows what a great teacher is? Not till years have gone by. Abolish comparison of schools on the basis of scores. The aim is to get a high score, not to learn, but to cram your head full of information. Abolish gold stars for athletics. Indeed, we're worse off than we thought we were.

If our future lies in specialty products and services, as mass production moves to automation and to other countries, then improvement of education in this country is even more vital than hitherto supposed. We must from now on live by services that bring money into the country, and by high-value, high-profit machines and apparatus. One of them was aircraft engines. Another one was aircraft. High value, high profit. We're doing pretty well. We ought to have more. American movies bring in lots of dollars. There was a time when this country did very well on insurance and banking. I'm afraid those days are submerged, at least for quite a long time. The biggest American bank is something like number twenty on the list of world banks. The Japanese have overtaken us. Have far outdistanced us.

Our schools must preserve and nurture the yearning for learning that everyone is born with.

Joy in learning comes not so much from what is learned, but from learning. It's fun to learn, if you learn knowledge. Not fun to learn information. The joy in the job comes not so much from the result, not from the product, but from contributing to optimization of the system in which everybody wins.

A grade is only somebody's assessment of a pupil's achievement on some arbitrary scale. Does the scale make any sense? Will high achievement on this scale predict future performance of the pupil in business, government, education, or as a teacher? Some other scale might be a better predictor. Some other pupil, low on the prescribed scale today, might perform better than the one that made a high grade on it today.

A grade given to a student is nevertheless used as prediction that he will in the future do well, or do badly. A grade is a permanent label. It opens doors, it closes doors. How may a teacher know how someone will do in the future? If a student seems to lag behind other members of the class, it may be the fault of the teaching. Or maybe the pupil is acquiring knowledge and not information. Does not show up so well compared with the others. Grading in school is an attempt to achieve quality by inspection. Very interesting. Quality by inspection is not the way to get quality.

Because of such folly, I do not give grades to my students. They all pass. Who am I to predict what somebody will do?

I read the papers that my students turn in. A whole stack of them. That's 435 students at Columbia University last semester and 150 at NYU. A lot of papers to read. But I read them. Not to grade them. No, I read them to see how I am doing. Where am I failing? What don't they understand? Why do they give wrong answers? Why do they have some point of view that I don't think is right? Where am I failing? Where do I need to build up. And I'm looking for somebody, anybody, who is special, in need of special help. I'll try to see that he gets it. And who, if anybody is extra-well prepared. Would relish some extra work. There was one such woman in my class. Extra well prepared. I gave her extra work to do.

Where's all this come from? Maybe from games. I have nothing against games. There's a scarcity of winners in a game. Only one player can come out on top. The human race has somehow, for reasons unknown, carried the pattern of games into grades in school and on up through the university, gold stars for school athletics, the merit system (putting people into slots), ranking groups and divisions within the company. All these practices induce competition between people. Negative interactions. Destroying us!

Grading and ranking produce scarcity of top grades. Only a few students are admitted to the top grades. Only a few people on the job are admitted to top rank.

This is wrong. There is no scarcity of good pupils. There is no scarcity of good people. Why don't we use our heads? There is no reason why everyone in a class should not be in the top grade, nor at the bottom, nor anywhere else. Moreover, a grade is only the teacher's subjective opinion. This is so even for the result of an examination.

What is the effect of grading and ranking? Humiliation of those that do not receive top grades or top rank. Demoralization. Even he that receives top grade or top rank is demoralized.

Four widely held myths regarding competition: (1) That competition is an inevitable part of human nature. It is not. (2) That it is more productive than cooperation in promoting success.

Wrong again. (3) That competition is more enjoyable. Wrong again. (4) That it builds character. Wrong again.

People say to me, "Don't students in Japan get grades?" Well, yes they do. There are Japanese people in this room. And they can attest to what I say or they can correct me. But I wish they would take the platform and tell us more. Let me tell you something. A Japanese child is never humiliated, either in school or at home. He's never humiliated. He's trusted. He's never made to feel inferior no matter what be his grade, which puts on him a tremendous responsibility.

But, what do we do? Here I copied from *The Washington Post* a little before Christmas, this clipping. One hundred and ten thousand children in Baltimore took home with them, on the Friday before Christmas, a printed leaflet, printed by the school board directed toward the parents, a plea, in effect, please do not beat your children for low grades. Think of the difference. A plea of the school board to parents: "Please don't beat your children for low grades." What have we come to? Think of the difference. Are children humiliated? Yes. Here they are humiliated with a low grade. Or even if somebody got an A-plus, now he gets only an A or an A-minus. He's humiliated. Parents wonder what happened. What's the matter with him? Think of the harm done.

From a presentation at a CEO seminar,
Quality, Productivity, and Competitive Position,
1992.

Deming often wrote notes to himself about topics that occurred to him as he was sitting in a meeting, or at his desk at home. The ideas in his notes often provided fodder for future letters and articles. The notes below, titled by Deming, "Notes on Teaching in a School of Business," were handwritten on January 24, 1988. He describes the nature of purpose and quality in an academic institution.

Notes on Teaching in a School of Business

Constancy of Purpose: to help industry to improve our economy.

Our customers are U.S. industry. Better: our customers are industry the world over. The material that we work on is our students. We can also work directly with management through seminars and special lectures.

What will our students need to know so that they can help our economy in the future? How ought we to modify our teaching?

Do we teach students to conform? To learn how business is done, and how to carry on in the same channels?

Again, how ought we to modify our teaching? How can we give to them a smattering of the profound knowledge that they will need if they are to help our economy?

The intent of quality is dictated by top management. Quality can not be better than the intent.

Innovation is necessary:

For design of product and of service
For improvement of processes

Good operations are essential, but will not ensure quality.

Chain reaction: improve process → costs decrease → capture the market with better quality and lower price → stay in business → provide jobs.

Improvement of a process requires improvement of incoming material, more reliable service (e.g., transportation).

Some negatives:

- The President of one of our largest companies put quality in the hands of his plant managers. What went wrong?
- Hard work will not ensure quality.
- Best efforts will not ensure quality.

- Good intentions will not ensure quality.
- Experience by itself teaches nothing.
- Examples by themselves teach nothing.
- Investment in gadgets, computers, automation, or new machinery will not ensure quality.

Follow me around. Most of the new machinery that I see is a source of poor quality, frustration, increase in costs.

Wrong. The future belongs to him who invests in it.

How much of the student's time is spent in learning skills that could be learned better and with good pay on the job?

A necessary ingredient for improvement of quality is knowledge. I call it profound knowledge.

Improvement of design and of quality in all its aspects requires knowledge of variation. How may we reduce variation?

Strange it is that a lot of practices of management serve to increase variation, a barrier to better quality, and a guarantee of high cost.

Funnel [just the word, Deming didn't complete the thought]

Handwritten notes
on teaching in a school of business,
January 24, 1988.

What Should We Be Teaching Students?

(A Memorandum to the Dean of a Business School)

I come now with boldness to ask you to share with me a few ideas that have occurred to me in respect to committees of the GBA [Graduate School of Business Administration]. Please, whether you agree or are shocked at my ideas and temerity, remember

that my only purpose here is to help the GBA to move upward
and to be a leader amongst schools of business.

1. It seems to me that most of the committees in your memoranda of the 6th July do not tackle issues of chief importance.
   Your memoranda, as I see it, aim at short-range satisfaction
   of students instead of positive recognition of our mission
   here on earth.
2. Our mission is of course to serve students. I have nothing
   in mind except service to students. What we should try to
   do, however, is to serve their needs 10 or 20 years from now.
   This we can do by building a greater university. We can not
   accomplish such aims by vacating our responsibilities, which
   the list of committees and the terms of reference appear to
   me to do.
3. One question is how to serve our students better with what
   we have. Are we making the best use of our great men?
   (Later on, I shall enquire why we don't have more of them.)
   It seems to me that all our students should have a taste of the
   best that we have to offer. I propose that a course of lectures
   be arranged for day students, and for night students as well,
   to be given by our six greatest men, two lectures each, any
   subjects that they choose to talk on; and that attendance at
   these lectures be required for a degree (any degree). Such
   lectures might be a great service in adult education as well as
   to our regular students.

How many of our students ever heard a lecture by Peter
Drucker? It is unfortunately possible for a student to get
a degree at the GBA, yet never be exposed to men whose
thinking could influence him the rest of his life.

We should not make it difficult for a student to get an
education along with his degree.

4. By my criteria, there is too much emphasis at the GBA on filling the catalog with courses, lots and lots of courses, articulated with prerequisites like stair-steps, with little regard to the competence of the men that give the courses.

   a. To illustrate, the catalog of the GBA shows for each course the title and content but NOT WHO WILL GIVE IT. All that will matter to the student, 15 years from now, is WHO GAVE THE COURSE, not the title of the course nor its alleged content. How can a student prepare his curriculum, or how can anybody help him, if the names of the instructors are not shown? Is the student, in planning, to trust that the School will somehow dig up an instructor when the time comes? We should make it clear to students that we don't just offer courses: WE OFFER MEN.

   b. Or do we? The catalog of the GBA would compare favorably in number of courses and in description of content with the courses offered at the University of Chicago. Is the reader to assume that the GBA is equal to the University of Chicago? Are we trying to keep up with the Joneses? Are we fooling anybody?

5. a. For myself, I should rather take six courses, all listed and described identically in the catalog and all given by six great men, than to take six courses, all written up differently and articulated, given by six different men of mediocre calibre. A great man gives himself, not a course. What we need is more great men, fewer courses, and less emphasis on articulation of courses. Our students need teachers that are thinking and doing things, who know what it is to face a board of directors, or a cross-examination, and to take a beating now and then.

   b. There was a time, years ago, when the GBA was noted for its great men. Are we on a downward incline? Why?

6. a. As Peter Drucker pointed out, a lot of people in universities, and a lot of students, are looking backward, not forward in their plans. No one can see the future, but we must try. Communication between different economic and social layers of people looms up as one of the main problems of the future.

b. There are new principles in management and administration that emanate as logical consequences of statistical methods and knowledge of psychology. The outstanding example is Japan. Our students in business administration should have a chance to learn about these new principles. Much of the traditional learning and teaching in administration and management is out-moded and has been for years. The new principles throw light on enrichment of jobs; they achieve more economic production, improvement, of quality and dependability of product, and better competitive position in the marketplace.

c. Certainly American industry needs these improvements.

d. How many M.B.As. could define in a scientific or legal case such qualities as on-time performance, reliable, safe, satisfactory, polluted? How many know the distinction between the specification of a unit of product, and economic principles for acceptance of lots?

e. Why should our graduates be handicapped?

7. a. It is necessary for the administration of a university, if service to students be the goal, to differentiate between teaching knowledge and teaching information. A teacher that is competent in his line will teach knowledge. Less competent men will teach information and hardware. There is an old Chinese proverb that applies here: "Give me a fish, and you feed me today: teach me how to fish, and you feed me for life." We should teach students how to fish. We are not in business to produce whiz kids.

Information systems, however marvelous and glamorous they be, and the hardware that they employ, are fish for today. They tell management where they are very important of course.

b. But what management needs to know also is how to improve. Not only where are we, but how to achieve a goal, is the problem.

c. If this assertion be worth consideration, then what our students of management, administration, and accounting need is cross-fertilization with theory for detection of causes of trouble and for indication of the level of responsibility for improvement. Should we grant an M.B.A. without this requirement?

d. There will be a revolution in management and in administration when these principles become known. It started in Japan in 1950. The whole world knows about the results.

8. What could be more important in industry than population research or demography? Where are our courses in population research? Changes in the age–sex pyramid, by income level, by type of residence, and by level of education, along with changes in productivity, are of paramount importance in business. Demographers and economists make predictions of these changes with range and accuracy that are very useful to the man in business provided he is aware of their usefulness. Examples of failure to look ahead with the aid of demographic research lie close to home—our railways, the New York Telephone Company, Con Edison.

Think what a man like Phil Hauser could do at the GBA, even if we saw him only once a month (which is incidentally all that his students at Chicago see of him, but they do see him!).

9. Where are our courses in the theory of knowledge? If any group of people needs theory of knowledge, it is men

in business. They go forth with degrees from schools of business without knowing the difference between formal knowledge and empirical knowledge; nor the dangers, hazards, and limitations of inductive logic, the very thing that a man in business must live with day by day the rest of his life. What are we doing about it? The only place where our students learn anything about the theory of knowledge, so far as I know, is in some of our courses in statistics. Are we being fair to our students?

10. A committee of men who are willing to try, versed in the frontiers of economics, statistical methods, psychology, theory of law, theory of knowledge, sociology, whose terms of reference would be to look ahead and try to assess the needs of business and government, would be one of the most important activities of administration at the GBA, I should think.

11. Our job is education, not to train people in the trades and skills. Education means understanding of theory, and the interlocking of theories, the history of the development of thought in a discipline, the limitations of theory. Education is partly but not entirely memory with storage and retrieval. Education means theory and research, unfolding of questions and answers, with more questions than answers as the cloth comes off the loom.

12. The GBA faces a fork in the road: (a) take steps to attract great men, and thus move upward; or (b) let nature take its course, and its toll. Where are our Milton Friedmans, our Simon Kuznetses, our Arnold Webers, our Henry Kissingers, our George Schultzes, our Churchill Eisenharts, our Herman Wolds, our Phil Hausers, our Joe Jurans, our J. Tinbergens, our Margaret Meads?

13. a. How can we attract distinguished men? I don't have all the answers, but there are two requirements: (a) a firm policy on the matter; (b) a fresh look at salaries.

b. Policy toward elevation must come from the top authorities of the University, with tangible evidence of intent and means.

c. As for salaries, the GBA must compete with industry and with government. We need teachers with experience in industry and in government, men who can step at will in and out of industry, in and out of government, in and out of any school. We must face the fact that the GBA can not command the major portion of the time of a top man for less than treble or quadruple the salaries paid now. We can not expect a man in his right mind to give up, for the privilege of being a professor at the GBA, fees of $50,000 to $100,000 per year that he could be earning, and building up a research-record besides, by putting in a few days per week with private industry. Wishful thinking will not change the pull of gravity.

d. A way out, and a good way, is to attract more part-time teachers of renown. The GBA can take on full-time only a limited number of men of stature, because of the cost. The remaining great men will be part-time teachers, with allegiance to the GBA but not on call four days a week. They will spend a good share of their time in private research and writing. Such men bring to their students what no other teachers can bring. Recruitment of men of renown, on this basis, should be pursued actively, I submit.

14. In this connexion, we must be aware of a strong centrifugal force by which the research and creative writing of our best men is already being done more and more in their homes and in offices of clients. The centrifugal force that I refer to arises not alone from a desire of these men to supplement their salaries, but from opportunities in business for high grade research. Another contributing factor is impoverished office

space and facilities at the GBA, especially secretarial service and assistance; also library. It is so much easier and more satisfactory to work elsewhere.

For example, in my own case, I have spacious offices at home, a fine library, big blackboard, superb secretary on duty Saturdays, Sundays, and holidays, and nights as needed (high-priced but worth it), Xerox machine and other equipment including coffee. Clerical work, summaries, computations, are done in offices of clients or in my home. I put out several papers a year on this basis: now and then a book.

Preparation of papers and notes for my teaching, and the printing thereof, are also done at home. The GBA has no facilities for typing mathematical manuscripts to my satisfaction, and has cut out printing of notes for trial in class, in preparation for papers and books.

It would cost the GBA something like $50,000 per year to supply the clerical help and computations that go into my own papers, and this is just one man. Summed over the whole GBA, the whole amount in effect donated to teaching by clients of our top teachers would run into a magnificent sum.

I offer the thought that we should accept this centrifugal force as a way of life, and be deeply appreciative of the contribution that clients and teachers make to our students and to the stature of the GBA. This thought leads back to my earlier suggestion to recruit more part-time teachers of renown.

15. What the proportion of distinguished men should be in a university is one of the problems for a committee to think about. And just what is a distinguished man? These are

tough questions, but not too tough to cope with. Contributions to knowledge, usually through publication, honors bestowed by learned councils and societies, offers from other schools and from industry and from government, are time-honored criteria.

16. Not all the men on a faculty will be distinguished, nor need they be. (An exception would be an institute like the Institute for Advanced Study at Princeton, but this, I take it, is not our aim at present. The thought crosses my head, though, that perhaps we ought to establish such an institute in business.) Any school, including the GBA, must then of necessity have as assistant professors and as instructors a number of lesser men. But these lesser men should be on their way up, not stationary. Every man now in first rank on any faculty worked his way up. A man is not born famous.

    How may we recognize in a young man the potential for growth? There is no sure way, but a man's goals for research, and his performance (record or promise of publication) in research are the most important criteria. Love of teaching and personality are necessary but not sufficient.

17. The man who improves himself weekly by carrying on research, and who has an interest in his students, is the man we need at the GBA. Quality of teaching will take care of itself. If a teacher is doing research, and cares for his students, his enthusiasm for depth of study will be contagious, and students will learn.

    The teacher we don't need is the popular man with lustre of personality, who holds students spellbound, teaching what is wrong. In the absence of research, a teacher can only teach what is wrong. Without research, a man can not appreciate the limitations of his knowledge, and certainly can not impart these limitations to students. The limitations of knowledge are the most important ingredient of knowledge itself. Only he who does research can know this.

18. The plea that the University can not afford more great men and better facilities is a dud. The University is spending munificent sums of money. It is spending money to fill our catalog with a plethora of courses with a trend toward more than our share of [second-string] men and more courses. What is needed is reversal of this trend, with an avowed policy toward goals that will build a greater University. The first step is determination to reverse the trend. Money is not the problem.

19. There are two problems in respect to finances: (1) how to get money; (2) how to spend wisely what we have. This memorandum deals only with the second problem. Perhaps, however, if we worked seriously on the second problem, there would be less trouble with the first one.

20. A concomitant problem is research carried on at the GBA. I can only touch on this problem here, but some principles seem clear.

    a. The only legitimate reason why a school should ask for or receive funds for research should be to provide instruction and internships for students.

    b. The GBA should accept a grant for research only if no person or firm in private enterprise could take on the job and do it satisfactorily (sometimes a touchy problem in subjective judgment). Tax shelter, library, working space, and help at the GBA should not be permitted to under cut the prices that private enterprise would have to charge.

    c. Methods, results, and data may all be published, with no restrictions.

    d. Any research project at the GBA should be in the charge of a man of stature. The students on a project should have the advantage of seeing how a great man works. The man in charge of a research project at the GBA must be paid for this work on a scale that attracts him in competition with industry. On this basis, research at the GBA would be beneficial to both industry and students.

e. Students do not learn much by participation in [second-grade] research, which is all that it can be if headed up by a man who can not hold his place in industry or in government, whose only qualification is that by undercutting prices through tax shelter he can scare up funds.

21. It is desirable to distinguish between (a) research carried out officially by the GBA and (b) research carried out privately by teachers for their own clients. Private consultation and research should be completely independent of the School except for its impact on teaching. Private consultation and research should not in any way make use of the School's facilities. Results of a study should be typed on the teacher's personal stationery, not on NYU stationery, and not signed by him as a professor in some department. It is wrong to involve the School in any expense, methods, conclusions, or recommendations that involve only a private connexion. (I know of no instance here of trespass on these principles, but I have seen it in other schools.)

It would be ethical nevertheless, I believe, for a professor to state in his qualifications in a legal case that he holds or has held certain academic ranks, and where, with dates.

22. In closing, let me repeat that my purpose here is only that we take action to reverse downward trends before it is too late. Drastic surgery may be required. A lot of the economic ills that beset this country (and some others) are chargeable to management in business and in government that in years past vacated their responsibilities to let other forces rush in and take over the job. The same thing can happen in a university. It is in fact taking place under our noses.

23. What committee or committees are studying the problems raised here? If we don't do the job, somebody else will, in his own way. Or am I just seeing things and hearing voices? Perhaps the problems and suggestions that I raise are not for your committees at all, but for the Dean alone. As I said at the beginning, I beg you to forgive my intrusion with ideas.

From a Memorandum to Dean Dill,
New York University,
originally dated January 3, 1972;
slightly revised December 18, 1972.

In an interdepartmental communication at a business school, Deming questions whether a credible job is being done in the design of quantitative courses. This memorandum might well have been sent to any graduate-level business school. He questions whether courses teach techniques at the expense of helping students understand how to uncover what the problems are in a business, how to work with subject-matter experts, how to conduct analyses that include non-normal situations, non-response, outliers, and the limitations to techniques taught.

Memorandum on the Teaching of Statistics, Operations Research, Quantitative Analysis

I

Is it correct to say that we in our department are teaching Quantitative Analysis? Are we teaching Operations Research? Or are we teaching theory that may at times be useful in the design and analysis of quantitative studies? This is in itself a noble pursuit, but do we explain to our students what it is that we are doing?

We of course illustrate theory with application, but our applications are aids to the teaching of theory, not ends in themselves. The most difficult and most important step in operations research is to decide what the problems are in a business or in a branch of government or other endeavour that have a chance of solution, immediate and long range, and thereupon to decide what information or calculations might be helpful. At that point, techniques come into play, and that is what we teach, techniques. In a school of business administration, knowledge of the limitations of techniques is as important as knowledge of the techniques themselves.

Ability to perceive what the problems are in a business or in any other endeavour rests in knowledge of the subject-matter—economics, marketing, production, transportation, accounting, law, medicine, psychology, sociology, agriculture, finance, or something else.

The job of the statistician is to work with experts in the subject-matter to help them to solve their problems. It is the responsibility of the substantive expert to decide with or without help of the statistician, what problems are important and what information or tests or comparisons or other spade-work, resulting in statistical information, might be helpful, and to arrive finally at a meaningful (statistical) statement of the problem and what might be done about it. Of course, he can not do this without some superficial knowledge of the techniques that might possibly provide help on his problem. The statistician works with the expert in the subject-matter, assisting him to formulate the problem in meaningful terms, and to broaden the scope or to limit the scope of possible courses of solution, in an attempt to reap the greatest economic or scientific benefit from any expenditure to be put forth.

Knowledge of techniques alone does not enable one to go into a company to find out what is wrong there and what the problems are, any more than a teacher of marketing could teach statistical methods.

Techniques we can teach: subject-matter we can not: subject-matter is the specialism and obligation of other departments.

One can only learn theory; one can only teach theory. Illustration on a practical problem sometimes helps both teacher and student to understand the theory better, and its limitations. In my own courses, for example, I use illustrations in inventory-policy, measurement of inventory, consumer research, government statistical series, psychological tests, medical treatments, transportation, agricultural science, accounting, costs, production, reliability, failure, complex apparatus, amongst other applications. It is not necessary for the statistician to decide whether the applications that he uses for illustration in his teaching of theory are important, nor to explain much about the subject-matter. Someone skilled in the subject-matter brought a problem to me. To him it was important. It is my place to teach the statistical methods that I prescribed, and why, and the statistical interpretation of the results: also what statistical methods might have been better under the same circumstances and under different circumstances.

It is important to know and to teach where the statistician fits into a problem and how necessary it is to require the expert in the subject-matter to accept the responsibilities that are rightfully his and which he is fitted for, or should be, if he is worth working for.

Possibly some members of this department have the knowledge that is required in economics, consumer research, psychology, management, transportation, manufacturing, to take on the responsibilities of the expert in subject-matter as well as to teach the mathematical techniques.

It is also important to teach the limitations of our methods. The limitations are as important as the methods themselves.

Only we who know theory can perceive the limitations of the theory that we teach.

Statistical work, or operations research, by whatever name, is team-work. None of us can be a whole team. A man learned in statistical theory, for example, and applying statistical theory to motor-freight, will not also be learned in the economics of transportation. It is enough to be a statistician.

For example, in Japan in 1950 and after, what I tried to teach to top management was not management but *Some statistical problems in the management of quality*. They knew enough of the substantive part of management to weld statistical techniques into their thinking. I did not teach consumer research, but *Use of Statistical Techniques in Consumer Research*. The whole world knows the result.

II

None of the foregoing thoughts is intended to play down the importance of techniques. We may all swell up and gloat over the contribution that statistical methods have made to understanding of subject-matter, and to the improvement of information that goes into subject-matter. I may enumerate a few here.

a. Comparison of our Census of Population, 1970, with that of 1930, provides a good example of the impact of the statistician on the scope, content, speed, economy, and accuracy of our Census.

b. Government statistical series (monthly or quarterly) on employment, unemployment, housing starts, home repairs, health statistics, and a host of other subjects

c. Optimum inventory-policy

d. Measurement of inventory

e. Theories of response. Theories of non-response

f. Randomization of questions to reduce bias of response to embarrassing questions

g. Theory of optimum investment (queuing theory)

h. The distinction between special causes and common (general) causes of excessive variability in dimensions, performance of workers, performance of field-workers, performance of salesmen, performance of a portfolio manager. Statistical signals detect, with a specified probability of being wrong, the existence of either of these types of cause, and indicate the level of responsibility for correction.

i. Operational definitions of a host of adjectives used in reliability and in measures of performance. "On time," for example, can only be defined statistically.

j. Distinction between enumerative and analytic studies, with improved economy in the design and use of quantitative information

k. Optimum policy for maintenance and replacement

l. Psychological terms. (Many psychological traits are based on mean and standard deviation—I.Q., for example.)

m. Speedy development of a process

n. Capability of the process. (A process can be developed to a stable and identifiable state only by statistical methods. In this state, statistical methods provide objective measures of the precision, uniformity, quality, speed of the process, and the cost per unit, all of which are vital for *economic* production and for rational conduct of business.)

o. Capture–recapture method of counting bats, rats, fish, nomadic people

p. Distinction between (a) the specifications for a single unit of product, and tests by which a single unit will be accepted or rejected; and (b) the specifications for lots, namely, the rules by which a lot, in a succession of lots, will be accepted or rejected (acceptance sampling)

q. Use of statistical techniques to arrive at economic and enforceable standards and specifications of performance, behavior, dimensions, refinement of tests

r. Refinement of standards of weights and measures through interlaboratory testing. Refinement of instruments and use of instruments

s. Design for optimum balance between sampling variation, errors of response, nonresponse, and cost

Any of us could go on and on. The sum of these contributions, however, does not alter the importance of knowledge of subject-matter nor the basic principle of the division of responsibility between subject-matter and techniques.

No one, more than the statistician, reaches into a wider variety of man's quantitative activity. Statistical theory is scholarly, and important discipline. The impact of statistical theory should be part of a liberal education, and studied for an understanding of man and nature, not just as a tool of research and management.

III

We have a heavy responsibility to teach students of business administration what no other department here can teach. Perhaps a few questions would give some idea of our responsibility and opportunity here.

a. How many students in the GBA, handed the results of a study, could interpret them in a form useful to management, without losing information in the report, and without overstepping the inherent accuracy of the data?

b. How many of them would be alert to the various types of uncertainty and sources of misinterpretation that afflict any data?

How many would have an idea on how to go about it to detect and measure the main possible sources of uncertainty in a batch of figures on sales, consumer research, tests of a product?

c. For example, how many students here, in order to understand what certain data mean, could ask appropriate questions about the way the data were collected? How many would enquire into the proportion of non-response? How many would enquire what classes of people failed to respond? or what training and supervision there was over the field-work and the coding? How many would ask for a copy of the questionnaire? How many would wish to see some of the completed questionnaires (or raw results of tests)? How many would appreciate the difficulty or impossibility of answering or measuring certain very important items of information (such as, "Have you ever heard of Brand X of oven cleaner?")?

d. How many of them appreciate the futility of increasing the size of a study in which the main items of investigation are difficult to measure or to answer? How many students appreciate the futility of great precision for use in an analytic study?

e. How many of them would enquire into the difference in results obtained by seasoned interviewers and new interviewers?

f. How many of them could lay out a simple plan of selection and computation by which one could readily estimate (i) the variance of the result for a given question, and (ii) the variances between interviewers? How many know that it can be done (even if they don't know how to do it)?

g. How many of our own students would know how to specify appropriate tabulations and make statistical tests in an attempt to discover whether some spurious looking results may be attributed (a) to the environment (the questionnaire, administration of field-work, season of the year), or (b) to variable performance of the interviewers?

h. How many of our students would make the mistake, in an analytic problem, of calculating by probability-methods the risk of committing an error of the second kind? How many know about the limitations of estimates and statistical tests?

One might enquire whether anyone should consider himself a master of business administration if he is lost in questions like the above.

Estimates and standard errors and statistical statements of probability are not the whole of analysis of data. They are sometimes helpful, but almost never sufficient. One usually needs much more statistical information and a lot of substantive information to understand and use the results of a study.

How many of our students are aware that calculation of confidence intervals and likelihood-ratios and the like are in most studies inefficient methods of analysis? Are we teaching better ones? Are we teaching our students anything about tests to help one to arrive rationally at a decision to accept use of the standard deviation of a set of results, or whether to dig further into the data for hidden sources of information that would help to evaluate the precision and accuracy of the results?

IV

So, are we teaching statistics, operations research, quantitative analysis? Are we doing a creditable job in teaching analysis of data? Or are we merely teaching some selected techniques used in design, in analysis? Does it make any difference what we call ourselves or claim to teach?

Should the teaching of quantitative analysis include at least one attempt during the student's career at the GBA to dig out the meaning of some actual data? Are we teaching the limitations of our techniques? Are we teaching efficient methods of analysis in the face of non-normality, moving frame, non-response? Are we teaching how to use outliers effectively?

A university-wide department, charged with the obligation to prepare students for the doctorate and with the power to recommend to the authorities of the university the conferment of a degree, will perhaps call for a bit more responsible consideration than we would give to the matter were we isolated among understanding friends.

The teaching and the work that we do would be called by some people the mathematical techniques of operations research; by others, design and analysis of studies; by others, systems analysis; by others, the statistical control of quality; by others, statistics. To me, it is just the work of a statistician trying to do his job, and trying to learn day by day how to do it better.

Whatever be the comments and criticisms of this memorandum, the writing thereof, over a space of many months, has profoundly affected my own teaching and work.

From an Interdepartmental Communication at NYU (typed and printed at private expense) for circulation to colleagues, July 24, 1971.

In this article Deming proposes to the statistical community that they need to keep up with the demands of industry for statistical knowledge. He makes some specific recommendations for material to be added in statistical courses.

Changes Required in the Teaching of Statistics

Respect for the statistical profession amongst scientists, engineers, and professional people has followed a monotonic decreasing sequence for 40 years. At the same time, industry has ever-increasing need for statistical help. Unfortunately, the gap between supply and demand for statistical work widens by the month.

What is wrong? The answer lies in the teaching of statistics. Here are some suggestions for change in the teaching of statistics to engineers and to students of the natural sciences and the social sciences, and in schools of business.

1. Distinction between enumerative studies and analytic studies. Error and loss from use of theory for enumerative studies for analytic problems
2. Distinction between common causes of variation and special (assignable) causes. For example, the distinction between common causes and special (assignable) causes of variation (i.e., between a stable system and an unstable system) is vital for improvement of quality. The responsibility for improvement of a stable system rests with the management, whereas identification of a special cause and its removal is usually best attempted at the local level.
3. Losses from tampering with a stable system. Examples: (1) worker training worker; (2) executives working together without guidance of statistical theory; (3) sharing ideas without guidance of statistical theory
4. Organization for statistical work

From "On the Statistician's Contribution to Quality," presented at the meeting of the International Statistical Institute, Tokyo, September 8–11, 1987.

––––––––––––––––

At NYU, as in most other universities in the United States, students are asked to evaluate content of courses and competence of teachers at the end of each term of study. Deming believed it a "reckless idea" and counseled himself and his colleagues "to take no notice of evaluations by students." And this he did. He couldn't stop the envelopes, filled with evaluation forms for distribution to students, from finding their way to his mailbox at the end of each semester. So, he had a box of "scrap" paper on his desk that got refilled at the end of each term.

Memorandum on Teaching

There is much discussion today about student participation in affairs of the university, even in respect to evaluation of teachers and content of courses. Here are some of my thoughts on the matter.

It seems to me that the prime requirement for a teacher is to possess some knowledge to teach. He who does no research possesses not knowledge and has nothing to teach. Of course some people that do good research are also good teachers. This is a fine combination, and one to be thankful for, but not to expect.

No lustre of personality can atone for teaching error instead of truth. One of the finest teachers that I ever knew could hold 300 students spellbound, teaching what is wrong. The two poorest teachers that I ever had (though a third one ran neck and neck) were Professor Ernest Brown in mathematics at Yale and Sir Ronald Fisher at University College in London. Sir Ernest will be known for centuries for his work in lunar theory, and Sir Ronald for revolutionizing man's methods of inference. People came from all over the world to listen to their impossible teaching, and to learn from them, and learn they did. I would not trade my good luck to have had these men as teachers for hundreds of lectures by lesser men but "good teachers."

It is too late when the student finds out that the foundation he built in college is shaky. He may fill in gaps by self-study, but the place to lay the sure foundation is in school. The best insurance that a student can take out is to make sure that his professors do research.

The student is at a disadvantage when asked to evaluate a teacher. On what basis? Lustre of personality? Knowledge of the subject? Content of course? The teacher's interest in making sure that he is communicating to the students whatever it is that he is trying to say? A student can possibly judge the teacher's knowledge of the subject, but he can hardly be a judge of the content of the course. Not even the teacher has dependable knowledge about what ought to be taught.

Learning today is preparation for 5, 10, 20 years in the future. A student naturally likes what he calls a good teacher, for whatever reasons. What use, then, could be made of students' evaluation of a teacher?

The problem of identifying a good teacher is not one in consumer research, though every statistician knows well the importance of consumer research. A university should be now, as in days gone by, a place where one may listen and learn from great men.

The only suitable judges of a teacher's knowledge are his peers. The only objective criterion of knowledge is research worthy of publication. Publication should of course be measured on some sale of contribution to knowledge, not by number of papers.

Suggestions from students concerning the content of a course or the competence of a teacher are accordingly, in my judgment, a reckless idea. I would counsel myself and my colleagues to take no notice of evaluation by students. For my own part, I could not teach under a system of evaluation by students.

Interdepartmental Communication, New York University:
Memorandum on Teaching,
January 4, 1971;
later published as a Letter to the Editor,
The American Statistician,
Volume 26, No. 1, February 1972.

7

Management Is Prediction

(Statistical Thinking Is Required)

———◆———

Deming was a leading expert on surveys, sample design, and design of statistical studies. His books Some Theory of Sampling *(1950) and* Sample Design in Business Research *(1960) remain today two of the best books available for the practicing statistician. They include some techniques he developed, such as the half-open interval, and numerous other methods for dealing with the practical problems that surface for the practicing statistician. Very few authors with strong theoretical statistics knowledge have had such an active practice in which to define, refine, and develop solutions for preserving statistical integrity while dealing with the problems of the real world. He was certainly one of the few.*

This chapter includes papers on administrative aspects of some key areas of statistical thinking that Deming believed managers ought to be familiar with.

———————

In this paper Deming discusses the need for statistical knowledge in assessing causes of defective products and services, setting specifications, creating testing procedures, and determining reliability of complex products.

The Need to Apply Statistical Principles

Engineers face today problems that were unknown in engineering a few years ago. Use of automatic machinery, complex apparatus, automation, can only be useful with better understanding of statistical methods.

The engineer needs education in engineering, but engineering itself can not solve the statistical problems that he faces. One important function of the engineer is to find and to remove special causes of variability; also common causes of variability. He needs the control chart to detect a special cause; then he needs engineering knowledge to remove it. He may need knowledge of design of experiment to find a common cause, and to distinguish between special causes and common causes, as confusion between the two leads to bad administration, variability of product, and loss of business.

A feed-back mechanism that supposedly makes automatic adjustment to maintain dimensions within prescribed limits should operate on statistical principles. Statistical criteria for action, as provide by the Shewhart control chart, must be built into the feed-back, else the mechanism will overcorrect or undercorrect, and will cause excessive variation. The product may meet specifications, but excess variation, even within specifications, may be costly.

Specifications have no meaning except in statistical language. For example, what meaning would there be to a specification that steel wires 6 cm in length must have tensile strength of 60,000 psi? How would one carry out a test to decide whether the lot of 10,000 wires meets the specification? The test is destructive. How is the sample of pieces to be drawn? How many pieces in the sample? Must every piece in the sample satisfy the specification, or will it suffice that [some prescribed number of] pieces meet specification?

Obviously the specification has no meaning except in terms of statistical criteria and interpretation of tests. The same may be said in respect to other tests used in engineering. The engineer must therefore follow statistical principles in writing a specification.

Parts are often assembled today from hundreds of manufacturers in various parts of the world. The problem of specification and production are enormous. They can be met best by statistical principles of specification and test.

The statistical control of quality becomes more necessary than ever with the introduction of automatic machinery. Delays are now expensive, as the cost of machinery continues minute after minute, whether the machine turns out product or lies idle. A tie-up in one stage of production may mean tie-up in succeeding stages. Tolerances from one stage to another must therefore be much more exact than ever, to avoid excessive costs of production.

The engineer needs to know today that there is no test-method at all unless the test-method shows randomness. If it shows a decided trend, any engineer would reject the method. But non-randomness is not always visible to the eye. The engineer therefore needs a test of randomness. The Shewhart control-chart provides one possible test. A run-chart provides another. There are still other statistical tests, as one may learn.

Engineering problems of air-frames, lift-mechanisms, and many other products, require close tolerances to lighten the load and to improve reliability. It will no longer suffice to cover up ignorance with a huge factor of safety. It is necessary to replace ignorance with engineering knowledge, supplemented with statistical principles of tests.

Consider the problem of reliability of complex apparatus. Reliability can be defined only in terms of statistical criteria and statistical tests. It will not suffice to say that something is extremely reliable, or is only moderately reliable, as such words will not suffice in modern industry. Reliability can be defined only by statistical criteria and statistical tests.

Message to Engineers for the
Union of Japanese Scientists & Engineers, Tokyo,
December 11, 1966.

Statistical studies are divided into two distinct categories, each with its own methodologies—not transferable to the other type of study. Deming provides here a description of the two types of studies and their use. To become proficient requires much more than is written here. Deming wrote two books, Some Theory of Sampling *(1950) and* Sample Design in Business Research *(1960), that contain statistical foundations for the category of studies known as "enumerative," where you are trying to count something, for example a census of people in the United States, a customer survey on your product or service, the level of damage in a warehouse fire. Analytic studies help us learn something that will help us improve future product or service.*

Enumerative and Analytic Studies

An enumerative study: A problem exists. In the opinion of experts in the subject-matter, study of a proposed frame would produce information that is needed. A frame is necessary for an enumerative study. A frame is composed of [products, people, services], any one of which may be drawn into the sample for investigation. A simple example is a list of accounts receivable on a certain date.

The second step is to understand the concept of the equal complete coverage, defined as the result that would be obtained by investigation of every [product, person, service] in the frame, by use of prescribed methods, definitions, and care. The aim of the sample drawn from the frame is to estimate what would be obtained were the equal complete coverage to be carried out [every product evaluated, every person queried, every service reviewed].

In an enumerative study, action will be taken on units of the universe. In an analytic study, action will be taken on the process that produced the material studied, with the hope to improve units yet to be produced.

An analytic study: A problem exists. It is thought by the management, or by the people on the job, or by experts in the subject-matter, that a change in procedure would bring better quality and higher yield in tomorrow's run, or in next year's crop.

An analytic study is one in which material made yesterday may furnish information by which to improve a process. A time-honored example is last year's crop, studied with the aim to improve next year's crop. In industry, one studies the performance of material made in the past, or service delivered in the past, with the aim to learn about the effect in the future of a proposed change in the process. A proposed medical treatment will be tested on human beings or on animals in an attempt to provide better treatment in the future.

When can we use probability? The theory of probability applies only to the random variation of a repeatable operation. This condition is met for practical purposes in an enumerative study if random numbers are used for selection of samples. A confidence interval has operational meaning and usefulness in an enumerative study.

In contrast, the economic and physical conditions that governed an experiment or test carried out last week, or the product of last week or last year's crop, will never be seen again. We must conclude that for an analytic study, any material that we test to aid us in planning is a judgment sample, not a random sample. There is, in an analytic study, no equal complete coverage, hence no random sample, error yes, but no standard error, no confidence interval.

Statistical theory for analytic problems has not yet been developed.

The only possible exception exists for performance or product that comes from a stable system, one that is demonstrable in statistical control. Prediction of the statistical characteristics of future product may then be calculated by the theory of estimation applied to last week's product as if it were a sample drawn by random numbers.

The aim of an analytic study is to aid prediction of the behaviour of a process, to aid plans for improvement of tomorrow's run or of next year's crop.

Planning requires prediction. One may have to plan with a little degree of belief in the predictions that he would wish to have in hand for planning, or he may be fortunate with strong degree of belief in some of the predictions. Degree of belief can not be measured in numbers.

Better knowledge of a process means enhancement of the degree of belief in the prediction of its performance, and a better basis for planning. There is no sure way to predict the results of a change. Empirical evidence is never complete.

Statistical theory, as used in an enumerative study, does not provide measures of degree of belief in a prediction. Tomorrow's run, or next year's crop, will be governed by conditions different from those that governed the data from a study of the past.

The only exception is data from the output of a stable process, one in statistical control. The theory of estimation, as used in an enumerative study, applies in all its glory to lots yet to come from a stable process, provided the process stays stable. Lots, and samples drawn by random numbers from lots, behave as samples drawn from a frame. A sample that is big enough will predict with a high degree of belief the statistical characteristics of lots to come tomorrow from the same process.

Unfortunately, a stable process must be created and demonstrated. Moreover, a process that is stable today may not be stable tomorrow. Stability must be charted, and any special cause detected by statistical signal should be identified and removed.

Data from an experiment can not qualify as output of a stable process. Last year's crop in a certain area did not come from a stable process. The environmental conditions of last year (rainfall, weather, soil) will never be seen again.

One may use graphical displays to look for repeated patterns of response to forces that by knowledge of the subject-matter may be suspected or expected to influence response. One may look for repeated patterns of reaction and interaction that seem to persist in replication after replication, and from trials under different environmental conditions.

From "On the Statistician's Contribution to Quality,"
presented at the meeting of the
International Statistical Institute, Tokyo,
September 8–11, 1987.

Deming describes the nature of statistical quality control with a few examples.

Making Things Right

What is the statistical control of quality? The statistical control of quality is the use of statistical methods in all stages of production—in design of product, in tests of product in the laboratory, in tests in service, for specifications and tests of incoming materials and assemblies, and for achieving economies in production, maintenance and replacement of machinery and equipment, economic inventory of parts for repairs of machinery, even for economic inventory to meet predicted demand.

Inspection is a very important function in production. The results of inspection are themselves products of human observation, uses of instruments, observation by machine, and transcription of figures onto forms ruled up for the purpose. Faults recorded in inspection may be in the product itself, or they may be the result of faulty instruments or gauges, or faulty use of them.

We must be content in this article to limit ourselves to a few simple examples of statistical control of quality drawn from the production line. In the first two examples the aim will be to detect the existence of special causes of trouble, for the operator to correct. In the third example the aim will be to measure the effects of common (environmental) causes of trouble, for management to correct. In the real world, we are always working on both kinds of cause. The reader will, we hope, see in the examples the distinction between special causes and common causes, and how they affect the variability of the process or cause other kinds of trouble.

Example 1. Fudging the data. [Figure 7.1] shows the distribution of diameters in centimeters, these being the results of the inspection of 500 steel rods. Such a graphic representation of a distribution is called a histogram. The lower specification limit, abbreviated LSL, of the diameter of these rods was 1 centimeter. Rods smaller than 1 cm will be too loose in their bearings, and the rod will be thrown out (rejected) in a later operation, when it is fitted to a hole. Rejection means loss of all the labor that was expended on the rod up to this point: also loss of material and of overhead expense.

The horizontal axis in [Figure 7.1] shows the centers of intervals of measurements; for example, 0.998 stands for rods that measured between 0.997 and 0.999 cm. The vertical axis is labeled to show the number of rods that fell into an interval of .002 cm on the horizontal axis. For example, about 30 rods were in the interval centered at 0.998. It appears from the distribution that 10 + 30 = 40 rods failed because they were too small.

A distribution is one of the most important statistical tools, when used with skill, yet it is extremely simple to construct and to understand.

[Figure 7.1] is trying to tell us something. The peak at just 1 centimeter, with a gap at .999 seems strange. It looks as if the inspectors were passing parts that were barely below the lower specification, recording them in the interval centered at 1.000. When the inspectors were asked about this possibility, they readily

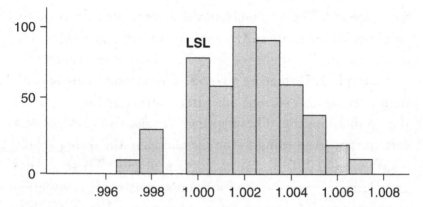

Figure 7.1 Distribution of measurements on the inside diameter of 500 steel rods. The chart detected the existence of a special cause of variation, a fault in the recording of the results of inspection.

admitted that they were passing parts that were barely defective. They were unaware of the importance of their job, and unaware of the trouble that an under-sized diameter would cause later on.

This simple chart thus detected a special cause of trouble. The inspectors themselves could correct the fault. When the inspectors in the future recorded their results more faithfully, the gap at .999 filled up. The number of defective rods turned out to be much bigger, 105 in the next 500, instead of the false figure of 10 + 30 = 40 in [Figure 7.1].

The results of inspection, when corrected, led to recognition of a fundamental fault in production, the setting of the machine was wrong. It was producing an inordinate number of rods of diameter below the lower specification. When the setting was corrected, and the inspection carried out properly, most of the trouble disappeared.

The upper specification limit had its problems also, but they were not so serious. A rod that is too large in diameter can be tooled off to fit. This is not the economic way to achieve the right dimension, but it is cheaper than to lose all the labor expended so far on the rod. The next problem was accordingly to work on the problems of uniformity and correct centering of the average diameter, to reduce the number of defectives from wrong diameters.

Example 2. Detecting a trend. The second example deals with a test of coil springs one after another as they come off the production-line. These springs are used in cameras of a certain type. According to the specification, the spring should lengthen by 0.001 cm for each gram of pull. These springs are relatively expensive, and are supposedly made to exacting requirements. The length of any horizontal bar in the histogram at the right in [Figure 7.2] shows how many springs the inspectors recorded with the elongation shown. We have turned it sidewise for convenience. This histogram represents measurements on 50 springs manufactured in succession. It will be noted that distribution is symmetrical and is centered close to the specification; furthermore that all 50 springs were within the upper and lower specification limits.

One might be tempted to conclude from this histogram alone (in contrast to the conclusions from that of Example 1), that the production of this spring presents no problems. However,

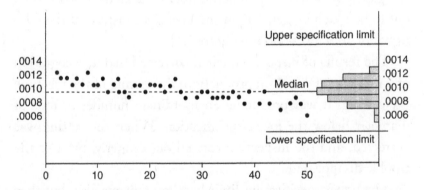

Figure 7.2 Run chart for 50 springs tested in order of manufacture. The chart shows a definite trend downward, and thus detects the existence of a special cause of variation, which is important to correct. The frequency distribution alone could not detect this trouble.

another simple but more powerful statistical tool, a run chart, indicates trouble, as we now explain.

A run chart is merely a running record of the results of inspection. The horizontal scale shows the order of the item as produced, and the vertical axis in [Figure 7.2] shows the measurement for that item. In our example, the elongations of the successive 50 springs are plotted on the vertical scale. A run chart has several simple uses. For example, (a) a run of 6 or 7 consecutive points lying all above or all below the median? the middle point in height? signifies with near certainty the existence of a special cause of variation, usually a trend: (b) a run of 6 or 7 points successively upward or successively downward has the same significance.

In no instance in [Figure 7.2] are there six consecutive points trending upwards or downwards. It so happens that the median of the 50 points falls midway between the upper and lower specification limits. This would be good, but we note that the opening burst of points at the left of the figure has 10 points in succession above the median. Fifteen out of 18 points after 29 fall below the median. These observations give a statistical foundation for the conclusion that, although the points vary up and down, there is a general drift downward. You may feel that your eye was good enough to detect this trend without knowing from theory that a run must have 6 or 7 points above or below the median to detect with near certainty the existence of trouble, and in this example you would be correct.

Knowledge of what lengths of runs are required to indicate trouble is also valuable but secondary in problems of production. Indeed, it is an important statistical point that some of the most powerful statistical techniques are simple, as in our examples here. It was their widespread use, beginning about 1942, that laid the foundation for the statistical control of quality, which of course has since grown into all phases of management.

In our example of the spring for the camera, either the production process is in trouble or the apparatus used for testing is giving false readings. Correction is vital, whatever be the source of the trend. If it is the tension of the spring that is drifting downward (and not the testing apparatus), defective springs will be produced in the immediate future. If the source of the trend is faulty testing, then the tests are misleading, and may have been giving faulty reports on all the springs produced during the past week.

In this particular case, the trouble turned out to lie in a thermocouple that permitted the temperature to drift during the annealing of the springs. The process was headed for trouble. The simple tool of the run chart detected the trend before trouble occurred. The operator himself, seeing the trend, was able to head off trouble.

The reader may note that the histogram and the run chart in [Figure 7.2] were plotted from the same data, yet they tell different stories. The histogram by itself gives no indication of anything wrong. The run chart (again, plotted front the same data) leads us to suspect the existence of something wrong, which unless corrected, would soon lead to the production of defective springs.

Knowledge of statistical theory, coupled with practice, leads the statistician to use whatever technique will lead to the correct conclusion about the process, with the smallest probability of being wrong.

It is interesting to note that if the points in [Figure 7.2] had been plotted in random order instead of one after another in the order of production (1, 2, 3, and onward to 50), the run chart would have lost its power to detect a trend. Statisticians are thus not only concerned with figures, but with the relevant figures. In this instance, the order of production was relevant—very relevant—and was used to make the run chart. The distributions in [Figures 7.1 and 7.2], on the other hand, do not make use of the order of production. They would remain unchanged, regardless of order: they depend only on the figures recorded as results of inspection. The distribution in [Figure 7.1] nevertheless did its work: it told us that something was wrong (namely, in the inspection itself). A run chart in connexion with [Figure 7.1] would not have added any information. The distribution in [Figure 7.2], however, was helpless to detect the existence of anything wrong. Judging by it alone, without the run chart, we could not have detected impending trouble.

Example 3. Measurement of common (or environmental) causes. The first two examples dealt with special causes, specific to a designated worker or to a machine, or to a specific group of workers. Statistical techniques point to specific sources of trouble when the process is non-random. The same statistical methods also tell the worker to leave things alone, do not over-adjust, when attempts at adjustments would be ineffective or even cause greater variation than now exists.

There is another kind of problem that faces the management of any concern. No matter how skilled be the workers, and no matter how conscientious they be, there will be at least a bed-rock minimum amount of trouble in production, owing to common or environmental causes. All the workers in a section work under certain conditions fixed by the management, or one might say by the environment, which only the management can alter. For example, all the workers use the same type of machine or instrument. They are all doing about the same thing, and are using the same raw materials (which might be semi-finished assemblies). They must put up with the same amount of noise and smoke.

It used to be supposed by management that all troubles came from the workers: that if the workers would only carry out with care the prescribed motions (soldering a joint, placing a part and turning a screw), then the product would be right with no defectives. This kind of reasoning does not solve the problem. Alert management can now look into the problem with infra-red vision, supplied by statistical techniques.

An example was a small factory that made men's shoes. The machinery that sews soles is expensive. Time that an operator spends re-threading the machine and adjusting the tension after a break in the thread is lost time. Minutes lost may add up to hours and even days in the course of a month. There is not only the loss of rent on the machine, and wages of the operator, but loss of labor and materials, non-productivity of floor space, light, and increases in general over-head expenses. In this factory about 10% of the working-time was being spent re-threading the machines and adjusting the tension. Management was rightly worried. The trouble became obvious with a bit of statistical thinking. Observations on the proportion of time lost by the individual workers provided data for a chart similar to [Figure 7.3]. This figure showed that all the operators were losing about the same amount of time re-threading their machines. In fact, the time lost per day per man showed a pattern of randomness. This uniformity across operators could only point to the environment. What was the trouble?

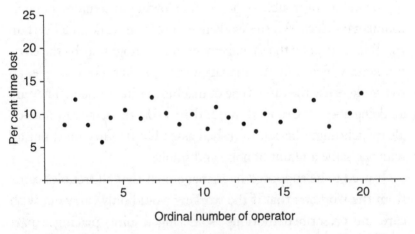

Figure 7.3 Time lost by each of 20 operators

The trouble turned out to be the thread. The management of the company was trying to save money by buying second grade thread, which cost 10 cents per spool less than first-grade thread. Penny wise and pound foolish. The savings on thread were being wiped out and overwhelmed many times over by troubles caused by poor thread.

A change to thread of first grade eliminated 90% of the time lost in re-threading the machines, with savings many times the added cost of better thread.

What is the distinction between this example and Examples 1 and 2? In Examples 1 and 2, the workers themselves could make the necessary changes, and did. In this example, the operators were helpless. They could not put in an order for thread of first grade, and scrap the bad thread. Their jobs were rigid—work with the materials and machines supplied by the management. They all worked with the same bad thread. That is, they all worked under a common cause of trouble. Management is responsible for common (environmental) causes; only management could change the thread.

But how is management to know whether there are common causes of trouble? The answer is simple: common causes are always present, but management needs a better answer: management needs a graphical or numerical measure of the magnitude of the trouble wrought by common causes. Without statistical techniques, the management can have no accurate idea about the magnitude of the trouble being caused by conditions that only the management can change.

Charts like [Figure 7.3] tell the management that management has a problem: that the time lost on re-threading will not go below 10% until management makes some fundamental change. Change in thread in Example 3 was a fundamental change. What to change is not always so easy to perceive as it was in this example. Sometimes a series of experiments is required to discover the main causes of trouble. Statistically designed experiments have led to the identification of common causes such as these:

Raw materials not suited to the requirements

Poor instruction and poor supervision (almost synonymous with unfortunate working-relationships between foremen and production-workers)

Vibration

Shift of management's emphasis from quantity to quality is one common environmental cause of trouble. The production-workers continue to work with emphasis on quantity, not quality. Methods by which management may direct the shift from quantity to quality, however important, is beyond the scope of this paper.

Written during 1970–1972, this appeared as one of 44 essays in J. Tanur, et al., eds. (1972), Statistics: A Guide to the Unknown, *Holden-Day, San Francisco. (There are newer editions, but only the first contains Deming's essay, "Making Things Right.")*

Deming discusses six uses of statistical quality control and then follows up with some examples.

The Statistical Method of Quality Control

A.

Not how much product, but how much *acceptable* product is what counts. The statistical method in a quality control program can be made a potent factor in assisting the manufacturer and the purchaser in meeting the demands for increased safety, performance, and quantity of product, because it has the effect of

1. increasing the safety and performance of product, at the same time often greatly;

2. decreasing the amount of inspection required in many operations, yet attaining better quality assurance;

3. decreasing the production of defective material by attaining greater uniformity at a safe distance from the tolerance;

4. giving early warning on changed conditions of manufacture that may cause trouble or require increased inspection;

5. improving vendor-purchaser relations by providing better records; and by

6. providing a rational basis for setting tolerances with regard to requirements in service, and economies of production.

B.

The only way to get a critical dimension right, and to know that it is right 100 percent, is to know that it is being made at a safe distance from the required tolerances in the first place. The only way to know that it is being made right is through knowledge of the manufacturing and testing, and through statistical control of important stages of the process. Inspection is then used—eyes—not for sorting, but for assurance that the required quality is being maintained. The control chart will tell how much inspection is needed. Get the method of production right, and the results obtained by valid inspection procedures will afford real protection to both producer and consumer. Get the method of production right, and you will have no fear of your purchaser's inspection. If you fail to get the method of production right, then a sound acceptance procedure will reject a large portion of your material (that is the purpose of an acceptance procedure).

C.

Safety, economy, and quality assurance all require specification in terms of a distribution. The mere specification of tolerances is not enough because it is also necessary to specify how much of the product is to conform to the tolerances. The control chart record of important stages of the manufacture is needed in order to attain stability of the distribution, to put it at the right level and spread, and to provide assurance that the required operating conditions are being maintained. This is particularly important for safety in the performance of critical parts which must be 100 percent conforming, as was emphasized in Part B. It is also important for economy in the manufacture or purchase of material that is allowed to contain a certain fraction defective. The control chart records are needed as evidence of stability by both the manufacturer and the purchaser, particularly when the testing of the product is destructive. They should be required in the specifications as part of the product for the improvement of vendor-purchaser relations.

D.

How much variation can you take out of your product, and how much improvement can you achieve without making expensive changes in your equipment or raw material? The statistical method helps to answer these questions.

E.

Statistical control furnishes a rational basis for deciding whether specifications should be changed.

F.

Two problems are always present in the production or purchase of materials;

Problem A. What to do with *this* lot? (Accept it, reject, pass, scrap, rework, regrade, or further inspect it before deciding which to do.)

Problem B. What to do with the *process*? (Leave it alone; or look for some identifiable cause, make some adjustment, use different raw materials; carry out more or less inspection than you have been doing on previous lots.)

Both these problems are always present, whether you are manufacturing or purchasing; and action, intelligent or otherwise,
is continually being taken one way or another, lot by lot, hour
by hour. The control chart helps to formulate rational courses
of action by showing when the variations in the inspection
results may safely be left to chance, or whether it will pay to
assume the existence of an assignable cause and do something
about it.

G.

There are two kinds of mistakes occasionally made in any quality
control program:

1. Looking for an assignable cause of variation or increasing the
   amount of inspection, when the variations in quality are only
   random.
2. Failing to look for an assignable cause of variation, or failing
   to increase the amount of inspection, when an assignable cause
   actually did exist.

We must expect to make these mistakes once in a while, even
when using the statistical method, but we try to *keep their costs at
a minimum*. The Shewhart control chart was designed to answer
the question, when to look for an assignable cause, by striking an
economic balance between these two kinds of mistakes.

H.

Each point on the control chart is derived from inspection tests
carried out on a supposedly homogeneous batch of product.
The batches are selected in some rational manner, the purpose
being to disclose assignable causes of variability. Often it turns
out that small samples selected in order of production is proper.
The points will show variation in the quality of the product,

batch by batch, hour by hour. Control limits are placed on the chart. The rules for placing them are astonishingly simple. The control limits provide a basis for action. When a point falls outside the control limits, it will pay to assume that some assignable cause produced the variability. Whether you are manufacturing or buying, lack of control indicates a spotty or variable condition, and the need for increased inspection to maintain protection.

I.

It is the responsibility of every industrial executive to acquire an appreciation of the fundamental principles underlying the statistical method. Then when statistical methods are used in. his plant the organization must be such that action can and will be taken when need is indicated by the control chart.

J.

Control chart uses include the following problems: Mass production in the usual sense is not necessary to their use. Most of them can be handled satisfactorily in no other way.

Testing the uniformity and accuracy of check inspection
Testing flaws in riveting or welding, to discover whether assignable
    causes of variability are to be sought
Standardization of testing
Standardization of personnel performance
Inspection of finished assemblies
Administrative action on the variability of error and production
   · rates in office processing
Standardization of foods and drugs
Setting piece rates
Standardization of machine performance
Discrepancies in inventories and performance accounting

For class use at Temple University Engineering, Science, and Management War Training; excerpts from papers on The Statistical Method of Quality Control Bureau of the Census and Bureau of the Budget, January 11, 1944.

In this excerpt Deming discusses the causes of variation in products and services, distinguishing between differences that result from inherent characteristics of the processes delivering the products and services and those differences that have a specific cause. Failure to identify the cause-type by use of statistical methods can lead to inappropriate actions. He then describes statistical techniques for other types of problems.

Different Statistical Methodology for Different Problems

One of the important uses of statistical techniques is to help an engineer or scientist to distinguish between two types of cause, and hence to fix (with adjustable risk of being wrong) the responsibility for correction of undesired variability or of undesired level.

Confusion between common causes and special causes is one of the most serious mistakes of administration in industry, and in public administration as well. Unaided by statistical techniques, man's natural reaction to trouble of any kind, such as an accident, high rejection-rate, stoppage of production (of shoes, for example, because of breakage of thread), is to blame a specific operator or machine. Anything bad that happens, it might seem, is somebody's fault, and it wouldn't have happened if he had done his job right.

Actually, however, the cause of trouble may be common to all machines (e.g., poor thread), the fault of management whose policy may be to buy thread locally or from a subsidiary. Demoralization, frustration, and economic loss are inevitable results of attributing trouble to some specific operator, foreman, machine, or other local condition, when the trouble is actually a common cause, affecting all operators and machines, and correctible only at a higher level of management.

The specific local operator is powerless to act on a common cause. He cannot change specifications of raw materials. He cannot alter the policy of purchase of materials. He cannot change the lighting system. He might as well try to change the speed of rotation of the earth.

A mistake common amongst workers in the statistical control of quality, and amongst writers of textbooks on the subject, is to assume that they have solved all the problems once they have weeded out most of the special causes. The fact is, instead, that they are at that point just ready to tackle the most important problems of variation, namely, the common causes.

Special Causes of Variation

Variation of any quality characteristic is to be expected. The question is whether the variation arises from a special cause, or from common causes. A point outside limits on a control chart indicates the existence of a special cause. Special causes are what Shewhart called assignable causes. The name is not important; the concept is.

Statistical techniques, based as they are on the theory of probability, enable us to govern the risk of being wrong in the interpretation of a test. Statistical techniques defend us, almost unerringly, against the costly and demoralizing practice of blaming variability and rejections on to the wrong person or machine. At the same time, they detect almost unerringly the existence of a special cause when it is worth searching for.

What statistical tests do, in effect, is not just to detect the existence of a special cause, or the absence of special causes; they do more: they indicate the level of responsibility for finding the cause and for removing it. The contribution that statistical methods make in placing responsibility squarely where it belongs (at the local operator, at the foreman, or at the door of higher management) can hardly be over-estimated.

This aspect of the statistical control of quality was not appreciated, I believe, in the earlier history of statistical methods in American industry, and is even now neglected. The Japanese had the benefit of advanced thinking on the matter.

Common Causes of Variation and of Wrong Spread, Wrong Level

If we succeed in removing all special causes worth removing, then henceforth (until another special cause appears), variations in quality behave as if they came from common causes. That is, they have the same random scatter as if the units of product were being drawn by random numbers from a common supply. The remaining causes of variability are then common to all treatments, to all operators, to all machines, etc.

Some common causes are in the following list. The reader may supply others, appropriate to his own plant and conditions.

- Poor light
- Humidity not suited to the process
- Vibration
- Poor instruction and poor supervision
- Lack of interest of management in a program for quality
- Poor food in the cafeteria
- Inept management
- Raw materials not suited to the requirements
- Procedures not suited to the requirements

- Machines not suited to the requirements
- Mixing product from streams of production, each having small variability, but a different level

Common causes are usually much more difficult to identify than specific causes, and more difficult to correct. In the first place, carefully designed tests may be required to identify a common cause. Then problems really commence. Would it be economically feasible to change the specifications for incoming material; to change the design of the product, to install new machinery? to change the lighting? to put in air-conditioning? Only management can take action on these things. If the trouble lies in management itself, who is going to make the correction?

Although the detection and removal of special causes are important, it is a fact that some of the finest examples of improvement of quality have come from effort directed at common causes of variation and at causes of wrong level. One example, interesting because it is outside the usual sphere of industrial production, is the improvement of quality and decrease in the cost of statistical data put out by the Census in Washington. For many years, effort has been directed at common causes of the system that lead to error and to high cost, as well as elimination of special causes. The result today is quality, reliability, and speed of current statistical series that are the envy of other statistical organizations in the U.S. and abroad, and at costs that are about a third of what private industry in this country pays out for similar surveys in consumer research.

Other Statistical Techniques

Acceptance sampling [is] a scheme of protection (provided one will really reject and screen a lot when the sample contains more than the allowable number of defects). The specification of a unit of product is of course vital. However important it be, a vendor does not know how to predict the cost of making a product unless he has in hand, in addition, the plan by which his lots will be sampled by the purchaser and accepted or rejected. How big is a lot? What is to be done with pieces found to be defective? Answers to these questions are a necessary part of any plan of acceptance, if vendor and purchaser understand each other. The plan of acceptance sampling is a necessary specification of a contract for lots.

Acceptance sampling was frequently at first confused in America with process control. Some people looked upon it as a detector of special causes. Other people supposed that acceptance sampling furnishes estimates of the quality of lots. Still others supposed that it separates good lots from bad.

Problems in statistical estimation are very important in industrial production, as in decisions on whether one type of machine is sufficiently better than another to warrant the cost of replacement, or to warrant the higher cost of purchase of a better machine. Consumer research presents hosts of problems in estimation. Determination of the iron content of a shipload of ore is a common problem in estimation.

In a problem of estimation, one is not seeking to detect the existence of a special cause. He is not trying to discover whether there is a difference between two processes, or between two machines, standard and proposed. One knows in advance, without spending a nickel on a test, that there is a difference; the only question is how big is the difference?

Statistical calculations using data from two samples (coming from two treatments, two operators, two machines, two processes) provide a basis on which to decide, with a prescribed risk of being wrong, (a) whether it would be economical to proceed as if the two samples came from a common source, or (b) whether it would be more economical to assume the converse, and to proceed as if the difference has its origin in a special cause, not common to the samples, which makes one of the treatments, operators, machines, or processes different from the other. Essential considerations in fixing the probability of being wrong lie in the economic losses to be expected (a) from the failure of being too cautious—failure to make a change that would turn out to be profitable, or (b) from making a change that turns out to be costly and unwarranted.

Many people, in America as elsewhere, in a burst of enthusiasm, confused statistical methods with engineering or with other subject matter. They would substitute statistical calculations for knowledge of engineering, and then try to solve statistical problems by consulting their own knowledge of engineering.

Power and Limitation of Statistical Techniques

No amount of statistical theory will generate a problem. To find problems is the responsibility of management or of the expert in subject-matter (engineering, production, consumer research, medicine). A problem in industry might be simply to enquire whether it would be possible to decrease the variability of some quality-characteristic, and if so, how? The problem might be more complex, such as to question the basic design of a product. It might be comparison of two or more processes or machines. It might be a new idea in a chemical process.

Which quality characteristic to test and to use in a Shewhart chart, or what questions to ask in a comparison of products in a study of consumer research, is fundamentally a problem in subject matter. No statistical theory will tell anyone which quality characteristic to test, although it is necessary to use statistical theory for reliability and economy in the design and interpretation of tests.

Statistical theory, like any other theory, is transferable. The symbols don't care what the problem is, nor what the material is. Therein lies the power of theory: the solution to one problem may aid in the solution of many other problems. Our words *theory* and *theater* come from the Greek *tha* to see, to understand.

There is not one distinct theory of probability for process control, another theory for acceptance sampling, another for reliability, another for problems of estimation, another for design of experiment, another for testing materials, another for design of studies in statistics, another for engineering. Instead, there is statistical theory.

Statistical work, in the hands of a statistician, means optimum allocation of human skills and of machines to provide and interpret with speed and reliability as aid to administration, management, and research, the results of tests and of other observations. Other professions (e.g., management, administration) have the same goal, but the statistician is the one that has the skills and tools for accomplishment of the goal.

An essential requirement of the statistician working in industry is to know statistical theory, and to continue to learn more. He must learn something about the subject matter, of course, in order to work in it, but his contribution will be more successful if he will enhance day by day his knowledge of statistical theory, instead of trying to become expert in the subject matter. Thus, the statistician need not be an expert in a production process in order to make a contribution to production. He works with people that know production; what the statistician needs to know and do is his own job, statistics, not someone else's job.

Of course, in a small plant, the same man must sometimes work both as statistician and as engineer. He must nevertheless observe the same rules. He should, to be effective, use only the statistical theory that he understands, and he should use it for the statistical aspects of problems. He should not try to substitute statistical techniques for the basic input of engineering that must go into a problem.

From "What Happened in Japan?,"
Industrial Quality Control, Vol. 24, No. 2,
August 1967.

As early as 1948, when Deming was an Adviser in Sampling at the Bureau of the Budget of the Executive Office of the President of the United States, he wanted businessmen to understand the role and importance of sampling, as well as what it could and could not do. This personal, eight-page letter was written by Deming in response to an inquiry from a New York publishing company executive about why so many opinion polls failed to accurately predict an outcome.

Letter from W. Edwards Deming to Printers Ink

I am happy to accept your invitation to express a few views regarding the techniques of sampling, particularly with reference to the recent failures of the major opinion polls. As a preamble it must be admitted that a forecaster has more trouble than a physician burying his mistakes.

In order to understand what has happened, it is important to recognize at least four distinct steps in any survey. For convenience I shall state these four steps as they occur in opinion polling. *First,* comes the *definition of the universe.* If a complete canvass were to be made (i.e., if there were no problem of sampling), who would be canvassed? All adults? All people who will be legally eligible to vote on election day? All heads of households? A decision on these very important questions, in technical language defines the universe of enquiry. *Second,* a meaningful *questionnaire* must be devised to throw light on the aims of the survey—in this instance, prediction of an election. *Third*, the sample—how to do the job without canvassing everybody. In this case the sampling problem might be how to estimate with sufficient accuracy from a relatively small sample how many people or how many voters in the whole country or perhaps in the several states would, if canvassed, say in response to a particular questionnaire that they voted this way or that way or no way in the last election, and now express this or that preference, intensely or apathetically. *Fourth*, the *interpretation* of the results. In election forecasting, this step requires a prediction, on the basis of an inventory of opinion, and *with the aid of any of the relevant knowledge or judgment, how the election will turn out on Tuesday*. Besides the steps specifically enumerated here, there are a host of others also, such as the selection, training, and assignments of interviewers; the control of the field work; the definitions and classifications to be adopted; the coding.

It is interesting to note that the definition of the universe, the questionnaire, the procedure for conducting an interview, the definitions, and the coding are the same whether the survey is to be accomplished through a sample or a complete canvass. The interpretation of the results, however, is tied up in a complex manner with the procedure of sampling and everything else.

Inferior workmanship in any one of the major steps impairs the reliability and the usefulness of the results, and invites failure of a prediction based on them. In which one or ones did the recent failures occur? Well, obviously the last step failed (it is only the last battle that counts), but the question is *why*? Were the methods of prediction unreliable or were the predictions based on poor data, or both? The whole matter has been reviewed by a committee appointed by the Social Science Research Council and it is not necessary to repeat their report here. I shall nevertheless offer some further statements that may be helpful in understanding the nature of the problem, and in particular how the prediction of an election differs from many other statistical surveys.

Probably the most important observation, if I were allowed but one sentence, is that prediction of how people will vote is a step in opinion polling which presents difficulties that are not common to all surveys. The interpretation and use of data giving census information, pantry inventories, purchases, expenditures, prices, and employment as of a past date are certainly not the same problems as forecasting an election. I believe that publicity emphasizing the difficulties of forecasting an election, and making a clear separation between forecasting and eliciting information on which to forecast, will go a long way toward restoring public confidence in sampling surveys if not in opinion polling as well.

The definition of the universe is always a tough problem, even in such an apparently simple task as counting the number of people in an area. Does one count transients, visitors, temporarily divided families, and if so, how and where does one find then? Given $30,000,000 and unlimited manpower for an opinion poll so that I could take a complete census of the Continental United States, I should still wonder how to instruct interviewers in the art of recognizing every eligible voter in a household. Yet neither a complete count nor a sample in a public opinion poll can be taken until this problem of defining the universe has been satisfactorily solved. Without implying that the results of a complete census of opinion could be processed in a day, even a complete census on Monday would still not solve the problem of predicting how the voters will vote on Tuesday.

Thus any sample however good still leaves a gap between the census of opinions and the prediction of the net effect of all actions (voting behavior). This gap, which relates to either the stability or the net shift in total behavior, may eventually be completely bridged by the fruits of further research in social psychology, but it is important to make clear to the public that at the present time this gap is filled in large measure by judgment and subjective methods.

This assertion, however, is not meant to imply that forecasting is not necessary or respectable, but only that frequently the methods that must be used are simply *not statistical.* It may well be that the most important problems of market research and of administration, both in government and industry, require prediction of what people are going to do—what they will purchase, where and how long they will live, and even how they will vote. In fact, I have a suspicion that the social and economic problems that require prediction of what people are going to do are in general the really glamorous and attractive ones—also the dangerous ones.

In the previous paragraph, I have tried to emphasize the fact that sampling is only one of the links in forecasting an election. However, it is an important link, and it is still more important in statistical surveys not aimed directly at forecasting what people will do. Hence I shall devote the rest of my space to sampling. A number of points should be asserted. As the poll masters and much but not all market research have depended on quota sampling, a few words should be said to distinguish quota sampling from the statistician's probability sampling.

First, quota sampling is accomplished through exercise of the interviewer's judgment, and. it is therefore subject to the biases of selection, availability, and definitions of the quotas. The importance of these biases can only be conjectured; to date, no real effort has been made to measure them or to provide underlying theories for explaining them. Any attempt to correct them, as by "weighting" them out, is dangerous: I know of no statistical method for making good data out of bad. Increasing the number of interviews will not help. In a probability sample the biases just mentioned are avoided by mathematical design and careful execution of the field work. Another source of error in the quota method is its dependence on census and other information for controlling the proportions obtained in the sample: obsolescence of the controls is carried into the final results. A probability sample may be designed to walk on its own feet, without controls.

Second, when probability samples are used, the sampling errors are under control and are measurable. After the results of a probability sample are in, and the estimates made, the range of sampling variability may be calculated, *not* by comparing the results with known census figures or by observing whether they look to be about right, but by calculation from the returns themselves. If the results, from the point of view of sampling, are wide of the mark that would be hit by a complete canvass, this fact is clearly indicated, and the user is warned not to be cocksure of his interpretations. On the other hand, when the sampling variability is small, the user may have confidence in his basic figures. A probability sample may also be designed so that various other measures of quality are obtained at the same time, other than the sampling errors, such as the possible range of error arising from differences between interviewers, different methods of training them, or between different versions of the questionnaire.

Third, in a probability sample *predetermined rules* govern both the selection of the respondents *and* the procedure of computing the estimates for the universe. The results are not weighted this way or that way, according to judgment. Any method of survey into which judgment enters either in the selection of the respondents or the procedures of estimation will give results whose sampling precision can neither be controlled nor measured. Any such method is not safe where unbiased samples and an index of precision are essential.

Modern statistical research has disclosed some amazing facts about sampling. Filling quotas is not enough. It is possible, for example, by adding a few names here and subtracting some there, to build up a "perfect cross-section" in which various geographic, age, sex, economic, educational, and other classes agree very well with those of the whole population, but which is nonetheless a dismal failure with respect to the questions asked in a particular survey that someone is paying for. A way out is furnished by the statistical tools of randomization, stratification, methods of estimation, and design of experiment, as used in modern sample design.

The costs of two surveys cannot be compared merely by comparing the price per interview or by comparing total costs. There is no satisfactory measure of price without a simultaneous index of quality. A probability sample furnishes the required index of quality of the samples.

Clients can assist in improving the quality of statistical surveys by taking more interest than they have in the past in the techniques that are used in the research that is done for them. Good statistical surveys are not accidents, and there are no bargains. Because of the severe shortage of competent statisticians, some pooling of resources amongst commercial research organizations is probably expedient.

Although sampling problems require constant and competent statistical advice, yet it is not difficult to recognize dangerous procedures. There are criteria by which a layman may judge the quality of a survey. But unless full and complete statements regarding procedures accompany the description of a survey, criteria for judging its quality cannot be applied. The mere statement that "the sample was a perfect cross-section of the population," (or of housewives, or of any other class of people) is not sufficient; it is in fact a dead giveaway, however sincerely intended.

It is notable that the users of probability methods take the trouble to calculate and publish their sampling errors; also the theory and description of their methods so that the reader may recalculate the sampling errors, and judge for himself what the figures mean. Inclusion of a statement of the sampling error and of any particular difficulties encountered, instead of being a confession of weakness, is in fact a sign of strength because it indicates that the survey was in competent hands and its quality known.

Yet, however essential probability sampling may be for government statistics and for much private research as well, the poll masters, as I tried to indicate at the beginning, would still have had plenty of problems left over even if they had used probability samples.

There is no reason to be discouraged about future opportunities for the use of sampling surveys. Without sampling surveys, administrators in government and business would have to make decisions without the aid of periodic information on the labor force, volume of employment, turnover, prices, sales, cause of death, and a host of other population and agricultural characteristics that are considered vital in the administration of government and private business. No one is in favor of making decisions in a vacuum.

Letter to Mr. Herbert L. Stephen,
Printers Ink,
November 26, 1948.

This paper, more statistical than the others in this chapter, gives details on conducting a sample survey. Deming includes the requirements for reliability placed on the survey, characteristics of a well-designed sample survey, steps in taking a survey, and some remarks on how data are collected, sampling variation, and biases. Written around 1948, this early paper may have been the genesis of Deming's two later books on sampling and design of statistical surveys.

Some Administrative Aspects
of Sampling

I. Requirements Placed on a Survey

The requirement of reliability. Rational planning and action in meeting both business and governmental problems require the collecting of current information. This need for information is often met by the use of surveys. A properly designed survey provides the desired information with known and calculable reliability, and does so within the limitations of time and cost and whatever other restrictions are imposed.

> This is not the place to give a complete description of what is meant by reliability, but briefly it is the absence or near-absence of bias coupled with narrowness of sampling variation. The outside practicable limits of sampling variation may be taken as thrice the standard error, which will not be defined here.

Every survey has its own peculiar difficulties and requirements. An important aspect of a properly-designed survey of today is that it possesses a known and controllable degree of reliability; in other words, in a professional job of sampling the guesswork in regard to reliability is removed. Aside from reliability there is another point in regard to surveys which is often overlooked—the survey should provide information that will actually be used. It is possible to design and carry out perfectly good surveys yielding results with speed, low cost, and reliability, yet perfectly useless. Common sense argues against the collecting of information that cannot or will not be used.

Professional sampling requires extensive studies in mathematics and statistics, coupled with several years of experience in the design of samples under competent leadership. It is nevertheless possible to describe many of the aspects of sample design in nontechnical language, and such is the aim of this paper.

Information, if it is to be of real use, must be reliable, and as intimated above, one of the most important features in modern sampling is that the reliability of a survey can be controlled and determined. It is in fact the control of reliability that brings forth one of the most important aspects of surveys, namely, its proper cost. The statistician's problem in sample design is to meet the requirements of reliability, but not to exceed them, for to do so entails wastage of funds or resources.

A decision on the desired degree of reliability beforehand is an important part of any survey and should be worked out with the administrators in charge of the program that the survey is to serve. Every problem has its own requirements of reliability. The population count of a city might require a standard error of 2 percent. An inventory of some commodity, such as wheat, might require a standard error of 10 percent; while an estimate of the number of vacant apartments might be useful even if it has an error as large as 20 or 30 or even 50 percent. The reliability of a professionally designed survey is under control and can be made as great as desired simply by taking a bigger and more complex sample, and accordingly spending more funds, and usually requiring more time.

A survey may cover, completely or incompletely, a population of people, farms, farmers, prospective purchasers, business establishments, voters, etc. The proper procedure to use varies greatly with the problem and with the type of population to be covered; also with the facilities that are available, such as the condition of the roads, whether the population can all be reached by trains or automobiles or donkeys, whether trained or untrained personnel can be obtained to do the job, or whether there are detailed maps and statistics from some recent survey covering the population.

The more information that is available concerning a population, the less the cost of conducting an additional survey for providing new information with a specified degree of reliability; however, no attempt will be made here to describe the manner of using maps and detailed census information in sample design, for to do so would broaden the scope of this article too far.

Questionnaires and interviewing. Before any survey can be expected to give useful results, the problem that it is intended to help solve must be explored to the point where questions can be framed in such fashion that answers are possible and useful. In other words, aside from the proper design of the sample, there is an equally important question involving the construction of the questionnaire and the conduct of the interview. The procedure of sampling, the construction of a satisfactory questionnaire, and the proper procedure for interviewing, all require thorough knowledge of the subject and of the difficulties that are to be met in carrying out the survey. This is why it has been stated that applied statistics is 90 percent knowledge of the subject matter and only 10 percent statistics; it was Shewhart who first made this statement with regard to statistical work in engineering and manufacturing. It will not suffice merely to send people out to explore the subject at their own discretion, no matter how clever they may be. Useable quantitative results cannot be obtained unless there is a fairly uniform pattern of questions and procedure, and some system for cataloging the answers. Requisite knowledge of the subject for developing the questionnaire and interviewing technique means knowledge of the actual population of people, farms, or business establishments that are to be covered; it means knowledge about them from the standpoint of the personalities involved, the facilities for travel, whether the people in the sample can supply the information that is needed, and whether they will. How are you going to find them; will they be at home? How are you going to select the sampling unit; will it be a small area, a small cluster of households, a single dwelling unit, or an individual? The answer depends on many characteristics of the population; involving the variance (or degree of variability) between areas and within areas, between households and within households. How much is it going to cost to send your interviewer to the people, farms, or business establishments which are in the sample? How long will it take them to get three? How can you instruct them so that they will draw the sample and conduct the interview the way you want it done?

One should remember that aside from a few professionals who have a hand in designing the survey, the main part of the work is carried out by people who are not experts. Will such people carry out the survey in the way intended? The question is not only whether they *can* but whether they *will*. Accordingly, the procedure must be outlined in such language that it will be carried out in a manner that is known in advance; otherwise the mathematical calculations that have been made by the sampling experts with regard to the expected reliability may be invalidated, and serious biases may be introduced. Actual field tests are usually required in order to reach the desired degree of conformance with intentions.

It is important to recognize the phenomenon called variability of response. One may obtain different answers from a man concerning himself than one will get from other members of the family. This will not seem surprising if one is asking questions concerning a man's political views, different answers concerning a man's age, education, occupation, and— believe it or not—sometimes even his marital status, by questioning other members of the family, or even the man himself on two different dates, perhaps a week or two apart. Many questions, such as whether a man is employed, or whether a woman is a housewife or employed, or how much education a man has had, are indeed difficult for one reason or another.

Tricks of memory and misunderstanding of the question play their roles. Part of the variability in response undoubtedly lies in carelessness of the people that the interviewer talks to, and partly from his own carelessness in recording the results, but the main point is that variability exists. Such phenomena are not to be regarded as mere exhibitions of falsification or carelessness but rather as a useful piece of knowledge regarding human behavior.

In spite of such peculiarities in the problem of response, plans of enquiry can usually be devised that will yield useable quantitative results. Experience in considerable amount has demonstrated that costly enterprises can be a failure if the sampling is inexpertly designed and if certain elementary principles of response are disregarded. When a plan of enquiry has been decided upon, it is extremely important that it be followed faithfully by all the interviewers who take part in the project.

II. Characteristics of a Well-Designed Sample Survey

From what has preceded it is possible to specify three characteristics that mark a professional job of sampling:

1. The particular elements of the sample are selected automatically in accordance with mathematical principles. If this method of selection is embodied in the sampling plan it is not to be modified by the interviewer, or anyone else. Every household in the area that is to be covered has a chance of being included in the sample; these chances are known, and are used to compute the precision of the survey.
2. The procedure for utilizing the data obtained from the survey and for computing the characteristics of the whole population are carefully laid out in advance as part of the sampling plan.

3. The precision of the results (the standard error of sampling) can be calculated pretty accurately beforehand, and with certainty afterward. There is no guesswork regarding the sampling errors.

These characteristics bear the implication that the sampling will be carried out according to certain rules. There can be no error-formula for the precision of the results and the control of biases unless the rules for automatic selection are followed faithfully. If, to the contrary, the selection of a sample were left to the interviewer's judgment or convenience, or to the desire of people to respond or not to respond to the question, then the rules of selection would be out of control, and there would be no way of calculating the expected reliability. It would instead, be a matter of judgment. Unfortunately, if the experts disagree, the reliability of the survey is undecided and remains in doubt until resolved.

The economics of a proper sample design. The statistician does not take unnecessary chances with sampling errors; he cannot leave them to judgment. He has them under control and knows how much it will cost to reduce them to any desired degree. He knows that reliability beyond what can actually be utilized in formulating decisions on the basis of the data is sheer waste of resources. His guiding philosophy is a very practical one, namely, to minimize, in the long run, the net losses arising from two kinds of mistakes:

1. Trying to cut corners, by taking too small a sample, or a sample not of the best possible design, often running into sampling errors that are troublesome
2. Being too sure, by taking too large a sample, and too often getting more precision than is needed, thus wasting funds and slowing up the work, running into errors and biases that often beset large operations

It is possible to avoid either of these mistakes completely, but only by running headlong into the other. Thus, one could always avoid the first kind of mistake by making a practice of taking samples that are much bigger than necessary. Likewise one could always avoid the second kind of mistake by making a practice of cutting corners too close and taking samples that are too small. Even a sampling expert will occasionally commit one mistake or the other; but his net losses over a long period of time will be at a minimum. He strikes these minimum losses by means of his error-formulas and by developing new and more efficient sample-designs.

III. Steps in Taking a Survey

An outline of the steps that are ordinarily met in planning and taking a survey will be attempted here. First, it should be recalled that a problem must have arisen in administration, policy, design, or research, and the proposal has been made that data from a survey would provide new information that would be helpful.

1. State the problem and what is wanted from the survey.

   Define the universe to be studied, and draw up some specimen tabulation plans. Consider the resources for carrying out the work: office, field-force, maps, lists, instructions and experience in similar work, and approximate cost, and decide whether it is possible to go ahead. Consider the difficulties of definition and interviewing, availability of the information, difficulties of classification and interpretation. Decide what type of survey, if any, could possibly provide the information needed.

2. For the type of survey settled upon, lay plans for reducing all the errors and biases that will be encountered.

3. If the survey is to be of the probability type, decide the allowable sampling error (2, 5, 25, or 50 percent).

The decision on the allowable error is an administrative matter, but must usually be solved by the statistician in deliberation with the administration. The administrator who needs the information to be supplied by the survey usually thinks in terms of absolute and complete reliability. He has heard of sampling errors, but may be unaware of other kinds of difficulty in collecting or interpreting data. He may think of sampling as a game of chance, not appreciating the fact that sampling errors are under control. He is responsible for administering a program and cannot take unnecessary chances. He needs facts and not errors or guesses. It is therefore natural for him to demand too big a sample or even a complete count, thus committing the second kind of mistake mentioned above. The statistician, on the other hand, is fully aware of the fact that absolute accuracy is a myth, and should be realistic and stand his ground firmly on the actual requirements of the precision to be sought, and the costs. An administrator is sometimes content to go along on impressions of observers. There is an important distinction between qualitative exploration and the numerical results that a scientifically-designed survey is expected to produce, and the statistician must make this distinction clear.

4. Compute costs and decide whether the desired precision can be attained at the allowable cost, or whether it must be relaxed and a cheaper job done, or the survey abandoned or altered in character.

5. Construct and pretest the questionnaire. Write and revise the field-instructions and definitions. Hold schools of instruction.

Broad knowledge required. If the turn-down rate is too high, a probability sample will be impossible. The importance of the questionnaire and instructions cannot be over-estimated. They constitute a problem in validity, and are the same whether the survey is to be a small sample or a complete count. As a result of pretesting the questionnaire and instructions it may be decided that the refusal rate is so high, or the costs or burden of response so great, that the survey should be abandoned.

6. Draw up the sampling procedure. Provide maps, lists, and controls. Draw up the tabulation and other office-procedures; they are part of the sample-design.

   The aim in sample-design is to just meet the desired sampling tolerance at the least cost, or to obtain the best precision possible within the allowable budget. By modern sampling methods it is possible to control the precision and the costs pretty closely in advance.

7. Carry out the survey.

8. If it is a probability sample, compute the sampling errors that were actually obtained for some of the characteristics.

9. Interpret and publish the results.

   Publication may consist of a research paper on procedures, results, conclusions, and action recommended. It may be equally important to put forth summarily a brief report for administrative use, stating the action indicated.

   The conclusions and recommendations drawn from the data are a professional statistical job, because the errors and biases and other difficulties afflicting the data govern the meaning of the data, and these things are the special province of the statistician.

   Publication of a research paper should include a statement of the procedures, definitions, nomenclature, and difficulties encountered in field and office, and their effect on the data. Enough detail must be given so that the reader can derive or verify the formulas given for the variances of the results, and form his own opinion regarding the precision.

What did the survey teach us? In what ways did it enlarge our experience? Publication of some of the observed variances and correlations should be made as aids in future planning.

IV. Some Specific Remarks on Sampling

How information is collected. One's first impulse in collecting information is to go out and ask a few people what they think of the matter. This is indeed called for in Step 5, being necessary in carrying out Steps 4 and 5 above. However, the problem is not simple. Suppose you were interested in the attitude of people regarding the conduct of an election. What people do you talk to, and how do you go about asking questions? In many problems it would be disastrous simply to get information from a "typical" sample of households, business firms, farmers, or educational institutions, or to leave any part of the selection to the interviewer. In eliciting opinions, it may not suffice simply to talk with anyone that happens to be home, or with just any waiters, shopkeepers, vendors, coffee drinkers, taxi drivers, or police that one chances to meet. It might be a serious blunder to try to generalize from such observations. In the first place, any of the groups of people just mentioned are only part of the population of any city. In the second place, such a procedure does not make a systematic coverage by which numerical measures of characteristics of the population could be obtained. Third, it is necessary to have a systematic framework for questioning and for cataloging the answers. What one learns in a haphazard way may indeed make interesting material for a book, but it will not supply numerical information for making decisions.

A few words regarding basic principles of sampling. The people that someone talks to casually can in no sense be called a sample suitable to the rigid requirements of a scientific survey. They are only the people that someone talked to. The difficulty with just talking to people—any people whom you meet and who seem inclined to talk—is that such audiences are usually unrepresentative. People willing to talk, or who invite us to talk with them, and people on the street drinking coffee, or selling in their shops, are people, to be sure, and they are residents of Athens or some other city, but they represent only certain classes or segments of the population. They deserve representation in the sample, and they get it, but only in their proper proportions.

To do a job of sampling that is to possess objectively known reliability, one must use what is called automatic or random selection. In a scientific sample design, the interviewers are directed to certain business firms or to certain areas and particular households or addresses within these areas. These particular units fall into the sample, not because they wanted to be in it or out of it, nor—very important—because someone thought they looked like representative households. Neither the interviewer nor the selected households should have anything to say about whether they are in the sample or not. The selection of households should be very much like drawing marbles out of a bag. You may mix them thoroughly and draw out a few, blindfolded, and call them a sample. A ball must come when you take hold of it. It has no choice. This kind of drawing is called automatic selection. A sample of households must be drawn with similar disregard of the interviewer and the household.

You will find, if you examine carefully any sampling plans drawn up by experts that all business firms, all households, or all areas, have had a chance to come into the sample, and that the chance of any particular unit coming in is known. Not one business firm, household, or area will be left out of the reckoning. Of course, not all the firms or households need to be interviewed (as a matter of fact, only a small percentage of households will actually be interviewed, if the sample is small) but each one has its chance of being selected. None is excluded because of economic level, convenience, location, industrial occupation, willingness to talk, appearance, or anything else. This is what makes a good sample.

The selection of households in the sample area is the last step in the sampling procedure, but strangely enough, in much sampling practice, this step is the one wherein the most failures occur. As was stated earlier, departure from the rules lowers the reliability of the figures that will be obtained. It is therefore necessary to abide by the rules.

Sampling in which the selection of the households is random or automatic is to be distinguished from sampling in which the selection is in any way left to the discretion of the interviewer. The latter procedure has been used, apparently with success, in some of the polls of public opinion and consumer preference, but can not be considered adequate wherever control of reliability is considered essential.

Need for studying the instructions and being watchful of procedure. Because the calculations and conclusions depend on the faithful execution of the rules for drawing the sample, the utmost emphasis must be placed on procedure. An interviewer, however, will find situations in which it will be much more convenient to talk to people in households other than those that the rules lead him to. The rules may send him to households that are difficult to reach because of distance, or to people that do not wish to talk, or to people that wish to talk too much. He may have to go through mud and over trails. It is barely possible that he may be unwelcome in certain households. The rules may lead him to houses where no one is at home, or at least no one home who can furnish the information that he requires. These houses are nevertheless in the sample and he must return to them if at all possible or obtain the required information from a neighbor or find out from a neighbor when the people are likely to be at home.

It is important to record just what happened. Even the most conscientious worker will encounter an occasional refusal, and an occasional failure to get an interview because no one was ever home. Such events are part of a normal job. Perfect performance can not be attained, but nothing short of the best efforts of everyone taking part in the project will suffice.

Sampling variation and biases. In drawing up the procedures for selection of a sample, the statistician is guided by the principle of calculated risk. He knows that there are two types of errors in any survey and he knows how to control them, although he often can not do so as well as he would wish within the limitations of time, cost, travel, difficulties, personnel, and other considerations. One type of error is called bias and the other kind is called random error of sampling, or simply the sampling variation. One kind of bias has already been described—namely, the bias of selection. If one selects households according to his judgment, in an attempt to get representative households and hence representative opinions, he is very likely inadvertently running into the bias of selection. The best of intentions are not enough in sampling; as a matter of fact, the best intentions are almost a guarantee that the selection of households will be biased.

An afterthought concerning biases may be of interest. Biases that are present in the most elaborate censuses are not all removed by taking a complete coverage in which every family, every farm, or every business firm is included. It may be surprising that many biases are even made larger when the size of the sample is increased. This is particularly true of biases that arise from the sheer enormity of a complete coverage. Control of the work becomes difficult. When there are many workers turning in reports and waiting to have their work checked and be assigned new work, the job may well get out of hand, and frequently does. Then there is a further bias arising from the fact that as the size of job increases, more people must be hired, and a wider and wider range of variability will be encountered in their performance and ability. Training and supervision thus wax increasingly difficult and complex with the number of workers. Equally as important in an attempted complete coverage is the bias arising from incompleteness—that is, failure to get responses from all households, all farmers, all business men, or whatever the sampling unit is. This bias is often very serious in a large-scale enterprise. Ordinarily, the bigger the job, the bigger the percentage of incomplete interviews.

In contrast, when a small sample is taken, the number of workers is small, and the biases that arise from training, supervisions, lack of control, and non-response is diminished. Sampling, of course, introduces the random errors of sampling, but these are under control; they can be confined within as narrow a range as desired by making the sample bigger or smaller; also by adjusting the rules for selecting the areas and households, and by altering the procedure of estimation, which I can not touch here. The professional statistician is continually devising new mathematical theory and new physical equipment such as better maps, more complete lists of addresses, and new devices on tabulating machines, all to decrease the range of sampling error.

Believed to have been written in 1948.

For those readers who are familiar with statistical significance, this letter may provide an interesting perspective.

In a study that was reported in a bulletin issued by the U.S. National Center for Health Statistics, the conclusion was that white children had better hearing in the middle frequencies than African American children. Deming questioned why a study was necessary, when it was known in advance that there was a difference. The study would have been more useful if some level of difference had been tested in order to indicate a difference of importance to medicine, sociology, or learning, rather than just concluding that there was a difference.

Always the educator, Deming sent this letter to the Director of the National Center for Health Statistics:

Dear Ted,

Bulletin Series 11, Number 111, Hearing Levels of Children by Demographic and socioeconomic Characteristics records on page 3:

> White children on the average had better hearing than Negro children in the middle frequencies from 1000 to 4000 cps, mean differences being large enough to be statistically significant only at 3000 and 4000 cps (figure 2 and tables 2 and 3). At the extremes of the frequency range, 250–500 and 6000–8000 cps, Negro children tended to have just slightly more sensitive hearing than white. This pattern generally persisted throughout the age range but mean differences were not consistently significant throughout.

Is a study necessary to show that there are differences between white and Negro children? What I am driving at is that you could predict, before any study was made, without spending a dime, that there are differences between white and Negro children. All that you need to do to show that there is a significant difference between them in any characteristic whatever, is simply to carry out a survey that is big enough.

What is important is not whether white and Negro children differ (because it was known in advance that they do), but whether the difference exceeds some magnitude

D (which might be complex—as it would be in decibels and might vary with frequency). The magnitude D is some quantity fixed in advance by clinical knowledge, not by statistical knowledge. How big would D have to be in order to indicate something of importance to medicine, sociology, learning? Is this difference exceeded? That is the question that a survey should strive to answer. Until D is fixed, there is no point in carrying out a study. We never carry out a study to learn whether some difference is significant.

Would a seminar be helpful on some of these questions? I'd attend, if you hold it. Some Monday or Tuesday would be best for me.

Sincerely yours,
[W. Edwards Deming]

From a letter to Mr. Theodore D. Woolsey, Director,
National Center for Health Statistics,
April 3, 1972.

8

What Happened in Japan?

Under the auspices of General Douglas MacArthur, the Supreme Commander of Allied Powers (SCAP) during the occupation of Japan following World War II, Dr. Deming, as adviser in sampling techniques, visited Japan in 1947 and 1950 to help with the census of Japan. Apart from these activities, the Union of Japanese Scientists and Engineers (JUSE) formed in 1948 to provide statistical quality control services, as recommended by the Civil Communication Section of SCAP. JUSE held their first quality control seminar in September 1949. Although Dr. Kenichi Koyanagi, chief organizer of JUSE, had not yet met Deming by early 1950, he was aware that Deming was one of the pioneers in statistical quality control and "thought that a lecture course by a famous statistician like Deming could bring about epochal results." This led to Koyanagi's request of Deming to give lectures in Japan on statistical quality control.

On March 8, 1950, Koyanagi wrote a letter on behalf of JUSE to Deming asking "for two favors:

1. *To give a QC lecture course for several days to the Japanese research workers, plant managers and engineers who had just started learning or taking an interest in quality control methods, and*
2. *To contribute a message to the inaugural number of the monthly journal Statistical Quality Control to be published by JUSE." [from* The Deming Prize, *by Kenichi Koyanagi, Tokyo, 1960]*

Here is Dr. Deming's acceptance of Dr. Koyanagi's invitation from the Japanese Union of Scientists and Engineers to give a lecture course for several days to the Japanese research workers:

Washington
22 April 1950

My dear Mr. Koyanagi,

I feel deeply honored by your invitation to give lectures this summer and to assist with your proposed course in the statistical theory of control of quality and its applications. First of all, let me say that your plan for an intensive course lasting 5 to 7 days, 7 hours per day, is excellent. I myself have organized such courses in this country a number of times, and the results have been very good. Such courses enable people to attend who could not go to a regular university course.

It will be possible, I am sure, for me to assist you with this course by giving some lectures on statistical theory and demonstrations of applications, from 2 to 4 hours daily. However, I should explain before being too definite that my time will be under the direction of Mr. Kenneth Morrow, Research and Programs Division, Economic and Scientific Section, SCAP. I am sure, though, that Mr. Morrow will be delighted to have me give assistance to such a course in statistics in Tokyo while I am there. I shall speak to him about the matter and give you definite word as soon as possible.

In this country we found that 8 days was a minimum for people who had not studied elementary statistical theory. I should think that in Tokyo the 7-day period would probably be much better than the 5-day period. If possible you might even extend the time to 8 days.

Another suggestion which you might wish to consider is the possibility of requiring some preliminary study. Each student might be supplied with some preliminary papers to study before he comes to take the actual course. For example, the registration fee might be made large enough to cover a pamphlet like the one titled "Control chart method of controlling quality during production" which was published by the American Standards Association. I shall send a copy to you by sea. If students were thoroughly familiar with the contents of that article, and would also study something about statistical distributions, they could accomplish as much in 5 to 7 days as they could accomplish in 8 days without preliminary studies.

As for remuneration I shall not desire any. It will be only a great pleasure to assist you.

With regard to dates I might say that my ETA is about the 1st June. I am not just sure how long I shall be able to stay in Tokyo, but I hope to be there during June and July, and possibly a part of August. I believe that the best time for your course would be the last part of June or the first week in July.

I had wondered if I should give a general course in sampling while I am in Tokyo. It would cover the sampling of human populations, agriculture, and industrial product, including quality control. It might meet 3 times per week, and it would follow my new book, which will soon appear. Possibly this course should be given at the University. I shall attach an outline of the course in order to give you an idea concerning the type of course that I have in mind. As my stay in Tokyo would be short, some of the topics would be covered only briefly.

Please be assured of my earnest desire to help you in every possible way. Please accept my kindest regards and best wishes for the success of your course and for your journal.

Sincerely yours,
W. Edwards Deming
Adviser in Sampling

Dr. Deming gave more than a thousand talks about his work in Japan and wrote hundreds of articles, some just a paragraph or two, and others of considerable length. Below are some accountings written between 1958 and 1970, each with its unique focus.

Leap Forward in Quality

The meteoric rise in quality and efficiency of production of most Japanese products began in 1950 and is still gaining momentum. The success of Japanese manufacturers is an example of what can happen when a whole nation submerges itself in a determined, enthusiastic, methodical effort in the study and use of statistical methods in all stages of production, from specification and testing of raw materials to the final product, supplemented by consumer research and innovation aimed at design of new products and new levels of dependability.

The leap forward in quality that took place in Japan in 1950 was no accident; it was not accomplished by resolution, nor by cost-benefit analysis. It was the result of concerted effort of management, engineers, and production-workers, throughout all Japanese industry, company-wide and nation-wide, to put statistical methods to work immediately. The invitation came to me from Japanese manufacturers through the Union of Japanese Scientists and Engineers. The first seminars in statistical methods in production were held in June, July, and August 1950, for the teaching of engineers and men in top management. Return visits, along with the unsurpassed spectrum of courses in statistical application offered by the Union of Japanese Scientists and Engineers, for management, engineers, and foremen, welded and continued these efforts.

It is interesting to note that some service industries in Japan have been active in statistical methods from the start, for example, the Japanese National Railways, Nippon Telephone and Telegraph Corporation, the tobacco monopoly, the post office.

From "New Principles in Administration for Quality and Efficiency,"
presented in Manila,
July 2, 1979.

Quality Control Experiences Abroad

The Japanese have advanced to first position, I believe, in the intelligent use of statistical methods in all stages of manufacture, as a tool of management from raw material to consumer. The impact of these methods is now felt all over the world. Japanese articles of quality are unsurpassed, and are in good demand.

Method. My work in Japan commenced in 1950. I emphasized to Japanese statistical societies and to individual statisticians that their knowledge constituted one of Japan's most important national resources; that the saving of coal, iron, petroleum, cotton, machinery, copper, and other scarce materials through the use of statistical methods was the exact equivalent of going out and finding water power, coal in the ground, oil in the ground, fields of cotton, or a shipload of machinery. This is true in any country, but it is a special point in Japan where all of these things have to be imported to fill out their needs.

Success arose from the fact that the people I worked with in Japan were Japanese. Let me remind you that education in Japan includes calculus and physics, so the Japanese people have a superb foundation for any kind of study. In the second place, there was the magnificent organizing ability of Mr. Kenichi. Koyanagi, Managing Director of the Japanese Union of Scientists and Engineers, who arranged my lectures and visits to plants, and lectures before groups of executives. The lectures to groups of executives were convened by Mr. Ichiro Ishikawa, President of the Japanese Union of Scientists and Engineers, and at that time President of Showa Denko, one of the great manufacturers of commercial chemicals. He is now chairman of the Atomic Energy Commission.

Although the words statistical quality control were known in Japan prior to 1950, and there were a few spots here and there where something had happened along that line, application was only spotty. There was, nevertheless, great activity in theory, so the foundation was there.

Lectures to executives. When Mr. Ishikawa would invite a dozen or 50 top executives to come to a meeting they came. He could get acceptance from anybody in Japan. The main meetings of executives took place as shown below:

- July 1950: 50 top executives, dinner at the Industry Club, with a lecture on the power of the statistical method in industry
- August 1950: All-day meeting with 60 top executives on Mt. Hakone
- July 1951: Luncheon and meeting with 60 top executives in the mountains above Nikko

The rapid acceptance of statistical methods in Japan arose, in large part, from the fact that top management had exposure to the methods and were somehow convinced that these methods were vital to survival. This meant that younger people who learned statistical methods had a chance to try them.

I am no economist, nor even less an expert in marketing, but I can add and subtract, and it seemed to me that if Japanese wares could find markets in various parts of the world, there should be no worry about raising enough food in Japan to live on. It might be smart to import even a greater proportion of their food than they do now, and to export Japanese wares to pay for it. The people in Chicago don't raise their own food; they export their product and buy food with the returns. Switzerland is an example of a country that imports a good fraction of its food and exports watches and other products that are in demand all over the world. I tried to raise a little kitchen-garden myself once. I spent 80 cents for seed, ruined a lawn to turn it into a garden, and reaped somewhere between 5 and 6 cents worth of product out of it, and thereupon decided to import my food.

One point of emphasis to executives was the fact that the days were gone when Japan could manufacture goods of any quality and sell or barter them in other parts of Asia at prices dictated by Japan. Their wares must now make their way to all parts of the world on the basis of quality and price. With the great skill and productiveness of Japanese workers, there could be no doubt about the possibility of success.

Then, too, was the point that it would take a long time to overcome the bad reputation that Japanese products had built up before the war. It would he necessary to export better quality, and never again to damage with shipments of defective and low-grade articles the reputation of Japanese manufacturers and workers. The effort would have to be unanimous. The Japanese themselves did the rest.

Statistical methods could help Japanese manufacturers to raise the quality and dependability of their product, and to put it out at competitive prices. This was my story, and top management believed it.

Incidentally, if some manufacturers in this country would meet competition with effort, and spend less time on lobbies to boost tariffs and to lower quotas, they might not worry so much about Japanese competition and could give some of the rest of us the benefit of better quality and lower prices. Many people say that they believe in free enterprise and in competition, but what they mean is competition for the other fellow, not for themselves. Now in my own case, I believe in free enterprise, and I am not afraid of Japanese statisticians, English statisticians, French statisticians, or any others. If one of them is doing a better job, then the thing to do is to go over there, or bring him over here, and find out how in the hell he does it. I don't know of any statisticians' lobby to try to keep out Japanese statisticians, English statisticians, or any others. The more of them we import, the better off we are.

I'd like to mention also the fact that the Japanese manufacturers did not look to their government nor to ours for assistance. Instead, they raised the money themselves through the Union of Japanese Scientists and Engineers and paid for the consulting services that they required. An invitation enclosed a ticket and a cheque.

It is this same voluntary system that supports the courses arranged by the Union of Japanese Scientists and Engineers, on which I may add a few words later.

I can not pass up the opportunity to mention the deep gratitude of Japanese manufacturers for the help that they have received from statistical methods. They have always been very outspoken about the benefits that they have received. More than one managing director or president of a large company told me that he saved millions of yen through application of these methods. I may say in passing that one weekend of entertainment up in the mountains where the president of a large company requisitioned a hotel, imported 5 geisha girls, and made everything as comfortable as possible for his guests overwhelmed me when I thought of his expense account, and that is about all I could think of, until he took me through 2 or 3 of his factories and showed me what they had been doing with statistical methods. It was obvious that the savings that he was making in only a few days in those plants would settle his expenses for the weekend, and I worried no more about it.

Lectures to engineers. The first courses were modeled after the 8-day courses that brought statistical methods into use in industry in this country, the first of which took place at Stanford University in July 1942, at the suggestion of the author.

Some idea of the number of people trained in Japan in rudimentary 8-day courses may be had from figures like these:

Summer of 1950
  Tokyo 220 students
  Osaka 110 students
  Fukuoka 110 students

Summer of 1951
  Tokyo 220 students
  Osaka 110 students
  Fukuoka 110 students

I believe in using statistical theory where it will work, but I don't use it to solve problems of subject matter, such as chemistry, industrial chemistry, production, marketing, psychology, use of machinery, accounting, medicine, or anything else. The only thing that the statistical method can do is to point out the existence of special causes, for which there are a good many methods available—the Shewhart charts, test of significance, runs, being the most notable. A point out of control or a significant result indicates almost certainly the existence of a special cause. The statistical method does not find the cause. This is the responsibility of the expert in the subject matter, which in many cases is the operator of a machine.

Whether the elimination of a special cause is economical or possible is usually the responsibility of someone higher up. It is certainly not a statistical problem.

When you find most of the special causes and eliminate them, you have left common causes of variability, which may be any or several of various types—poor light, humidity, vibration, poor food in the cafeteria, absence of a real quality program, poor supervision, poor or spotty raw material, etc.

The removal of common causes calls for action by administration at a high level. The workers and foremen can not change the lighting nor put in air conditioning nor institute a quality program. These things can be done only by administration higher up. Statistical techniques turn the spotlight on the responsibilities for action in various levels and positions. It improves the use of substantive knowledge by directing it to the problems where it can be most effective. If one understands something about the power of the statistical method, and understands where it will work, why it will work, and where it won't work, he has a good start. The rest is up to the individual student to educate himself from then on in various ways.

It is important, as I said, to use statistical theory for problems that statistical theory can solve, and not to use it to solve problems in subject matter. If an engineer in production understands what the statistical method can do for him by pointing out almost with certainty the existence of special causes only when they exist, and that it is his job (a) to decide what quality characteristics are important to test; (b) to find the special cause when statistical techniques indicate the existence of one; (c) to decide on the basis of economics whether to remove it, then he can perform in his chosen field with new vigor and confidence. He will not misuse statistical theory nor his substantive knowledge if he understands these principles of statistical practice.

I believe that a clarification of responsibilities helped the Japanese a great deal. They did not expect statistical methods to do the impossible, yet they saw that some very important problems of production could be solved in no other way. It is this state of mind that is most important, I believe—more important than profound knowledge of statistical techniques.

It was only necessary in Japan to teach these principles of understanding, and enough rudimentary techniques to start some work. The Japanese did the rest.

Additional courses arranged by the Union of Japanese Scientists and Engineers. Mr. Koyanagi arranged at once after the first lectures a magnificent array of many types of courses to follow up the initial lectures. These courses have continued and have expanded to take care of various levels of statistical learning and circumstance. Some of the courses are concentrated into a week or two, especially for men who live away from Tokyo and must leave their jobs in order to come.

Other courses assemble weekly after regular hours for people in the area of Tokyo. These courses have assisted many hundreds of people in Japan to acquire fundamental training and to continue their statistical education on up through high grade work in mathematical statistics. No other institution in the world offers such opportunities for study. The monthly journal, *Industrial Quality Control*, Kenichi Koyanagi editor, which commenced in 1951, contains an account of theory and applications. The 100th issue has just appeared. The journal *Reports of the Statistical Applications of Research*, T. Kawata editor, which commenced publication in 1953, carries some of the research in theory that this organization is sponsoring and teaching.

Several of the universities offer excellent work; in fact, some of the first chairs in mathematical statistics were established in Japanese universities.

Results. I am not so foolish as to think that everybody was successful who tried, but there were scores of successes within a few months, and they grew and branched out to other types of statistical effort. By the summer of 1951, a year after the first lectures, tangible results were already in evidence. For example, at the Toyo Cotton Spinning Company, near Nagoya, there were in one of their plants 450 spaces vacant out of 600, where girls were at work the year before correcting flaws in the yard goods that came off the looms. These 450 girls were now in production. There were 9000 workers in the factory. The movement from correction to production meant 5% more effort on production. The result: not only greater production, but obviously a better product able to hold its own in competition and in price. The Fuji Steel Company reported that they were saving 20% of the coal used previously to produce a ton of steel. The Tanabe Pharmaceutical Company reported quadruple production of para-amino salycilate, and of several other products. The Furakawa Electric Company in its Yokohama plant was already turning out considerably more wire and cable, with greater uniformity. All these increases in production came without new machinery, and with no increase in floor space.

An account of the uses of statistical methods in industry in Japan appears in a pamphlet by Mr. Koyanagi, his speech before the American Society for Quality Control in Rochester, 1952. This is the best account of case histories in statistical method that I know of. An equally informative document, Quality Control in Japan, Japan Productivity Center, 1958, has just appeared. Some people that read these articles might exclaim that the Japanese, in order to make such great savings and improvements, must have been very inefficient to start with, but all of us have seen equal experiences in this country and we continue to see them day after day.

All this means that the statistical method today is not something that you install like a carpet or a new Dean, and then forget it. The statistical method is something that one uses day after day, in its proper place, and that we never reach a stage where there is nothing more to improve. The increased use of automatic machinery emphasizes as never before the need of uniformity and of proper design, attainable only with the aid of statistical methods.

From Speech before the Metropolitan Chapter of the
American Society for Quality Control, United Nations,
March 25, 1958.

Some Remarks on Recent Advances in the Statistical Control of Quality in Japan

Introduction and Purpose of This Paper

To speak of recent advances in anything, one must first of all decide what is recent. Ten or 15 years are insignificant in the history of man, but they may be a very important period in modern industry.

One must also decide what it is that has advanced, and how. In speaking of recent advances in the statistical control of quality in Japan, does one mean an enumeration of new competitive products that are frightening American and British producers, and others too; or does one mean new methods, new points of view emanating from Japan? Enumeration of competitive products would require a definition of competitive that only the Federal Trade Commission would dare to attempt; certainly not I.

What is really important, in my opinion, about advances in the statistical control of quality in Japan since 1950, is their competitive position in techniques and the lessons that we could learn from the contributions of the Japanese. The success of their efforts is well known. Reasons for the effectiveness and speed of their efforts are not so well known.

The first lecture was held with leaders of industry assembled at the behest of Mr. Ichiro Ishikawa, President of the Union of Japanese Scientists and Engineers, at the Industry Club in Tokyo in June 1950. There was a further session next month at the Yama-no Hotel at Hakone, and meetings for study in subsequent visits, in various cities in Japan. The lectures charged management with the responsibility to optimize the use of statistical methods in all stages of manufacture, and to understand the statistical control of quality as a never-ending cycle of improved methods of manufacture, test, consumer research, and re-design of product. They described in simple terms management's responsibility to understand the capability of the process, and the economic loss from failure to take due regard of it.

Obviously, the Japanese never had need of adjectives to describe the statistical control of quality. It was never anything but total.

The lectures emphasized the economic loss of confusing a specific cause with a common cause, with illustrations. Confusion between common causes and specific causes is one of the serious mistakes of administration, in industry and in public administration as well. The natural reaction to any event, such as an accident of any kind, stoppage of production (of shoes, for example, because of breakage of thread, is to blame a specific operator or machine. The real cause may, however, be common to all operators and to all machines, namely, poor thread—a fault of management, whose policy may be to buy thread locally or from a subsidiary. Demoralization, frustration, and economic loss are inevitable results of attributing a common cause to some specific local operator or condition.

One of the main functions of statistical techniques is to distinguish between the two types of cause, and hence to fix (with adjustable risk of being wrong) the responsibility for variability and for undesired level.

This aspect of the statistical control of quality was not appreciated, I believe, in the earlier history of statistical methods in American industry. The Japanese had the benefit of advanced thinking on the matters.

Statistical education in Japan. The program of education in techniques commenced in June 1950 under the auspices of the Society of Japanese Scientists and Engineers. In all, 500 engineers attended the technical lecture courses of 8 days during 1950, and literally hundreds more attended every year thereafter. Additional courses in sampling for studies in consumer research were held in 1950 and 1951, and in later years.

The effectiveness of such beginnings in mass education was more pronounced and more rapid than results observed from the 8-day courses that commenced in the U.S. nine years earlier. In the first place, Japan was in 1950 in desperate circumstances. Every minute must count. Second, management became aware of the possible results from use of statistical techniques, simultaneously with the commencement of education for engineers. Third, practically everyone in attendance at technical sessions in Japan knew calculus. One might argue that calculus is not necessary for productive applications of statistical theory. True enough, but it helps.

There were further reasons. Most important was a vigorous system of courses for continuation and advancement in theory, instituted by the Union of Japanese Scientists and Engineers.

Courses in statistical theory at various levels were held, and are still held, the duration, days, and hours being varied from time to time to meet the requirements of engineers who must come from distant points, as well as for those that live in or near Tokyo.

An additional point of strength came from the formation of committees to work on new theory and to investigate various areas of application, such as the sampling of bulk materials (mainly ores), design of experiment, queuing theory, and other problems. The impact of the work of these committees has substantially changed much industrial practice in Japan.

Publication of a journal *Industrial Quality Control* was started by the Union of Japanese Scientists and Engineers, in Japanese: the journal is now in its 14th year. *Research Reports*, a journal now in its 13th year, has a high reputation amongst mathematical statisticians the world over.

Another reason for speedy results in Japan was that statistical methods had the benefit of nearly three decades of experience in the western world. There were naturally, at first, inevitable misunderstandings in America, and undue emphasis on certain aspects of techniques. For example, the control chart was at first used only as a tool to help weed out specific (assignable) causes that remain (*vide infra*), and little attention was given to common causes. That statistical methods separate, almost unerringly, special causes from common causes is important, and that their removal rests with management, was by no means fully appreciated. Acceptance sampling was frequently at first confused with process-control. Some people looked upon it as furnishing estimates of the quality of lots. To others, it separated good lots from bad. Many people, here as elsewhere, in a burst of enthusiasm confused statistical methods with engineering or with other subject-matter. They would substitute statistical calculations for knowledge of engineering, and then try to solve statistical problems by consulting their own knowledge of engineering.

Some clarity of vision had pierced through the mist by 1950, and it was possible to make a fresh start in Japan. Such principles were woven into the teaching in Japan.

From an address delivered at a meeting of the American Society for Quality Control, Stanford University, September 12, 1964; expanded upon and published in Sankhya: The Indian Journal of Statistics, Series B, Vol. 28, Parts 1 & 2, 1966.

What Happened in Japan?
Introduction and Purpose of This Article

The competitive position of many Japanese products, according to the testimony of their own manufacturers, has been achieved largely through understanding and use of the statistical control of quality in the broad sense *(vide infra)*. Statistical techniques were not wholly responsible for what happened, as deeper perspective of later paragraphs will bring forth, but statistical techniques certainly played an important role in the miracle. The first step was to fire up desire on the part of management to improve quality and to impart confidence that improvement was possible; that utilization of statistical techniques would help.

The purpose of this article is to offer some observations on the causes of success in Japan, from the viewpoint of the statistical control of quality, with the thought that energetic application of statistical techniques in other parts of the world, including the United States, might have healthy impact. Appreciation of what happened in Japan might also be taken seriously on programs of scientific and professional societies that are interested in statistical methods applied to production.

Nine Features of the Statistical Control of Quality in Japan

As I see it, there are nine main reasons for the success and speed of application of the statistical control of quality by Japanese manufacturers:

1. Genuine and resolute determination on the part of management to improve quality.
2. Confidence in their ability to lead Japanese industry forth from the bad reputation that Japanese products had built up in the past, confidence in Japanese scientific ability, and confidence in Japanese skills. Confidence also, I might add, in statistical methods.
3. They were Japanese, with industrial experience, and with an inbred pride of workmanship.
4. Japanese top management, statisticians, and engineers, learned the statistical control of quality in the broad sense of Shewhart, as defined further on.
5. Management took immediate interest and learned something about the techniques of the statistical control of quality as well as about the possible results, and still more about what their own responsibilities would be. Proper arrangements for contact with top management, at the outset, was one of the fortunate features of statistical education in Japan.
6. Statistical education became a continuing process. Statistical methods cannot be installed once for all and left to run, like a new carpet or a new dean. They require constant adaptation, revision, extension, new theory, and new knowledge of the statistical properties of materials. Perhaps the main accomplishment in the eight-day courses that began in 1950 was to impart inspiration to learn more about statistical methods.

7. The Japanese learned the difference between a statistical problem and one in engineering, chemistry, management, or marketing. They learned that statistical knowledge is not a substitute for knowledge of engineering or of other subject-matter, and that knowledge of engineering does not solve statistical problems.

8. Japanese manufacturers took on the job themselves. They did not look to their government nor to ours for help. When they arranged for consultation, they sent a ticket and a cheque. They gave financial and moral support to statistical education, mainly through the Union of Japanese Scientists and Engineers.

9. Suggestions and technical information have a fairly clear channel from lower to higher levels of supervision and management. A Japanese executive is never too old or too successful to listen to the possibility of doing it a better way.

One ought also to mention the stimulus of a prize offered annually in the name of an American statistician [WED is that statistician] to the Japanese manufacturer who, in the opinion of the Committee on Awards, has made the greatest advance in quality of his product during the past calendar year. Many companies compete for the prize, often laying plans years in advance. Although only one company, or at most two, can receive the prize, the continual competition of many companies has had an important leavening effect in quality.

Lectures to Top Management

Lectures to management, beginning in 1950, brought up a few simple questions to think about. I am not an economist, nor a businessman, only a statistician, but some conclusions seemed inescapable. Why was it necessary to improve quality of Japanese products? Because Japanese products must now become competitive: the market in Asia was lost. The market for poor quality in the Western world is a losing game.

It is not necessary to raise all your own food, it seemed to me. Chicago doesn't. Switzerland doesn't. It may be smarter for Japan to import food and pay for it with exports. There is a market for quality. How do you build quality, and a reputation for quality?

No country is so able as Japan, I pointed out, with its vast pool of skilled and educated industrial manpower, and with so many highly proficient engineers, mathematicians, and statisticians, to improve quality. Statistical methods could help: in fact, realization of any goal to raise quality to a sufficiently high level would be impossible without statistical methods on a broad scale. Seeing their serious determination, I predicted at an assembly of Japanese manufacturers in Tokyo in July 1950 that in five years, manufacturers in other industrial nations would be on the defensive and that in ten years the reputation for top quality in Japanese products would be firmly established the world over.

Statistical techniques became a living, vital, and essential force in all stages of Japanese industry. The whole world knows how well Japanese manufacturers met the predicted time-table.

Management must assume the responsibility to optimize the use of statistical methods in all stages of manufacture, and to understand the statistical control of quality as a never-ending cycle of improved methods of manufacture, test, consumer research, and re-design of product. Lectures described in simple terms management's responsibility to understand the capability of the process, management's responsibility for common causes (vide infra), and the economic loss from failure to accept these responsibilities.

Japanese manufacturers took these arguments seriously to the point of doing something about them with concerted effort. A little fire here, and a little there, would be too slow. Concerted effort meant cooperation amongst competitors, assistance to vendors, and—probably for the first time in Japan—immediate attention to the demands of the consumer, and need for consumer research on a continuing basis, with feed-back for re-design.

Results were spectacular, even after only one year, especially in productivity per man-hour, with little new machinery. One steel company saved 28 percent on consumption of coal per ton of steel. A huge pharmaceutical company put out three times as much finished product per unit of input of raw material. A big cable company reduced greatly the amount of paper and re-work on insulated wire and cable. Many companies reduced accidents to a permanent low level. Improvement in quality and dependability came in due course, and in five years, as predicted, many Japanese products had earned respect to the point of fear in markets the world over.

Definition of the Statistical Control of Quality

The Japanese never knew the statistical control of quality in any way but in the broad sense introduced by [Dr. Walter A.] Shewhart. The statistical control of quality was defined in plain English in 1950 and ever after in big letters like this:

THE STATISTICAL CONTROL OF QUALITY IS THE APPLICATION OF STATISTICAL PRINCIPLES AND TECHNIQUES IN ALL STAGES OF PRODUCTION, DIRECTED TOWARD THE ECONOMIC MANUFACTURE OF A PRODUCT THAT IS MAXIMALLY USEFUL AND HAS A MARKET.

Translated into action, this definition of the statistical control of quality means

1. Use of statistical methods to construct meaningful specifications of raw materials, piece-parts, assemblies, and performance of finished product, by appropriate statistical design
2. Assistance to suppliers. Any raw material or piece-part is someone's finished product. Improvement of quality of incoming materials from vendors or from a previous operation is one of the most important requirements in a program of quality.
3. Control of process. Detection of special causes by statistical methods (X-bar and R-charts, run-charts, design of experiment, and other techniques). Distinction between special causes and common causes, with examples. Separation of responsibility for finding and removing
   a. special causes of variability (local),
   b. common or general causes of variability (upper management).
4. Use of acceptance sampling where appropriate
5. Consumer research. Test of product in service
6. Re-design of product
7. Tests of new product, in the laboratory and in service
8. Use of proper theory for finding optimum levels of inventory, and for economy in distribution

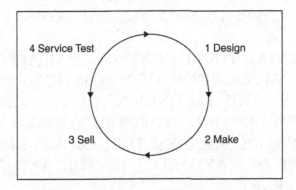

Figure 8.1 Cycle of Applied Statistical Methods

Cycle of Applied Statistical Methods

The statistical method shown in the figure was taught as a continuing process, in a never-ending cycle:

1. Design a product.
2. Make it.
3. Try to sell it
4. Test it in service.
5. Repeat Step 1. Re-design the product on the basis of tests in service.
6. Repeat Step 2.
7. Repeat Step 3, etc.

The contribution that statistical methods make in placing responsibility squarely where it belongs (at the local operator, at the foreman, or at the door of higher management) can hardly be over-estimated. [See chapter 7 for detail on statistical methods.]

This aspect of the statistical control of quality was not appreciated, I believe, in the earlier history of statistical methods in American industry, and is even now neglected. The Japanese had the benefit of advanced thinking on the matter.

Other Statistical Techniques

Consumer research was taught as an integral part of the statistical control of quality. In fact, small surveys of household inventories and requirements of pharmaceuticals, sewing machines, bicycles, and the like, constituted part of the course in sampling in the summer of 1951. [This course was taught by Deming.] These have been designated by the Japanese as the first studies in consumer research to be carried out by Japanese companies with the aid of modern methods of sampling.

Shewhart charts were taught in Japan as statistical tools for the economic detection of the existence of special causes of variation, not as tools that actually find the cause. However, emphasis was on action, find the cause and remove it, once a point goes outside limits. Once statistical control is established, then do something about common causes.

Acceptance sampling was taught as a scheme of protection (provided one will really reject and screen a lot when the sample contains more than the allowable number of defects). The specification of a unit of product is of course vital. However important it be, a vendor does not know how to predict the cost of making a product unless he has in hand, in addition, the plan by which his lots will be sampled by the purchaser and accepted or rejected. How big is a lot? What is to be done with pieces found to be defective? Answers to these questions are a necessary part of any plan of acceptance, if vendor and purchaser understand each other. The plan of acceptance sampling is a necessary specification of a contract for lots.

The effectiveness of mass education in statistical methods in Japan was more pronounced and more rapid than results observed in the U.S. In the first place, Japan was in 1950 in desperate circumstances. Every minute must count. Second, management was more responsive. Third, practically everyone in attendance at technical sessions in Japan had studied calculus.

A vigorous system of courses for continuation and advancement in theory was instituted by the Union of Japanese Scientists and Engineers. The levels are varied. The duration, days, and hours meet the requirements of engineers who must come from distant points, as well as for those that live in or near Tokyo.

An additional point of strength came from the formation of committees to work on new theory, and to investigate various areas of application, such as the sampling of bulk materials (mainly ores), design of experiment, queuing theory, and other problems. The impact of the work of these committees has substantially changed much industrial practice in Japan.

Publication of a journal *Statistical Quality Control* (in Japanese) was started by the Union of Japanese Scientists and Engineers; the journal is now in its 18th year. *Research Reports,* a journal now in its 17th year, has a high reputation amongst mathematical statisticians the world over. A journal specifically for foremen has been started, and one for engineers.

Power and Limitation of Statistical Techniques

Advances in uses of statistical techniques would come, the Japanese learned, not by searching a manufacturing plant for a chance to apply this or that technique, but to search the plant for problems, and then to enquire what statistical techniques might be helpful.

Statistical teaching in Japan put emphasis on the responsibility of management and of the engineer to foresee problems and to state them explicitly. Statistical techniques were taught, not as a kit of tools to try out here or there, but as an aid to solution of problems, aids to knowledge and creativity.

The Japanese learned something about what statistical techniques can do, and what they can't do.

From "What Happened in Japan?,"
Industrial Quality Control,
Vol. 24, No. 2, August 1967.

An Account of the Work of the Union of Japanese Scientists and Engineers in Quality Control

Introduction

As I understand it, the Union of Japanese Scientists and Engineers (JUSE hereafter) is one of the activities of the Federated Economic Societies of Japan. My first contact with JUSE was a letter that came in 1949 from Mr. Kenichi Koyanagi, for many years its Managing Director until his death in 1965. The letter asked me to come to Japan and to give lectures on the statistical control of quality. This I did in June, July, and August 1950. This first engagement in Japan was carried out by an appointment with the Economic and Scientific Section under General MacArthur's occupation. But my ten subsequent engagements in Japan were private with JUSE. In fact, an invitation to return to Japan always contained thereafter a ticket and a cheque. In other words, after the first visit, Japanese manufacturers never asked their government nor ours for a dollar toward the cost of engaging me. There may be a moral there.

It was the untiring efforts and. skillful ability of Kenichi Koyanagi that perhaps more than any other factor that put Japanese manufacturers in touch with statistical methods in consumer research and quality control.

Mr. Ichiro Ishikawa

My first contact in Tokyo with Japanese management was through Mr. Ichiro Ishikawa who was President for many years (until his death in 1970) of the Federated Economic Societies of Japan. Mr. Ishikawa's English was in 1950 almost non-existent, but he somehow understood what statistical methods could do for industry in Japan. He was a wealthy Japanese man, president of the great Showa Denko Company, a respected public spirited man who headed many movements for improvement of smooth running of civil and industrial affairs. When Mr. Ishikawa sent telegrams to call a meeting of the leaders of industry at the Industry Club in Tokyo for the evening of 25 July 1950, everybody showed up, a tribute to his leadership. Incidentally, he pursued English and became very good in it.

Lectures to Management

I was teaching or going to teach simple statistical methods to hundreds of engineers in Tokyo, Osaka, Nagoya, and Fukuoka that summer of 1950, but the horrible thought came to me that no matter how well these engineers might put their new knowledge to work, their efforts could not be fully effective and might even be a disappointment unless management also understood something about statistical methods, and about their responsibility to reduce common or environmental causes of poor quality and of low productivity.

Statistical techniques became a living, vital, and essential force in all stages of Japanese industry.

A little fire here, and a little there, would be too slow. The movement must have the force of an earthquake, and cover the whole of Japanese industry. The first step was to fire up desire on the part of management to improve quality and to impart confidence that improvement was possible; that utilization of statistical techniques would help.

Japanese manufacturers took these arguments seriously to the point of doing something about them with concerted effort.

Anyone who has had the chance to observe first hand the detail with which the Japanese plan any project will understand how thoroughly Japanese management went into the matter of their own responsibilities for design of product, reduction of common (environmental) causes of trouble, and into the problems of marketing. Armed with a good product, they invented economic and effective organizations for trade in the markets of the world.

Brief Description of Courses Given by JUSE

The main source of income of JUSE is mostly, I believe, from educational courses in quality control. Naturally, most of the courses are in statistical theory and application. However, JUSE has never lost an opportunity to branch out into other activities of education such as research by computers. It was JUSE, under the leadership of Dr. Kaoru Ishikawa, that established in 1955 the QC-Circles; more on them later.

Courses in statistical theory and application given at the JUSE are of many kinds, depths, and variety. Educationally, one might say that JUSE provides continuing education for all levels of management and production. It fills the gap between (a) statistical theory given in the universities, and (b) application in industry. It also provides introductory courses in statistical methods. There are lectures and courses for management, and they are difficult. I have seen them and have been amazed to see how many managers take five days off to work just as hard at JUSE as they do in their own plants, learning techniques of the statistical control of quality. Japanese management never made the mistake of assuming that they are good enough, or that subordinates can take over the job of quality. Japanese management took the trouble to find out what statistical methods are, why they are necessary, what they can mean to a company.

JUSE gives high-level theoretical courses in statistics, middle-grade courses, elementary courses. There are courses at night for people that work in Tokyo. They are intensive courses of 5 days, 10 days, and sometimes longer for people that come from outside Tokyo.

The QC-Circle Movement

This movement is frequently confused with quality control in Japan. The QC-Circle Movement is one of tremendous impact, but it is only one of the facets of quality control in Japan. The QC-Circle Movement is Japan's way of enlisting the aid of workers in the reduction or elimination of common or environmental causes of trouble.

The Japanese worker was always ahead of his American counterpart in a feeling of responsibility for the product and for the company. I need not rehearse here all the possible reasons for this, even if I understood them. Workers in Japan always had the privilege not only of making suggestions, but of trying them out. For example, a suggestion on a change in sequence of operations could be tried out in an autonomous group. The QC-Circle Movement is a wide development of group-participation. There are probably three million production-workers in organized Circles. Three hundred thousand production-workers are registered with the JUSE. The journal *Quality Control for the Foreman*, the official journal of the QC-Circle Movement, has a circulation of 90,000—about the highest circulation of any professional or scientific journal in the world.

The average age of the young men and women in the QC-Circle Movement is, I believe, around 24. It is indeed an experience to attend one of their conventions and listen to youngsters as they tell how they reduced defectives and increased output before an audience of perhaps 1800 other youngsters. Interchange of ideas between companies, including competitors, is the Japanese way of life.

Lectures by Foreign Experts

Management of JUSE has never lost a chance to invite a foreign expert to hold one or more seminars and to talk to top management; also to visit a plant or more if interested. One of the great achievements in this connexion has been the repeated visits of Dr. Juran to Japan. We in America who know Dr. Juran can well understand the powerful impact that he made in Japan. Acheson Duncan gave lectures, and there must be other names that do not come to mind.

International Convention, November 1969

This was the first international convention in Quality Control. People came from all over the world. Over 1000 papers were presented. The Proceedings were published by JUSE. The arrangements were superb, an adjective that can hardly be appreciated to its full depth except by people that have attended an international meeting in Japan, and have attended also, for comparison, a convention in some other country. This convention was the dream of Kenichi Koyanagi, who did not live to see it.

Working Committees

JUSE established shortly after 1950 a number of committees to work on various difficult problems in industry. There was the committee on the sampling of bulk materials, under the leadership of Dr. Kaoru Ishikawa. Some of the results of the work of this committee are Japanese Industrial Standards on the sampling of coal and various ores. The care, knowledge, and skill that went into these standards are obvious to anyone familiar with this field, and it is no wonder that these standards have been widely admired and copied.

The K-Committee (K for Professor T. Kawata) undertook to foster and coordinate high-level research in mathematical problems. The journal *Research Reports* was formed for publication of relevant theory and application. The excellence of this journal is recognized worldwide.

Publications

JUSE publishes the journal *Statistical Quality Control, Quality Control for the Foreman*, and *Research Reports*. The last one is in English, and contains mathematical papers with illustrations of application. The Publications Division of JUSE has published also a large number of books on quality control and related subjects.

Prizes

JUSE administers several annual prizes, and awards them in a national convention each year, usually in November. Public interest is manifest; the ceremonies are broadcast. These prizes provide strong propulsion throughout Japanese industry toward improved design, quality, and economy of production. The main prizes are the two Deming Prizes, one a sum of money to an individual statistician, the other citation to a company. The committee on the Deming Prize listens to presentations from various plants and corporations and makes site visits. They faced long ago the problem where one plant of several belonging to a corporation for affiliation of some sort does outstanding work, far ahead of other plants in the same corporation or affiliation. They have also the problem of general excellence of an entire corporation, and comparison thereof with some single outstanding plant also belonging to a large corporation.

They give consideration, of course, to small concerns and sub-contractors. Quality Control Month is observed annually, with flags flying.

Summary of Accomplishments

Japan is today the country that one should visit for study of the control of quality. Japanese management, in my estimation, is far ahead of the management of industry in any other country.

American management and our experts in quality control can no longer bury their heads in the sand with the old excuse that the Japanese can only copy models and methods. Whom did SONY copy? Whose trains did they copy? What sociological phenomenon anywhere did they copy to build the QC-Circles? What trading organizations did they copy to market their products here and in other countries?

Renewed efforts in statistical methods in Japan, along with their skillful management, may overcome the upward evaluation of the yen, and advance even further the competitive position in foreign markets.

An Account of the Work of the Union of
Japanese Scientists and Engineers in Quality Control,
1969.

Twenty years after his pivotal lectures in Japan, Deming reflected on the establishment of the Union of Japanese Scientists and Engineers, and the effect his lectures had on their working capital.

Some Early History of JUSE

A windfall from my visit to Japan in 1950 was to put JUSE [Union of Japanese Scientists and Engineers] on its feet. JUSE, up to the time of my visit to Japan in 1950, had been a group of men, held together by Kenichi Koyanagi. The group had been formed, nameless, by Mr. Koyanagi during the War to help Japan in its war effort. The aim of the group, after the War, was the reconstruction of Japan. The aim was clear, but the men had no plan.

The group received some precarious financial support from the government. They had office space in the Osaka Shosen Building, long ago demolished, not far from Tokyo Central Station. Mr. Koyanagi provided for me, out of his space, an adequate office.

Attendance at my 8-day course in June 1950 in the auditorium of the Medical Association brought in money. The cost was 15,000 yen per person, attendance 235, mostly engineers. My services were free, paid for by the Occupation. Attendance at Osaka a few weeks later was 150, at Nagoya 125, at Hakata 85. JUSE was on its feet financially, a going concern.

A return visit six months later, and another six months after, with further return visits, swelled the working capital of JUSE. It was now established.

Notes written ca.
1970.

In 1955, Dr. Kenichi Koyanagi wrote in a little booklet, "The Deming Prize," that the Prize was instituted in 1950.

> *with gratitude to Dr. Deming's friendship as well as in commemoration of his contributions to Japanese industry.... Most of the Japanese were in a servile spirit as the vanquished, and among Allied personnel there were not a few with an air of importance. In striking contrast, Dr. Deming showed his warm cordiality to every Japanese whom he met and exchanged frank opinions with everybody. His high personality deeply impressed all those who learned from him and became acquainted with him. He loved Japan and the Japanese from his own heart. The sincerity and enthusiasm with which he did his best for his courses sill lives and will live forever in the memory of all the concerned.*

From 1950 through 1993, Deming prepared speeches for the Annual Deming Prize Ceremonies in Japan. He delivered his speech in person when possible, through one of his daughters at other times, and sometimes by another representative. His speeches always included praise for what the Japanese had done, encouragement for the future, and a lesson to be taken away. Some of these speeches and excerpts from others have appeared elsewhere in this book. Here is Deming's 1974 speech for the Deming Prize Ceremonies. His great affection for the Japanese and pride in their accomplishments comes through clearly.

Message from W. Edwards Deming to the Ceremonies for the Deming Prize, November 1974

I appreciate much the honor to send this message to the ceremonies for the Deming Prize to be held in November 1974. All people should give thanks to the first committee on the Deming Prize for their wisdom and effort to establish the ground rules for winning the prize. The ground rules have created healthy yet fair competition amongst Japanese companies for the prize.

I send hearty congratulations to Mr. Koji Kobayashi, President of the Nippon Electric Company, Ltd., for being the Prize Medalist this year. I send also congratulations to the Kyodo Survey Company, Ltd., and to Horikiri Spring Manufacturing Company, Ltd., for winning the prize for application in small enterprises.

Many companies compete for the Deming Prize. Unfortunately, only one or a small number can be chosen each year. However, all the companies that strive for the prize contribute to the quality of Japanese products and to the reputation for quality that Japanese products have established the world over, to the good name of Japan.

As I pointed out to Japanese management and to engineers in 1950, when Japanese quality was at a low level, Japan had a bountiful supply of important national resources in the form of (1) well-educated engineers, (2) the world's most industrious production-workers, and (3) skill and creative ability in management that is admired the world over, and which management in no other country has been able to approach.

All variation in dimensions and in other quality characteristics of product should be studied, even though 100% of the product meets specifications. Variation impairs dependability and reliability, represents loss of output, and waste of materials, fuel, machines, and human effort.

The problems of achieving dependability, low cost, and high output, are threefold:

1. The disposition of product already made. Should it be shipped out to the consumer? Should incoming materials be accepted? Japanese manufacturers have built up a reputation for high quality and have sustained it by permitting only the best quality for export. The chief tools for this function are (a) statistical plans of acceptance, with calculable, governable risks to the consumer and to the manufacturer, (b) tests of prototypes, (c) calibration and maintenance of instruments and standards of measurement. Statistical plans for inspection and acceptance provide a basis for calculation and control of the risks to the consumer and to the manufacturer. They provide an operational definition for the quality of lots, and a basis for carrying on business.

2. There are special or specific causes of variation in the process, which the worker himself can correct through the use of statistical signals, common examples being X-bar and R-charts. Achievement of statistical control is the greatest contribution that a production-worker can make to the company.

3. The same statistical signals that detect the existence of special causes of variation also provide measures of the portion of variation that arises from faults in the system (the common causes, as I called them originally in my first talks with management in 1950). Change in the system is the responsibility of management. Changes in the system might be, for example, change in sequence of operations, change in raw materials or ingredients, more exact setting of machines, change in design of product, reduction of vibration, noise, confusion, etc.

Japanese management acted at once in 1950 on this advice. The first step was to understand how to achieve better uniformity by statistical methods. Then came new designs and new products. The Union of Japanese Scientists and Engineers instituted courses at many levels by which engineers, production-workers, and foremen throughout the plants, learned to use X-bar and R-charts and other techniques to detect the existence of special causes of variation, and to eliminate or reduce these causes. Seminars with top management, and short courses in statistical techniques and in statistical logic for management at various levels, were given by the Union of Japanese Scientists and Engineers. Quality became at once a vibrant, concerted, national effort.

One of the most important acts of management in Japan, toward improvement of the system, has been the establishment of the QC-Circle Movement, originated by my good friend Professor Kaoru Ishikawa. This is one of management's answers to improvement of the system. It is a stroke of good management to make use of the specialized knowledge of the worker on the spot to improve the system.

The greatest satisfaction of my life is to have so many friends in Japan, and to work since 1950 with Japanese industry through the great Union of Japanese Scientists and Engineers.

The revolution in quality in Japan which began in 1950 is the greatest demonstration yet carried out of the power of statistical methods in production.

Index

competing for, 155
cost of living and, 106
Monopolies, 2, 10
automobile industry, 34
diamond, 34
myths, 31–35
optimization and, 71–72
service as obligation of, 32
telephone system, 33
Morale, 5
Moriguti Sigeiti, 152
Morrow, Kenneth, 278
Motivation
extrinsic, 81–82
of people, 11, 157
Mozart, Wolfgang Amadeus, 190–191
Myths
competition, 31–35, 201–202
Japan and economic, 3
monopolies, 31–35

Narcotics. *See* Drugs
National Center for Health Statistics, U.S., 274–275
"The Need for Change" (Deming), 38–40
"The Need to Change" (Deming), 40–42
Negative interactions, 155
Negotiation, 79
Nelson, Lloyd S., 14, 83, 170
New Principles in Administration for Quality (Deming), 174–178
"New Principles in Administration for Quality and Efficiency" (Deming), 280–281
New York University (NYU), 198–199, 223. *See also* Stern School of Business
The New Economics for Industry, Government, Education (Deming), 69
Newton, Isaac, 190
Nippon Electric Company, 310
Nippon Telephone, 281
Numbers
prime, 80
in statistical theory, 102
Numerical goals, losses and, 55–57
NYU. *See* New York University

Obligations
of customer and supplier, 126–128
with monopolies and service, 32
"Obligations of Management in the New Economic Age" (Deming), 7–15
Office, authority of, 164

Office of Education in Quality, 88
Office of Statistical Methodology, 86
"On the Statistician's Contribution to Quality" (Deming), 23–26, 223–224, 230–233
On-the-job training, 130–131, 175
Operational definitions, 65–66
Optimization, 58
cooperation with, 71–72
failures, 75–77
sub-, 15
of systems, 73–77, 154, 160
Organization chart, 153. *See also* Flow diagrams
Orsini, Joyce, 128, 178
Out of Crisis (Deming), 12–13, 57, 105
Overjustification, 178–180

Paperwork, as unnecessary, 52
Past, education and, 197
Pay
incentive, 11, 25, 39, 44–45, 76, 82
merit system, 2, 9, 14, 17, 25, 27–31, 39, 41, 75–77, 83, 84, 173
Payroll
cost of inspection in, 115–116
responsibility of, 186–187
PDSA. *See* Plan-Do-Study-Act Cycle
People
improvement and investment in, 46
knowing how to manage, 168–173
management of, 2, 75–76
merit pay system as destroyer of, 9, 14, 27–31, 39, 41, 75–77, 83, 84, 173
motivating, 11, 157
psychology and, 80–82
transformation for, 145–147
Performance
evaluation of, 17, 21, 25, 29, 53
explanations and excuses for poor, 2–6, 7
how to use, 31
pay for, 11
short-term, 75
Personal growth, 94
Personality, as power source, 164
Petersen, Donald E., 47, 86, 88
Philosophy, adoption of new, 110–113
Physics, 99
Plan-Do-Study-Act (PDSA) Cycle, 165–166
Planning, prediction with, 232
Plans, rational, 79
Positive interactions, 155

About the Editor

Joyce Nilsson Orsini, PhD, is an assistant professor of management systems at Fordham University, the director of Fordham's Deming Scholars MBA, and president of The W. Edwards Deming Institute.